HITLER'S FORTRESS CHERBOURG

Also by the author:

HITLER'S FORTRESS CHERBOURG

The Conquest of a Bastion

William B. Breuer

STEIN AND DAY/*Publishers*/New York

Author's note: See appendices for table of equivalent ranks.

Appendices I and II are reprinted from Samuel W. Mitcham, Jr.'s
Rommel's Last Battle; The Desert Fox and the Normandy Campaign
with the permission of Stein and Day/*Publishers.*

First published in 1984
Copyright © 1984 by William B. Breuer
All rights reserved, Stein and Day, Incorporated
Designed by Louis A. Ditizio
Printed in the United States of America
STEIN AND DAY/*Publishers*
Scarborough House
Briarcliff Manor, N.Y. 10510

Library of Congress Cataloging in Publication Data

Breuer, William B., 1923–
  Hitler's fortress Cherbourg.

  Bibliography: p.
  Includes index.
  1. Cherbourg (France), Battle of, 1944.   I. Title.
D756.5.C34B74   1984   940.54'21   83-40364
ISBN 0-8128-2952-2

Dedicated to
JAMES MAURICE GAVIN
Lieutenant General, U.S. Army (Ret.)
Paratrooper pioneer, gallant leader of stalwart fighting
men, beloved by his troopers, distinguished ambassador,
an American legend in his own time

CONTENTS

MAPS

PHOTOS

American assault troops head for Normandy beaches
Allied heavy bomber blasting German positions outside Cherbourg
Brigadier General Theodore Roosevelt
Lieutenant General Omar Bradley
Brigadier General James M. Gavin
Major General J. Lawton Collins
Lieutenant Colonel Robert H. Cole
Brigadier General Anthony McAuliffe
Field Marshal Gerd von Rundstedt
Field Marshal Erwin Rommel
Lieutenant Arthur Jahnke
German officers inspect Goliath pygmy tanks
A Utah Beach bunker
Plan of blockhouse W-5 at Utah Beach
Dead German defender of Blockhouse W-5
La Fière Causeway
Carentan Causeway
Hitler's Fortress Cherbourg before the Allied invasion
Cherbourg from the air
Lieutenant Colonel August von der Heydte
Men of the 87th Mortar Battalion fire in support of 101st Airborne
    Division troops at Carentan Causeway
A destroyed German coastal battery
American troops move through Valognes
Sherman tanks moving into Cherbourg
American infantrymen advancing toward an underground fortress
American troops on Fort du Roule in Cherbourg
General von Schlieben's force surrenders to 9th Infantry Division
Lieutenant General von Schlieben enters U.S. VII Corps headquarters
General von Schlieben and Admiral Hennecke brought before Major
    General Collins
German troops killed in the battle for Cherbourg

Introduction

On April 1, 1942, U.S. Army Chief of Staff George C. Marshall and an obscure subordinate, Major General Dwight D. Eisenhower, Chief of the War Plans Division in Washington, called on a beleaguered President Franklin Delano Roosevelt in the Oval Office of the White House. There they presented a plan code-named Operation Sledgehammer; it called for a massive assault early that fall across the English Channel against German-held northwestern France.

A pacifist America had been at war less than four months. Only a short time before, its understrength, ill-equipped, and inexperienced army had been forced to drill with broomsticks in lieu of rifles. But Roosevelt approved the plan.

Experienced British military leaders were aghast. Field-Marshal Sir John Dill, Great Britain's senior liaison officer in Washington, wrote home: "This country is the most highly organised for peace you can imagine. At present [the United States] has not—repeat not—the slightest conception of what the war means, and their armed forces are more unready for war than one can imagine. The whole organisation belongs to the days of George Washington."

American military leaders saw the British armed forces in an equal light. An American general, after a visit to England in early 1942, reported to his superiors: "The British army, after the mauling it received [in France] is fit only for defense. . . . It is not strong enough, confident enough or well enough equipped for an offensive in northwestern France at this stage."

Across the Channel the Germans had twenty-five fully equipped battle-tested divisions; they were far superior in every respect to any force the

11

Grand Alliance (the United States and Great Britain) could throw against them.

Yet, to relieve pressure on the Russian allies, Roosevelt and Marshall adamantly insisted that Sledgehammer be mounted, and a date was set: September 15. The British bitterly opposed the cross-Channel invasion "at this time."

"It would meet with total disaster," declared General Alan F. Brooke, a combat commander in two world wars and England's most decorated soldier since Wellington and Marlborough.

As a result of American determination to mount Sledgehammer in 1942, an operation code-named *Ritter* (German for "horse soldier") was conceived. Its origin and principal sponsors would forever remain cloaked in a thick veil of mystery.

Ritter, Later changed to Jubilee, would be a massive reconnaissance in force by about 6,000 troops (primarily Canadian) against the French port of Dieppe, reputedly to test Allied equipment and techniques as well as German defenses in France. It would not be an invasion, but rather a raid.

It would be alleged that Winston Churchill had ordered the Dieppe operation, knowing that it would meet disaster—that as many as five thousand men would be sacrificed to dramatize to the inexperienced American leadership the folly of a full-scale invasion in the fall of 1942. Better this tragedy, Churchill allegedly believed, than a premature all-out effort in which a half-million Allied soldiers, their equipment—and the war—would be lost.

Shortly after dawn on August 19, picked Canadian assault troops hit the beaches at Dieppe. From that moment on, chaos reigned. The German defenders opened up a crescendo of artillery, antitank, mortar, automatic weapons, and rifle fire. Few of the 6,058 invaders got past the sandy beaches, others were killed before they reached shore.

The raid was a disaster. Sixty percent of those who participated in the assault, 3,623 men, were killed, wounded, or captured. Of the 4,963 Canadians in the operation, 3,367 (or 68 percent) became casualties. The Royal Air Force had 106 badly needed airplanes destroyed, and the navy lost 550 men plus a warship and 33 landing craft from a flotilla of 252 vessels of all types. German losses were extremely light—591 casualties, 46 aircraft.

At 5:38 P.M. that day, Field Marshal Karl Rudolf Gerd von Rundstedt, German commander in France, wired a terse report to Adolf Hitler: "No armed Englishman remains on the continent."

The Führer was jubilant.

Two days after the Dieppe debacle, Prime Minister Churchill wrote to his deputy: "My general impression of [the raid] is that the results fully justified the heavy cost." He did not elaborate.

If the Dieppe raid was a sacrificial ploy to dissuade the Americans from a cross-Channel attack in the fall of 1942, it succeeded: Sledgehammer was quietly shelved.

Exultant as Hitler was over Dieppe, the Allied raid drove home to him the threat to continental Europe of invasion from England. Consequently, shortly after Dieppe the Führer decreed that an *Atlantikwall,* reaching from the snowy fjords of Norway to the Spanish frontier, be constructed with "fantastic speed."

Hitler ordered the building of fifteen thousand concrete and steel structures, immune to bombing and naval gunfire, to protect a continuous, interlocking belt of weapons commanding the major ports and potential landing beaches. This monumental construction project, the German dictator ordained, must be completed no later than May 1, 1943, a mere nine months away.

"An impossible task," fumed Field Marshal von Rundstedt, *Oberfehls- haber West* (Commander in Chief, West), to his aides. "It would take ten years to complete this project!" The aristocratic, sixty-nine-year-old von Rundstedt considered the Atlantic Wall an enormous waste of energy, time, and materials.

Nurtured in the traditions of the old Prussian armies, the commander in the west subscribed to the doctrine of Frederick the Great: "He who would defend all, defends nothing. . . . Little minds want to defend everything, sensible men concentrate on the essential." Von Rundstedt held the view that the Allies could get ashore on continental Europe at any point and time of their choosing along the twenty-one hundred miles of Atlantic and Mediterranean coastlines, that were his to defend. Instead of trying to meet an Allied amphibious invasion head-on at the beaches, he proposed holding strong armored divisions in reserve well inland to counterattack the principal landing areas.

But the Führer had spoken. Work on the immense project got underway. Progress was slow and methodical until November 1943 when Hitler, concerned over von Rundstedt's evident apathy about the construction of the Wall, transferred Field Marshal Erwin Rommel—the famed Desert Fox—from Italy to France. Rommel was put in charge of repelling the looming massive Anglo-American onslaught across the Channel against Northwest Europe.

Since the tragic Dieppe fiasco in August 1942, the western Allies had fought the Wehrmacht (German army) in bloody battles in North Africa, Sicily, Italy, and elsewhere. Now, in late 1943 and early 1944, the Allies were massing land, sea, and air forces for a cross-Channel thrust to reach the heart of the Third Reich and end the war.

Dynamic, dedicated, and indefatigable, Field Marshal Rommel plunged into the task of shoring up the Atlantic Wall. When the Allies struck, it would be an invasion obstacle to be reckoned with.

Tens of thousands of slave laborers from all over Europe, under the direction of the Third Reich's Todt Organization, toiled around the clock. Millions of tons of concrete were poured and orders placed for vast quantities of steel. The old French Maginot Line was raided for steel, and inside Greater Germany it was almost impossible for others to locate building materials—all of them were being rushed to Hitler's Atlantic Wall.

In keeping with Hitler's directive, the major ports along the English Channel received the highest priorities for manpower and materials. "If we can keep a major port out of the hands of the Allies, we can defeat any attempt to gain a foothold on continental Europe," Hitler said often.

The Führer proclaimed several major ports in France and the Low Countries "fortresses" and required their German commanders to sign declarations that they would defend the fortresses "to the last man and the last bullet" and then destroy the harbor facilities to render them useless to the invaders.

Across the English Channel, Eisenhower's strategists had reached the identical military conclusion as had Hitler: unless they could quickly seize a major port to rapidly bring in troops, guns, tanks, ammunition, fuel, and rations, the invading Allies would be in danger of withering on the vine and being cut to pieces by a Wehrmacht converging by land onto the Normandy bridgehead.

Hitler's hopes for an Allied invasion debacle and a subsequent negotiated peace with the British and Americans would focus on Fortress Cherbourg, an ancient, heavily fortified city situated in a bowl near the center of the north coast of the Cotentin Peninsula. If Hitler lost this port to the invaders, any hope of destroying the Allied army would vanish. It well could mark the beginning of the end for the Third Reich and its leader.

HITLER'S
FORTRESS
CHERBOURG

INTRIGUE, DECEPTIONS, AND DISPUTES

Rommel Plans
to Contact
Eisenhower

1

A bone-chilling wind was whipping across the wintry Cotentin Peninsula, the narrow mass of Normandy countryside that juts out northward like a thumb into the turbulent English Channel. On that gray dawn of February 15, 1944, Lieutenant General Karl Wilhelm von Schlieben emerged from an imposing Gothic chateau outside the small town of Valognes. The towering structure served as headquarters for the general's 709th Coastal Division.

Six feet three, wearing at his throat the Iron Cross he had won in Russia, and a high-peaked visored cap, von Schlieben looked at the overcast sky and turned up the collar of his gray-green leather greatcoat against the wind. As were all members of the Wehrmacht along the northern coast of France, the general was glad to see the murky weather. It would ground Allied aircraft in England.

In recent weeks increasing numbers of American and British fighter-bombers, knifing in low over the coast, had been strafing German vehicles on peninsula roads. On several occasions von Schlieben himself had been forced to leap from his moving vehicle and scurry for the cover of roadside ditches as machine-gun bullets thudded into the ground around him.

With a nod to his waiting driver, the general climbed into his aging brown, camouflaged staff car and settled himself in the rear seat as the vehicle edged slowly down the narrow Norman road, still hazardous from an overnight accumulation of a sheet of ice. Von Schlieben was starting another of his almost daily trips up and down the 50 miles of coastline that were his to defend, visiting scattered troop formations and assessing progress on coastal fortifications.

As the staff car inched along, the general's thoughts turned once again to the task to which he had been entrusted: the defense of the crucial port of Cherbourg, 10 miles north of Valognes, and a lengthy stretch of coastline along the northeastern and eastern portion of the Cotentin Peninsula. Von Schlieben was deeply concerned about several factors. He knew that German army doctrine called for a division to defend a sector six to eight miles wide, but his command was strung out over five times that distance. Most of his 11 battalions were deployed in concrete strong points to cover potential landing beaches, but there were huge gaps between units.

It was more than the undefended gaps in his sector that bothered von Schlieben. The quality of his troops was questionable. Grenadiers in the 709th Coastal Division averaged thirty-six years of age (compared to twenty-five in the American assault divisions), and interspersed among the German nationals were a wide variety of *Osstruppen,* Soviet prisoners of war who, considering their alternatives, had "volunteered" to serve in the Wehrmacht. These included Cossacks, Tatars, Armenians, Georgians, and Ukranians.

Some of his officers and noncoms, though battle-tested veterans, had been medically downgraded because of wounds or illnesses sustained in Russia. Many of the men suffered ear and stomach complaints.

However, the 709th Division had a cadre of experienced, dedicated, even enthusiastic officers and noncoms who, General von Schlieben believed, could hold the fighting formations together when the time came for action.

In the concrete dugouts, at gun emplacements and strongpoints along the many miles of Cotentin coastline, von Schlieben's fighting men arose to face another weary, boring day of gazing out across the frothy waves of the English Channel, keeping watch for the invasion that might or might not strike them. They had heard repeated rumors that the Führer expected the impending Anglo-American blow to strike at the Pas de Calais, only 20 miles from England and far east of the Cotentin Peninsula. And the Germans in the 709th Division still had great faith in the Führer and his conclusions.

The days and nights of watchful waiting were long and tedious. When not on guard duty, von Schlieben's men lay idly on wooden bunks in their concrete caves, talking of home, women, and the war and sipping long draughts of Calvados or wine. The bunkers were cold and damp, and the liquid diversion helped to overcome the homesickness and war-weariness many felt. Often at night the haunting strains of the popular German ballad

"Lili Marlene" wafted through the smoky concrete structures from a chorus of voices:

> In front of the barracks, before the heavy gate
> There stood a lamppost, and if it's standing yet
> Then we shall meet there once again
> Beside the lamppost in the rain,
> At once, Lili Marlene, at once, Lili Marlene.

While the average German soldier along the Cotentin coastline was toasting Lili Marlene with Normandy apple brandy, in Cherbourg Rear Admiral Walther Hennecke, commander of German naval forces in Normandy, was enjoying the finest French wines and living the comfortable life of a high-level commander long submerged in the relatively sedentary existence of a military occupying authority. Hennecke lived in a villa situated over his underground Navy headquarters. When Allied bombers appeared, seeking out the small, fast German torpedo craft that were based in Cherbourg, Admiral Hennecke merely had to go down the stairs from his villa to the absolute safety of the subterranean war room.

As Admiral Hennecke's aides drew open the blackout curtains with the arrival of dawn, they were afforded a view of a vast sweep of the English Channel from the spacious living room where the naval commander often hosted nocturnal champagne-filled parties for his officers and their wives or French girlfriends. Sumptuous meals (by wartime standards in Europe) were served in Hennecke's dining room, and talented guests would play the finely tuned piano that filled one corner.

But the German admiral did more than entertain himself and others. Several times each day he trouped into the underground tunnel which, although only partially completed, was an elaborate facility. In one tunnel running off at an angle from the main room was a fully equipped military field hospital, while another tunnel angling off in the opposite direction led to an assortment of command posts, situation and map rooms. There were direct telephone lines to each artillery and coastal battery on the Cotentin Peninsula—and even a direct line to the Führer's headquarters at *Wolfsschanze* (Wolf's Lair) near Rastenburg in East Prussia and to the Nazi leader's chalet at Berchtesgaden in the Bavarian Alps.

The direct lines leading to Adolf Hitler dramatized the curious German command structure in France. If need be, the Führer could bypass the other Wehrmacht levels of command.

Almost nightly Admiral Hennecke dispatched Cherbourg-based torpedo craft, called E-boats by the British, into the English Channel to raid Allied shipping. Most E-boats were 105-foot vessels of a type similar to the American PT boats that had been used with devastating effect against the Japanese in the Pacific.

Hennecke and von Schlieben in recent weeks had been reassured by the bustling construction progress on heavy concrete and steel fortifications guarding the harbor and its approaches. Large-caliber guns fairly bristled around the old port where in peacetime the great luxury ocean liners *Queen Mary, Queen Elizabeth,* and the *Normandie,* had discharged carefree passengers.

During the drab, melancholy days of February 1944, Field Marshal von Rundstedt, the German Commander in Chief in the West, was quietly enjoying the courtly life of a country gentleman at the ornate Chateau of Saint Germain, just outside once glamorous Paris. He had grown increasingly disspirited over Hitler's relentless demands from far-off Wolf's Lair, and with the arrival of the young and energetic Erwin Rommel in France, von Rundstedt had nearly abandoned attention to the strengthening of the Atlantic Wall.

Von Rundstedt did little to conceal his contempt for the German dictator. He referred to Hitler as "the Bohemian corporal" (from the Führer's First World War status as an infantry lance corporal) and to the Nazi Brownshirts as "those brown scum." Yet the dignified marshal held Hitler's respect—and his command in the West—due to von Rundstedt's exceptional performance in leading the German legions to smashing victories in Poland and France, and in the early days of the invasion of Russia.

When the weather was favorable, von Rundstedt enjoyed walks in his Saint-Germain gardens, and he was fond of long lunches in his favorite French restaurant, *Coq Hardi.* As time passed by, the old Prussian marshal slipped more and more into figurehead status.

"See that guard at the front gate?" a philosophical von Rundstedt observed to a visitor. "I cannot move him to the other side of the house without Hitler's personal permission."

At this time in late February, Erwin Johannes Eugen Rommel, *Der Junge Marschall* (the Boy Marshal), was taking a short leave at his home in the picturesque Swabian village of Herrlingen, perched on a hillside four miles outside Ulm, in southern Germany. Rommel had made the trip mainly to console his beloved wife Lucie Maria who was lonely, in common with millions of other wives and mothers in the Third Reich in its fifth year of war.

22

It was a particularly difficult time for Frau Rommel. The Rommels' only child, fifteen-year-old Manfred, along with others in his age bracket in a Germany rapidly dwindling in manpower, had recently been called up as a Luftwaffe Auxiliary and assigned to an antiaircraft battery. He and his youthful comrades, together with elderly men, were charged with shooting down the swarms of Allied heavy bombers that had been pulverizing the Reich with increasing intensity in recent months.

Blessed with boundless energy and enthusiasm, Rommel, who had become Germany's youngest field marshal two years before at age forty-nine, refused to admit it even to himself, but he was near exhaustion from the tremendous burden that had been placed on his shoulders—the responsibility for defeating the looming Allied assault. He knew in his heart that it was an impossible task. Only Lucie Maria knew the immense strain he had been under.

For weeks, in his Mercedes 230 sedan, Rommel had been dashing up and down the long coastline of Northwest Europe, at all hours of the day and night, seven days a week. He talked with generals and privates, praised, cajoled, or criticized, supervised the construction of beach obstacles and mine fields, helped set up artillery fields of fire, and shuffled troop dispositions. Rommel didn't believe he could halt the Anglo-American juggernaut at the shoreline; he hoped only to make the Allies pay a fearful price when they struck.

Now, on leave at his home in Herrlingen, Rommel greeted a visitor, Dr. Karl Stroelin, a long-time friend and *Oberburgermeister* of Stuttgart. Unknown to Rommel, Stroelin had long been a conspirator in an ultrasecret group known as the *Schwarze Kapelle* (Black Orchestra), a group of German officers and civilian leaders dedicated to overthrowing Adolf Hitler.

Rommel remained expressionless as his old friend outlined the work of the *Schwarze Kapelle*. Then Dr. Stroelin loosed a bombshell: the group intended to seize the Führer, bring him to trial or execute him, and seek a separate peace with the United States and Great Britain.

Such a drastic action, Stroelin cautioned, could result in civil war in the Fatherland and a bloody fight between the German army and the SS *unless* a widely respected, dominating public figure surfaced immediately to lend his name to the conspiracy. That dominating figure, Stroelin explained, had to be Erwin Rommel.

Old friend or not, it was a perilous proposal Dr. Stroelin was making—high treason to the Nazi state. Had he misjudged Rommel's moral fiber, Stroelin would have been in Gestapo custody by nightfall.

The young marshal sat in silence, deep in thought. Clearly he was agonizing. Stroelin continued his persuasive effort. "You are our greatest and most popular general and more respected abroad than any other," the Stuttgart mayor declared. "You are the only one who can prevent civil war in the Third Reich."

By now Erwin Rommel's mind was in a turmoil. Everything he was he owed to the Führer. He had taken a sacred oath of loyalty to Germany and to Hitler, had commanded the Führer's elite bodyguard, and had received his marshal's baton personally from the Nazi leader.

Yet, a statement once uttered by Adolf Hitler himself returned time and again to haunt Rommel: "When the government of a nation is leading it to its doom, rebellion is not only the right but the duty of every citizen."

As Dr. Stroelin looked on in silence, Rommel finally stated, "I believe it is my duty to come to the rescue of Germany."

Riding back to his headquarters at La Roche-Guyon the following day, the field marshal had time to reflect upon the extraordinary position in which he found himself. He was determined to contact General Eisenhower, the Allied Supreme Commander, at the earliest possible moment to forestall the bloodshed certain to erupt soon on the beaches and among the hedgerows of northwestern Europe. He was convinced that the Western Allies would promptly grasp any reasonable offer of peace.

Rommel felt that once Hitler was effectively neutralized, the United States and Great Britain would join with Germany against the Russian hordes who, at that very moment, were assailing the eastern gates of the Reich.

If the two English-speaking powers refused a negotiated separate peace with a Third Reich minus Hitler, then Field Marshal Rommel intended to inflict the greatest degree of carnage possible on the Allied invaders. Perhaps then Roosevelt and Churchill would listen to reason.

Only a couple of hundred miles north of Rommel's headquarters at La Roche-Guyon in the fashionable Mayfair section of London, another overburdened military commander was staying up late on a cold February night. General Dwight Eisenhower, the Kansas farm boy who in less than two years had risen from obscurity as a lieutenant colonel to world renown, was relaxing in his private quarters in a townhouse known as Hayes Lodge. A cheerful log fire was burning briskly at one end of the room where he sat at a small desk he used for personal correspondence.

Six weeks before, Eisenhower had slipped quietly into London after a flight from the United States to assume an awesome assignment—

Supreme Commander of Operation Overlord, the combined Anglo-American invasion of Nazi Europe and the most massive undertaking of its kind ever mounted. In his role as commander in chief of all Allied ground, sea, and air forces in Europe, the fifty-four-year-old, blue-eyed Eisenhower had become one of the world's most powerful men.

Although the affable, chain-smoking Eisenhower, who had a mule-skinner's vocabulary when angered, had been at his new post less than two weeks, he was already figuratively staggering under the tremendous burden. The Supreme Commander (known to fellow officers as Ike), disliked writing in longhand, but now took up his pen to reveal to wife Mamie, back in Washington, D.C., the exhausting scope of his office.

"If I could give you an exact diary account of the past week," he confided to his wife, mother of the couple's only child, son John, "you'd get some idea of what a flea on a hot griddle really does."

Spies Along the Atlantic Wall

2

On February 16, Supreme Headquarters Allied Expeditionary Force (SHAEF) in London was visited by a delegation of young officers from the War Department in Washington; they had arrived as special emissaries of the Chief of Staff, General George C. Marshall. The delegation came to do a selling job: an audacious proposal for the deployment of American airborne troops in the impending assault on Hitler's *Festung Europa,* Fortress Europe.

The co-architects of the daring plan were Marshall himself, who in a forty-year career had never commanded troops in the field, and General Henry H. "Hap" Arnold, the leader of the Army Air Corps.

The Marshall-Arnold plan called for a parachute drop and glider landing by the U.S. 82nd and 101st Airborne Divisions between Evreux and Dreux on the night of D-Day minus 1. In that region, 40 miles west of Paris and some 70 miles from the nearest Allied landing beaches along the Calvados coast, were four airfields. The parachutists and glidermen would seize the airfields, and two additional conventional infantry divisions would be flown in by transport planes before dawn on D-Day plus 1.

The logistical task would be enormous. Supplying the force isolated 70 miles inland would require twelve hundred and fifty tons a day; the material would be delivered by 600 C-47s flying by night and two hundred heavy bombers operating by day.

After consolidating its airhead, the American force would attack and seize crossings over the Seine River below Paris. The operation would, the plan pointed out, create another front in France besides the coastal landing.

Anticipating protests from combat commanders, General Marshall admitted that a mass parachute and glider operation so far from friendly ground forces had never been attempted before. "Frankly, that reaction makes me sick," the chief of staff declared.

On hearing of the proposed airborne operation near Paris, Lieutenant General Omar N. Bradley also became "sick"—and stunned. As commander of First Army, the mild-mannered, professorial Missourian held the direct responsibility for the prompt capture of the crucial, heavily fortified port of Cherbourg. He had long insisted that the crack 82nd and 101st Airborne Divisions should be dropped behind Utah Beach at the neck of the Cotentin Peninsula. The mission of these two outfits would be to help the 4th Infantry Division get ashore on Utah and to prevent the Germans from reinforcing the Cherbourg defenses.

If the enemy succeeded in pouring troops into the Cotentin Peninsula from other parts of France once the Allies were ashore, the port of Cherbourg, so desperately needed by the invaders, could hold out indefinitely, Bradley believed. If the Germans held onto Cherbourg until September, the unpredictable weather in the English Channel could create havoc with Allied supplies and reinforcements efforts, since those needs were being brought in over open landing beaches. Bradley was convinced that failure to rapidly capture Cherbourg could even spell disaster for the entire Overlord operation.

"I've got to have the 82nd and 101st Airborne Divisions in the Cotentin Peninsula or I'll propose calling off the whole Utah Beach assault," the spectacled First Army commander exploded to Eisenhower.

General Marshall's bright-eyed, zealous young officers from Washington ran into a stone wall at every turn in their effort to "sell" the Evreux-Dreux airborne plan. Outspoken, blunt British Field-Marshal Bernard Law Montgomery, commander of Allied ground forces for the assault, declared, "It's nonsense. A commander to win a battle must concentrate his forces. We need those airborne troops in Normandy, not off seventy miles."

At Braunstone Parke in Leicestershire, Major General Matthew B. Ridgway, commanding the veteran 82nd Airborne Division, and the leader of his parachute elements, 36-year-old Brigadier General James M. Gavin, studied the plan in wide-eyed amazement. "A suicide mission," they concluded.

As Ridgway and Gavin saw the plan, the lightly armed paratroopers and glidermen would be deposited in the midst of at least two German panzer divisions being held in reserve in the Paris region west of the Seine.

The American airborne men would have no artillery, armor, or antitank guns to ward off enemy tanks.

General Eisenhower, the supreme commander, had been placed in a delicate position. The airborne plan had been conceived and was enthusiastically endorsed by his boss and mentor, George Marshall. But after intensive discussions with his staff and battle commanders, Eisenhower joined in their unanimous rejection.

Responding frankly, but careful to direct his remarks to the co-architect of the plan, Hap Arnold, rather than to the chief of staff, the man to whom the supreme commander owed his meteoric rise, Eisenhower wrote: "It would be a good idea to ponder how long the airhead would last [70] miles from the nearest harbor and surrounded by German panzer divisions."

No more was heard of the Evreux-Dreux airborne plan.

Meanwhile an American parachute officer browsing through the bookstalls of a London store spotted a volume entitled *Paratroopers*. His professional curiosity piqued, the officer picked up the book and saw that its author was Major F. O. Miksche, a Czechoslovakian belonging to a unit of the Free French forces in England.

Leafing through the pages, the American noticed that it contained a summary of German airborne operations. As he continued to scrutinize the book, he felt his heart skip a beat as he stared intently at a full-page map. Major Miksche had drawn the map to illustrate a story on a hypothetical Allied airborne assault that would spearhead an invasion of continental Europe across the English Channel. The hypothetical plan, as dramatized by the map, showed the divisions landing in three zones, two of which were almost precisely where the 82nd and 101st Airborne Divisions would touch down in the D-Day invasion at the base of the Cotentin Peninsula. The third zone was only a few miles off target.

The chilling discovery sent shockwaves of concern through the American airborne encampments in England as well as the rarified atmosphere of SHAEF in Grosvenor Square. There was little doubt that Major Miksche's book *Paratroopers* was in the hands of the German high command. The question was: would the Wehrmacht consider the theoretical Cotentin airborne plan an incredible Allied security leak and would the Germans pack the peninsula with additional troops?

As high-level planning and troop training in the field continued at a constantly accelerated pace, a violent dispute erupted at the headquarters of 21st Army Group, which would command ground forces in Overlord, and which served as a planning center for the invasion. The argument was between two top commanders, one British and one American, and it threatened to shake the foundations of Allied solidarity.

Touching off the heated debate at an airborne planning session was a proposal by British Air Marshal Sir Trafford Leigh-Mallory, air commander for Overlord, who ranked just below Supreme Commander Dwight Eisenhower and his deputy. Leigh-Mallory's startling proposal: cancel the parachute and glider assault by the U.S. 82nd and 101st Airborne Divisions on the Cotentin Peninsula in support of the campaign to rapidly capture the crucial port of Cherbourg.

"I cannot approve your plans," Leigh-Mallory told General Omar Bradley. "Your losses will be far more than what your gains are worth. I cannot go along with you."

Bradley was stunned. "Very well, sir," the soft-spoken American replied, "if you insist on cutting out the airborne attack, then I must ask that we eliminate the Utah assault. I am not going to land on that beach without making sure we've got the exits behind it."

Now it was Leigh-Mallory's turn to be stunned. After a moment's silence, he responded, "Then let me make it clear. If you insist upon the airborne operation, you'll do it in spite of my opposition."

The British air marshal turned to Montgomery, "If General Bradley insists upon going ahead he will have to accept full responsibility for the operation."

Bradley quickly cut in: "That's perfectly okay. I'm in the habit of accepting full responsibility for my operations."

Montgomery, finding himself in the curious role of inter-Allied peacemaker, rapped for order. "That's not at all necessary, gentlemen. I'll accept responsibility."

The two-division American airborne assault behind Utah was still on—at least for the present.

Late in February, General Eisenhower summoned Bradley to his office. Air Marshal Leigh-Mallory had gone to the Supreme Commander to pursue his crusade to have the American parachute and glider attack cancelled. Now Eisenhower sought Bradley's view.

General Bradley, soft-spoken, rough-hewn, his features possessed a rare combination of deep feeling for his men and an inner strength to make difficult decisions affecting their lives. Hearing of Leigh-Mallory's refusal to accept the conference table defeat after the verbal fireworks at Field-Marshal Montgomery's meeting, the normally mild Bradley was furious.

"Of course the airborne attack is risky," the First Army commander agreed. "But not half so risky as a seaborne landing without it."

Bradley told Eisenhower that he agreed that Leigh-Mallory's lumbering, low-flying C-47s packed with American paratroopers would be fired on from the ground the minute they were over the Cotentin Peninsula, and he concurred with the Air Commander that the Normandy hedgerow country would make glider landings costly. But, Bradley stressed, those risks of war must be subordinated to the primary objective of the invasion—the early capture of Cherbourg.

"If we could accomplish the mission without them, I certainly would not risk the lives of seventeen thousand airborne men," General Bradley told Eisenhower. "But I will willingly risk them to insure against failure for Overlord."

General Eisenhower, confronted with divergent views from his air and ground commanders, debated the issue and ruled in favor of the Cotentin Peninsula parachute and glider attack ahead of the Utah Beach seaborne landing. That seemed to end the dispute.

It was a chilly day early in March as Jacques Bertin, a young member of the French aristocracy with the exalted title *Comte de la Hautière,* was pedaling furiously on his battered old bicycle northward along the eastern coast of the Cotentin Peninsula, bound for Cherbourg. Six feet two, blond haired and handsome, the count had urgent business to attend to in the bustling, German-occupied port city. He had something else, also—a price on his head, put there by the Gestapo.

For nearly two years the young aristocrat, whose code name was Jacques Moulines, had been a man without a home. He was constantly on the go, always in danger of being trapped, seldom sleeping in the same house two nights in a row. Moulines was in charge of operations on the Cotentin Peninsula for *Centurie,* a network of thousands of amateur spies in Normandy whose job it was to report on enemy defenses, installations, and troops.

Moulines, a carefree young pilot in peacetime, was wearing his customary old leather flight jacket and he was hatless. Of all the organizers for Centurie in Normandy, Moulines' task was the most difficult, and perilous. Cherbourg, and some 60 square miles around it, were saturated with fortifications; German vigilance was intense. There were nearly thirty-nine thousand troops in and around the city.

If the Germans were vigilant, the count was doubly so—his life depended upon it. On entering a bistro, Moulines had to loiter inconspicuously until he learned if local residents were ordering alcoholic beverages that day. On arbitrary occasions, the Gestapo, seeking to identify outsiders, would suddenly forbid cafes and bistros to sell alcoholic beverages, a fact known to natives of the community but not to outsiders. Bartenders, under threat of arrest, were forced to report anyone who ordered wine or beer.

Moulines always entered Cherbourg wheeling his bicycle, because on certain irregular days the German authorities would suddenly forbid riding two-wheeled vehicles (pushing a bicycle was acceptable). Entering a cafe to eat, the young aristocrat glanced furtively about to see if locals were ordering meat; on some days the Gestapo ordered meat withheld.

Admiring agents claimed that Jacques Moulines was devoid of nerves. One night he slept soundly on a cot in the back room of a dingy Cherbourg bistro, a rough drawing of a German gun position in his pocket, as German soldiers in the front room drank boisterously throughout the night. One factor kept him from a slow, agonizing death dangling by a piano wire noose in a Gestapo torture chamber: despite relentless efforts for two years to trap the underground "terrorist" named Jacques Moulines, the German's had not the slightest clue to his description or identity. Certainly a playboy member of the French aristocracy would not possess the gumption for such hazardous and demanding ventures.

Centurie had been founded in late 1942, one of the spy networks under General Charles de Gaulle, who led the Free French in England. It was known as the *Bureau de Contre Espionnage, Renseignements et d'Action* (BCRA) and was created and commanded by Captain Andre Dewavrin (code-named Colonel Passy, after a well-known Paris subway station).

Soon afterward a powerfully built former soldier named Marcel Girard, who worked as a traveling sales executive for a cement firm in Caen, the historic capital of Normandy, was recruited to head Centurie. Forty-one, graying, looking older than his years but possessing enormous energy and initiative, Girard (code-named Moureau) plunged into the prodigious assignment, using his job as a cover. Only his patriotic boss knew that the sales executive never sold one pound of cement.

Girard roamed the Normandy coast. From Ouistreham on the Calvados coast westward through Coursuelles, Arromanches, Colleville, Vierville, and Port-en-Bessein, then northward up the eastern coast of the Cotentin Peninsula to Cherbourg and on to the Cap de la Hague. Always he was under the threat of imminent arrest, but he continued to bring in new recruits—farmers, housewives, train conductors, plumbers, mechanics, government officials, policemen, secretaries—all of whom became instant spies.

No one in Centurie ever had an inkling that one day powerful Allied forces would storm ashore along these Normandy beaches to be code-named Utah, Omaha, Sword, Gold, and Juno. Many of the spies were sustained in their efforts by religious faith.

In late 1942, the innovative Marcel Girard startled other Centurie leaders with a proposal that they create a large map of the Atlantic Wall in Normandy. He proposed that thousands of ordinary French men and women along the coast serve as the eyes and ears for the map project and they pass their bits and pieces of information on the Wall to a central collecting point in Caen. There skilled cartographers belonging to the network would incorporate the thousands of scraps of data into a detailed map that would depict the entire area extending from Cap de la Hague at the northwest tip of the Cotentin Peninsula all the way to Ouistreham, 100 miles to the east.

A major impediment to the recruiting of operatives along the coast was posed by the *Zone Interdite* (Forbidden Zone) set up by the Germans; it ran inland for several miles. A liaison agent would have to have a legitimate reason for lingering around a restricted area. But this problem was quickly solved when each recruiting agent was furnished with a set of official German identity papers and passes—all painstakingly counterfeited by a thirty-eight-year-old Caen housewife.

As March 1944 arrived, the master map of the Atlantic Wall in Normandy was already incredibly detailed and precise. The Germans, too, had assisted the mapping project by unwittingly providing information on areas it was virtually impossible for agents to reach, the crucial ports. When the Germans built a new fortification in Cherbourg, they notified the French civilian agency responsible for operating the port. There, agents of Centurie surreptitiously traced the German drawings and within hours the new construction or gun battery was part of the master Atlantic Wall map.

Nearly every day bits of information on German defenses and troop dispositions arrived at a central collection point in Caen, a city of some forty-two thousand, a few miles inland. There a courier would collect the large bundle of notes, diagrams, drawings and other data and carry it, usually by train, to a dingy suite of rooms in an old building located in a rundown section of Paris.

These inconspicuous quarters were Centurie's central headquarters for the Battle of the Atlantic Wall. A bespectacled, round-faced young Frenchman named Jacques Piette (code-named *Colonel Personne,* French for "Nobody") directed the operation of the spy network's communications center. Here, dedicated checkers daily sifted through the mountain of material collected by the spies in Normandy and bundled it for transfer to intelligence agencies across the Channel.

Lysander aircraft, flown by Royal Air Force pilots, landed under a blanket of darkness at predesignated pastures outside Paris. The planes taxied up to signalling flashlights held by French Underground agents, collected the bundles of Centurie Atlantic Wall data and maps, sped down the grassy field, and lifted off for England.

On reaching London, the raw Centurie data was picked up by agents of Colonel Passy and was taken to a dingy basement in a dilapidated building. There the information was studied and catalogued; summaries labeled *Most Secret* were distributed to top military and government leaders.

Outside London, in a tightly guarded facility known as the Martian Room, a mammoth, detailed master map of 100 miles of Normandy coastline and the Atlantic Wall was being pieced together from thousands of scraps of information gathered by Centurie agents. The map, updated daily, showed an amazing array of German defenses between Cherbourg and Ouistreham.

Plotted in were the precise locations of coast and field artillery batteries, their caliber, ranges, and fields of fire and thickness of protective concrete covers; radar sites, machine-gun posts, flamethrowers, tank obstacles, and mine fields; blockhouses, command posts, tunnels, signal communications, barbed-wire entanglements, barracks, supply dumps, and vehicle parks.

Even the positions of defending German units, down to platoon and squad levels, were being inked in, together with the names of their officers.

When the time came for the Allies to strike, General Eisenhower and his commanders would have more detailed data on the Atlantic Wall at their fingertips than would German commanders in France.

Unwitting Treason in German High Command

3

Blacked-out, bomb-battered Berlin lay ghost-like and tense the night of March 20. Fearful citizens huddled in their homes, in concrete shelters, or deep in subway tunnels, straining to hear the first faint hum of powerful airplane motors and the eerie wail of sirens that would foretell the nearly nightly appearance of the Royal Air Force.

Safely inside a conference room in the subterranean chambers of the Oberkommando der Wehrmacht (armed forces high command), a gathering of top German military leaders in the West and their aides were idly chatting. They awaited the presence of Adolf Hitler.

They were all there:

Aristocratic, aging Field Marshal von Rundstedt, clutching tightly his gold, jewel-embedded marshal's baton. He was Commander in Chief, West, yet that position was now only titular.

Energetic, dashing Field Marshal Rommel, folk hero of the Third Reich. As commander of Army Group B he was technically subordinate to von Rundstedt. But he reported directly to Hitler. Rommel rarely carried his marshal's baton.

General of Panzer Troops Leo Geyr Frieherr von Schweppenburg, young, handsome, haughty. The commander of Panzer Army West, he was in charge of armored divisions in France and the Low Countries.

Bull-necked, red-faced Field Marshal Hugo Sperrle, resplendent in his blue Luftwaffe uniform with gold braid. Sperrle commanded Luftflotte 3 which consisted of all bombers and fighter planes in the West.

Admiral Theodor Krancke, commander of Naval Group, West.

Each of these leaders had an independent command. When the Allies struck, von Rundstedt and Rommel would have to "request" the deployment of tank, sea, and air forces. In the case of von Schweppenburg, he could not commit panzer units without the personal approval of Hitler, the supreme commander.

Hitler was aware of the built-in dangers of this overlapping and splintered command structure in the West. He knew that every minute lost in deploying German ground, sea, and air forces would make it more difficult to repel the Allied onslaught. But there was a greater danger he feared: concentrating too much military power in the hands of any one man. At this stage of the war the Führer trusted few of his generals and admirals.

Suddenly the buzz of conversation in the underground conference room subsided and all leaped to their feet. Hitler strode briskly into the chamber, followed by his two confidants, Field Marshal Wilhelm Keitel and Colonel General Alfred Jodl.

Keitel, aloof, haughty, and humorless, held the title of Chief of the Oberkommando der Wehrmacht (OKW), but that exalted title was deceptive. OKW in fact consisted of a number of high-ranking officers who clustered about Hitler. It was Hitler who made the decisions. Many of Keitel's officers, privately, called him "*Lackeitel*"—German for lacky.

Jodl had held his office, Chief of the OKW Operations Staff, since the beginning of the war. He was the officer designated to translate Hitler's strategic decisions into field orders.

A hush fell over the room as the fifty-five-year-old Hitler began speaking. He was a spellbinding orator. The galaxy of German military stars, sitting ramrod straight in wooden chairs, listened intently. As Hitler's recitation became more impassioned, his face turned crimson and tiny beads of perspiration dotted his forehead and upper lip around his black brush mustache.

"It is evident that an Anglo-American landing in the West will and must come," he declared. "How and where it will come, no one knows for sure. At no place along our long front is a landing impossible, in view of the Allies' control of the sea.

"The enemy assault must be liquidated within a few hours. Under no circumstances must it be allowed to last longer than a matter of hours or, at most, days. This would prevent the reelection of Roosevelt who, with luck, would finish up somewhere in jail. Churchill, too, has grown old and would be finished, because the Allies could never launch another invasion."

When Hitler resumed, he startled his commanders: "The first Allied objective would be to obtain a large port. The most suitable and hence the most threatened areas are the two west coast peninsulas, Cherbourg and Brest, which are very tempting and offer the best possibility for the formation of a bridgehead, which would then be enlarged systematically. . . ."

Cherbourg? Brest? That was the first the commanders in the West had heard of these priority targets in Wehrmacht projections. Up to that moment, opinion had been nearly unanimous that the Allies would strike across the narrow Strait of Dover at the Pas-de-Calais. Although German defenses and troop formations were stronger in the Pas-de-Calais than anywhere else in Northwest Europe, it was believed that the Allies would accept that risk in order to land closer to the crucial Ruhr industrial region and to the heart of Germany—Berlin.

The supreme commander had made his strategic views known. As soon as the meeting adjourned, work was intensified along the coast of Normandy—a fact promptly reported to London by Centurie. More troops were brought in. The crack Panzer Lehr Division was rushed to the Normandy area all the way from Hungary, and the battle-tested 21st Panzer Division was transferred from Brittany to Normandy, in the vicinity of Caen.

Word that the Germans were building up defenses in Normandy increased a subtle pall of deep concern that had started to haunt the higher councils of the Allied command as D-Day inched inexorably closer. It was seldom brought out into the open, but SHAEF officers knew that there was a real possibility that Overlord might have to be cancelled.

At a staff conference late in March, Major General Walter B. "Beetle" Smith, Eisenhower's Chief of Staff and alter ego, could not restrain the gloom he felt inside. As the others listened in astonishment, Smith observed solemnly that the Germans had 12 mobile divisions in the Normandy landing sectors, and suggested that a decision on bringing needed landing craft to England from the Mediterranean should be "held up." The startling inference was made by those present.

Smith's pessimism was still evident a few days later in a conversation over a scrambler telephone with a War Department general in Washington. "We may find that we can't do Overlord," General Smith confided. "The buffer of German divisions confronting us across the Channel is just now approaching the absolute maximum we can handle."

In a hushed tone, Smith added ominously: "Do you see what I mean?"

"Precisely," responded the worried voice on the other end of the line.

As March turned into April and the lush meadows of England were putting on their finest greenery, an epidemic was breaking out in the ranks of American assault troops—fear of enormous D-Day casualties. Doom and gloom had set in.

At an encampment of the 4th Infantry Division, which would hit Utah Beach at the base of the Cotentin Peninsula, one soldier completely went to pieces and was dragged away screaming, "We'll all be killed! They'll use our bodies to walk ashore over!"

It was a debilitating experience for other Ivy Division soldiers who had seen and heard the tragic episode. By nightfall, word of the youth's breakdown had swept through the entire division in Devonshire. Major General Raymond O. "Tubby" Barton, aware of the deteriorating morale in his division, tried to counteract it, in vain.

Major General J. Lawton "Lightning Joe" Collins, the youthful, indefatigable commander of the U.S. VII Corps, which was charged with the early capture of the port of Cherbourg, each day rode the narrow, twisting byways of southern England, visiting his troops. They were scattered all the way from an area southeast of London westward to Wales.

Each night the peppery, silver-haired corps commander returned to his headquarters in the port of Plymouth after an exhausting day of troop inspections with his aide, Captain John Walsh. One question tore at General Collins: "Will these green American soldiers be able to stand up to the challenge of the Atlantic Wall their first time under fire?" He shared this concern with no one.

First Army commander Omar Bradley was startled when he visited the 29th Infantry Division, which would assault Omaha: Virtually the entire fourteen thousand-man force talked of 90 percent casualties. Bradley ordered division officers and noncoms to gather around him.

"This stuff about tremendous losses on D-Day is a bunch of tommyrot," the soft-spoken Bradley stressed. "Some of you won't come back, but it'll be very few."

He had hoped to allay the intense fears that had hovered over the 29th Division like a thick pall. "I doubt that I did much good," he confided to an aide.

General Eisenhower himself returned to his quarters after a lengthy and exhausting visit to several assault elements. He was depressed by what he had seen.

"There's an absence of toughness and alertness on the part of the young

American officers I saw on the trip," the supreme commander penned in his diary. "They're as green as growing grass. How will they act in battle?"

Eisenhower was even more concerned about some of the senior officers who would command regiments in the invasion: "They are fat, gray and oldish. Most of them wear the Rainbow Ribbon of the last war and are still fighting it."

Meanwhile, more verbal fireworks broke out between two high-ranking commanders: one British, the other American. Allied brass had assembeled in Field-Marshal Montgomery's 21st Army Group headquarters in St. Paul's School, London, on April 7. As commander of initial ground operations in Normandy, Montgomery proposed to review Neptune in the plan's final version. Neptune was the code name for the assault phase of Overlord.

Even before the meeting convened, while the officers were milling about, a dispute erupted between General Bradley and Field-Marshal Montgomery.

A large relief map of Normandy and its landing beaches, all the way up the Cotentin Peninsula to the primary invasion target of Cherbourg, was positioned on a tilted platform. What caught Bradley's eye and raised his hackles were the neatly drawn phase lines on the map.

In keeping with his tactical concepts of a neat, set-piece battle, Montgomery had insisted that phase lines for expansion of the initial bridgehead, lines which should be reached on designated days, be part of the invasion plan. Bradley strongly opposed what he considered a timid approach to battle, believing that commanders should enter an action with the expectation of breaking through for long gains if the opportunity arose.

"At least I do not want phase lines in the American sector," Bradley had stressed previously. He thought that the British field marshal had reluctantly agreed with him.

Now, in St. Paul's School, Bradley spotted the phase lines drawn in. He approached Montgomery and angrily demanded that the lines be erased— "at least in the American sector." Montgomery, his face reddened with anger, finally agreed.

It was not the first Montgomery–Bradley dispute. It would not be the last one.

As the Allies in England continued to feud, at his chateau perched on a lofty Bavarian mountaintop, Adolf Hitler rejoiced. His scientists had just advised him that a new "secret weapon" had been perfected and was now operational.

Code-named V-1, the secret weapon would soon be crashing down onto London. The V-1 was a pilotless aircraft containing explosives equivalent to a four thousand-pound blockbuster bomb. Built by Volkswagen, the V-1 traveled at 440 miles an hour, far faster than any Allied fighter plane. Its engine would be timed to cut off over a target, after which it would crash to earth. It was believed that there would be no defense against the V-1.

"This will bring England to its knees!" Hitler jubilantly told his aides. "America then would never go it alone."

The precise time for showering London with the death-dealing pilotless bombs was a decision given to von Rundstedt. He set the initial launching for one minute past midnight on June 16.

Neither Hitler nor von Rundstedt had any way of knowing that by that launching date the Western Allies planned to be ashore in strength on continental Europe.

Although Hitler had told his generals on March 20 that the Allies probably would strike in Normandy to capture the crucial port of Cherbourg, he expected a second major landing in the Pas-de-Calais. That stretch of coastline, across from Britain's famed White Cliffs of Dover, was the most heavily fortified section of the Atlantic Wall. It was manned by the strong Fifteenth Army, commanded by Colonel General Hans von Salmuth. Under no circumstances, Hitler proclaimed, was Rommel to strip the Fifteenth Army of troops or weapons to strengthen Normandy if the Allies stormed ashore there.

The Führer had a second critical reason for strongly defending the Pas-de-Calais: it was in that region of France, only 20 miles from England, that most of the concrete launching pads for the V-1s had been constructed.

Hitler's determination to keep the powerful Fifteenth Army in place to repel an Allied assault, even if the invaders landed in Normandy, had been influenced by a highly complicated and ingenious Allied deception plan— a stratagem code-named Fortitude. Through a variety of means, Fortitude was intended to disperse German forces and delay their reaction to the only Allied main landing. To achieve this crucial goal, Hitler and his commanders would have to be convinced that the Allies planned other major landings.

The outcome of the war hinged on the success or failure of Fortitude. The massive deception plan would have to completely mislead Hitler and his generals. But the Germans were cunning, resourceful and long schooled in the nuances of intelligence. Should they see through the Allied stratagem, they would know that Normandy would be the focus of the Allies' main effort, and large elements of the Fifteenth Army would be rushed to the Normandy landing beaches to drive the invaders back into the Channel.

The centerpiece of the massive Allied plan to deceive Hitler was Quicksilver, the fabrication of an entire army group that was to appear to consist of more than a million men in 49 divisions. This phantom force was "stationed" in southeastern England, across from the Pas-de-Calais. Known as the First United States Army Group (FUSAG), this fictitious organization's mission was to keep the German Fifteenth Army in place at the Pas-de-Calais.

FUSAG was an elaborate deception, on a scale never before undertaken in warfare. The fictitious force was supplied with landing craft, tanks, artillery and trucks—all of inflatable rubber. Some facilities were discreetly poorly camouflaged to be photographed by Luftwaffe reconnaissance planes.

The air over southeastern England crackled with the flood of bogus radio messages which were passed back and forth between nonexistent command posts. Often a "careless" wireless operator would send a message in the clear. All of this immense amount of radio traffic was closely monitored by the Germans across the Strait of Dover.

Although Quicksilver was a clever stratagem, a crucial requirement to inject authenticity into FUSAG was that it had to have a real "live" commander. That commander was at hand—Lieutenant General George S. Patton, Jr. Not only was Patton in England, but he was "available" for the critical assignment; he had been in General Eisenhower's doghouse since the previous July when the impetuous, high-strung genius of armor had, in a moment of pique, slapped an American soldier who Patton thought was malingering.

The choice of Patton as commander of the phantom army group had a built-in advantage: the Germans regarded the hard-drinking general as America's most audacious and gifted combat commander. Steeped in the autocratic traditions of their own army, German leaders could not comprehend that the Allies would deprive themselves of a Patton for the impending assault merely because he had slapped a lowly private.

Patton was the key to pinpointing Allied intentions for the *Grossinvasion,* the German high command was convinced. Undoubtedly, Patton would command the main effort. The Allies would be foolish to leave their star player on the bench.

Tall, trim, devout, and at the same time profane, General Patton held mixed feelings about his Overlord assignment. On the one hand, he was despondent because he would not be leading assault elements ashore in history's most spectacular military operation. On the other hand, the fifty-nine-year-old general relished the role of intrigue to which he had been assigned. "I'm a natural born goddamned ham," he told aides.

Patton played his role to the hilt. He dashed about England and Scotland while presumably energetically preparing to lead Army Group Patton against the Nazis. With his ramrod straight posture; lacquered helmet liner; a total of fifteen stars gleaming from his headgear, shirt collar, and shoulders; boots polished to a high gloss; an ivory-handled revolver on one hip; and roaring out commands to all, Patton would have been difficult for even the most myopic and dull-witted German spy to miss.

In mid-April, Brigadier General James Gavin, parachute elements commander of the U.S. 82nd Airborne Division, strolled into fashionable Claridge's in London at noon one day. There he ran into General Patton in the crowded lobby.

"Hello, Gavin," the general called out. "How in the hell are you?"

After a two-minute chat, Patton began moving for the front door. "Well, I'll see you over in the Pas-de-Calais," he said to Gavin. Patton never could keep his big mouth shut, his colleagues always declared.

A number of means were employed to let the Germans know that Patton was in England. British double agents with such exotic code names as Garbo, Brutus, and Tricycle each independently informed their controllers in the Third Reich that Patton had arrived. These agents had been sent into the British Isles as German spies, caught, and given the choice of sending carefully contrived false information to their masters in Germany or being stood up before a firing squad.

The phantom Army Group Patton hoax was crowned with success when the German army's intelligence gathering and evaluation branch, on March 20 rushed out a bulletin to top Wehrmacht commanders: "It has now been established that General Patton, who is highly regarded for his proficiency, is now in England." Obviously, Patton would be employed to spearhead the looming invasion.

Hitler believed Quicksilver so thoroughly that six weeks after Allied forces stormed ashore in Normandy, Fifteenth Army remained idle along the Pas-de-Calais, a day's motor march away, intently watching for the powerful smash by Army Group Patton.

Skilled and imaginative as were the Allied operators who had conceived and orchestrated Quicksilver, the mammoth deception could not have been achieved without the assistance of a German officer, Colonel Alexis von Roenne. Von Roenne's military record had been impeccable. Yet his unintended complicity would one day allow the Allies to carve out a bridgehead in Normandy while General Hans von Salmuth's Fifteenth Army stood by as spectators.

Colonel von Roenne was chief of the intelligence office *Fremde Heere West* (Foreign Armies, West) (FHW), it was his task to ferret out the Allied order of battle in Great Britain prior to the invasion. If von Roenne were successful in his task, Hitler and his commanders could discern the most logical locale for the Allies' main effort.

Baron von Roenne had long been esteemed for his battlefield gallantry and for his shrewd intelligence evaluations that permitted the Germans to smash the vaunted French army in only six weeks in 1940. Von Roenne's contribution to that victory was officially recognized when Hitler personally awarded him the *Deutsches Kruez,* the German Cross.

Von Roenne appeared to be a natural choice for the crucial task of divining Allied capabilities and intentions. Yet he had grown increasingly disillusioned with the Führer and his clique in Berlin, and had become a conspirator of the Schwarze Kapelle, the secret organization of German military and civil leaders dedicated to overthrowing Hitler and Nazism.

As February 1944 arrived a power struggle erupted among German intelligence agencies; the conflict would play a major role in convincing the high command of the reality of Army Group Patton across the Channel from the Pas-de-Calais.

It had been the practice of von Roenne's FHW to pass its intelligence evaluations to the *Sicherheitsdienst* (SD), the security service of the SS, the elite formation whose members swore an oath of allegiance not to the German state but to Adolf Hitler personally. FHW and SD for months had been involved in a bitter conflict to prove to the Führer that each was the more capable agency.

Confident that they were better qualified to assess incoming information about the enemy than was von Roenne's FHW, the SD invariably cut in half FHW estimates of the number of Allied divisions available in Britain. Hitler believed that the estimates of Allied strength reaching his desk had come from von Roenne, whose evaluations he held in the highest regard. But the reports were von Roenne's strength estimates cut in half by the SD.

Von Roenne was deeply disturbed by the turn of events. Acting on the halved estimates, the Führer was withdrawing divisions from the West for employment on the Russian front at a time von Roenne thought that the

Atlantic Wall should be strengthened. Although a Schwarze Kappelle conspirator, von Roenne was dedicated to inflicting heavy casualties on the Western Allies so that when Hitler was arrested or executed, Field Marshal Rommel and other Schwarze Kappelle leaders would have leverage in seeking a negotiated peace with the United States and Great Britain.

The chief of FHW was at a loss about what to do to resolve the situation. His arch foe, the SD, was powerful. Eventually he decided to take a drastic course of action, one that could cost him his life. Knowing that the SD would halve the estimates in FHW reports, von Roenne began grossly exaggerating Allied strength. When his figures reached the Führer, after having been amended by the SD, the resulting numbers would reflect an accurate assessment.

Early in May von Roenne prepared an exhaustive assessment of Allied strength in Britain. It falsely stated that the Allies had eighty-five to ninety conventional divisions and seven airborne divisions available for the invasion. Actually, there were thirty-two infantry and armored divisions and three airborne divisions. The FHW had to produce evidence of the presence of these ninety-seven Allied divisions, so von Roenne embarked on another dangerous course of action: he used the hundreds of pieces of leaked information fabricated by skilled Allied operatives to substantiate his estimate.

Then an unanticipated event occurred: the SD, for unknown reasons put its mark of approval on the enormously exaggerated estimate of ninety-seven divisions. The report was forwarded to Hitler who, knowing it came from von Roenne, accepted the information as fact. The feud between two German intelligence agencies had fostered official acceptance of the Quicksilver stratagem. Fifteenth Army was pinned down in anticipation of the arrival of Allied divisions Hitler was sure would invade elsewhere than in Normandy.

4

Airborne
Prediction:
Mass Slaughter

I t was near midnight on April 27 as nine German E-boats slipped quietly out of Cherbourg harbor. The squadron was to patrol the English Channel under cloak of night to pounce upon any Allied shipping unfortunate enough to cross its path.

On this night the E-boats came across a target attractive beyond the wildest dreams of its commander. A large convoy of Allied vessels, many crammed with troops of the U.S. 4th Infantry Division, was burrowing through the dark waves on its way from Plymouth to Slapton Sands, an area on the southern coast of England. The convoy was engaged in Operation Tiger, a full dress rehearsal for the Utah Beach assault.

This was a top secret exercise. Aboard the vessels were the actual units to be employed in the Utah operation, as well as such secret weapons as "swimming" tanks and rocket boats.

It was nearing daylight 11 miles off Slapton Sands and almost time for the practice assault on the beach to be launched. The night was dark and clear, and the only sound was a mild rustling of the sea breezes. Suddenly a tremendous explosion erupted in the center of the Allied flotilla, and a brilliant orange flame shot into the black sky. A five-thousand-ton LST (landing ship tank), loaded with 4th Division troops, appeared to leap out of the water. It had been struck amidships by a torpedo fired by one of the Cherbourg E-boats that had silently slipped in among the blacked-out Allied vessels.

The LST caught fire, then exploded. In an instant 151 of the 282 troops and 94 of the 165 sailors on board were killed outright or tossed into the water where they drowned. As the men in a nearby LST looked on in horror, their vessel also was caught in its center by a torpedo; in moments it was blazing from bow to stern, and then it exploded. This blast killed 310 of the 354 soldiers and 114 of the 142 sailors aboard.

By now all was confusion among naval commanders in the Tiger convoy. In the darkness they were unable to determine if the attack was coming from E-boats or submarines. Then there was another loud explosion—a third LST had been struck, four men were killed, twenty-two were wounded, and eight were missing.

Having inflicted a disaster on the Allied convoy, the nine E-boats turned and fled for the protective cover of Cherbourg. News of the catastrophe sent shockwaves among top leaders at SHAEF. Survivors reported E-boats sweeping the waters with searchlights after the LSTs had been sunk and cruising among the wreckage before dashing for home. Had the E-boats fished Allied soldiers and sailors out of the water—including Bigots, the code name of those who had been privy to D-Day secrets? If so, the Germans undoubtedly would find means to make them talk.

The disaster off Slapton Sands less than six weeks before D-Day resulted in day-long discussions in the higher councils of the Allied command. Serious consideration was given to drastically altering the Utah Beach seaborne and airborne assault. As the days went by, General Eisenhower and his commanders became increasingly alarmed that the Tiger debacle could have furnished the Germans with vital information on Neptune. Through Ultra, the ingenious decoding machine, Eisenhower learned that Rommel, only one week after the Slapton Sands event, had rushed two divisions into the Cotentin Peninsula, both specially trained for antiparatrooper duty. Was this a coincidence, or had Hitler reacted to information gained from Tiger survivors fished out of the water?

German reaction to the Tiger catastrophe was not the only security worry to rack those in charge of protecting the D-Day secret. They were confronted with one of such a delicate nature that not even Dwight Eisenhower himself could be advised of it. The target of the security worry: Kay Summersby, a tall, attractive former model in her early 30s who, although a citizen of Ireland, held a lieutenant's commission in the American Women's Army Corps (WACs).

The reason for the intense indecisiveness on the part of Allied security officials was that divorcee Kay Summersby and Supreme Commander Dwight Eisenhower had formed a very close relationship. Since 1942 she had been the general's driver confidante, and social companion. How, perplexed and hard-wringing security agents asked each other, does one approach the Big Boss and tell him that his lady companion was being permitted to violate the strictest security regulations?

It was an open secret in SHAEF that Eisenhower was infatuated with the willowy, vivacious Kay Summersby. Even while wrestling with monumental problems for Overlord, the Supreme Commander had written Chief of Staff George Marshall that he was planning to divorce his wife of many years, Mamie, to marry Mrs. Summersby.

Never was Summersby's loyalty, discretion, or integrity under question by SHAEF security officers. Although Eisenhower had cut through red tape and neatly skirted tradition to secure a commission in the United States Army for a foreign citizen, Kay Summersby, army regulations specifically disqualified her, as a citizen of Eire, from any contact with Overlord information. Yet daily she was at Eisenhower's side and heard the most confidential matters being discussed.

Security officers were particularly concerned about what might happen if the Supreme Commander and his mistress were to break up prior to D-Day. What, if anything, would be the reaction of Mrs. Summersby if she were a woman scorned? That prospect sent shivers of concern up the spines of those charged with maintaining D-Day security.

As preparations for the mammoth invasion of Fortress Europe continued at a feverish pitch in the British Isles, across the Channel on the Cotentin Peninsula, the head of Centurie in the Cherbourg area had more than 1,100 part-time spies working for him. One of Moulines' most active cells was at Saint-Lô, a key rail and road center at the base of the Cotentin; there a male school teacher had 103 amateur agents spying out German secrets under his direction.

The Saint-Lô agents kept the Allies in England informed almost daily of Wehrmacht traffic rolling to and from Cherbourg. But unknown even to the audacious Centurie agents involved, early in May the Saint-Lô cell pulled off its greatest coup: stealing plans for the locks at nearby La Barquette, which controlled the tidal flow of the Douve River for 25 miles northward into the Cotentin Peninsula and behind Utah Beach.

The La Barquette locks were a priority objective of the U.S. 101st Airborne Division on D-Day. Prompt seizure of the locks was vital to keep the Germans from flooding the eastern half of the Cotentin Peninsula where American seaborne forces would storm ashore. The stolen plans would permit airborne engineers to rapidly manipulate the locks to keep flooding to a minimum.

On May 11, Field Marshal Rommel was speeding along a dusty

Norman road in his Horch with his long-time chauffeur Daniel at the wheel. In the trunk of his car were several accordians. It had been his custom to present these musical instruments to outstanding units along the Atlantic Wall.

Lieutenant Arthur Jahnke, the young commander of Strongpoint W-5, along the Dunes of Varreville at the base of the Cotentin Peninsula, looked up from his work as he saw Rommel's Horch speeding toward his position. The vehicle lurched to a halt, and Rommel briskly leaped from the car and strode toward a nearby blockhouse overlooking the sea.

It soon became evident that Jahnke's men would receive no accordian. Rommel was in a foul mood.

Rommel traipsed up and down the dunes, with his omnipresent aide, Captain Hellmuth Lang, and the unlucky Jahnke struggling to keep pace.

The field marshal's criticisms fell like hail: not enough obstacles on the beach, too few mines around the blockhouse, not enough barbed wire.

At the latter remark, Lieutenant Jahnke bristled. A decorated veteran who had been seriously wounded on the Russian front, the young officer was not awed by the presence of the legendary Rommel.

"Marschall, sir, I string all the wire I'm sent, but I can't do more than that," Jahnke protested in a firm but respectful tone. "As to the obstacles, we plant them on the beach but it takes only one strong tide to drag them out to the sea. The sand doesn't hold."

Rommel, in his zeal to strengthen the defenses, had played no favorites among those who felt the lash of his tongue. Earlier that morning the field marshal had ripped into a general who he thought was too casual in his efforts.

But he was not accustomed to such forthright responses from his officers. He stared stonily at Jahnke for a moment, then barked: "Your hands, lieutenant. I want to see your hands!"

Puzzled by this curious order, Jahnke removed his heavy-duty leather gloves.

At the sight of the deep cuts and scratches that disfigured the lieutenant's palms, Rommel visibly softened. "Very well, Jahnke. I expect my officers to get out there and string barbed wire with their men," he said with a trace of approval. "The blood you lost building the fortifications is as precious as what you may have to shed in combat."

There was a clicking of heels and saluting all around, and Rommel marched off at a rapid pace toward his vehicle. None present knew that Strongpoint W-5 would be the focal point of a looming massive Allied assault nor that the Allies had code-named this stretch of beach Utah.

Before Rommel sped off to his next inspection, chauffeur Daniel trotted up to Lieutenant Jahnke. Holding out an accordian, he said to the young commander of Strongpoint W-5, "The field marshal is presenting this to you and your men."

Meanwhile in Cherbourg, several bored German sentries looked on casually as a black-cassocked Catholic priest was enthusiastically engaged in an impromptu game of kickball with several youngsters. There was much laughing and shouting. The boys were happy to have a revered man of the cloth playing with them in the street.

How curious that a priest would be idly scampering about with youngsters, the sentries guarding a casemated gun position near the docks mused to themselves. "Ah, well, those French . . ."

Whatever his ecclesiastical talents, the perspiring priest was obviously not skilled at kickball. He drew back his foot and gave the oval a terrific, and errant, boot. The ball sailed past the youngsters and headed directly for the concrete enclosed gun position some 50 yards away.

"I'll get it!" the man of the cloth shouted, apparently embarrassed that he had performed so ineptly in front of the boys. He chased after the ball and up to the gun position where it had rolled. Now the German guards, who had been lulled into inattention while watching the kickball game, suddenly realized that an unauthorized person was trotting into the forbidden zone around the large-caliber gun in pursuit of the errant ball.

"*Verboten! Verboten!*" the alarmed Germans shouted as they chased after the priest, waving their arms frantically.

By this time the clergyman had reached the ball. He picked it up and started back with it, apologizing profusely for unwittingly intruding into a forbidden zone.

Minutes later the priest concluded his strenuous athletic activity and began to walk away. He was approached by two neatly dressed strangers. He took them to be French, but could not tell for sure. They might be Gestapo agents.

Without change of expression one of the strangers said to the man in the flowing black robe, "We know you're not a priest."

"Why, I don't know what you're talking about," the kickball player replied. "Of course I'm a priest."

"Look, we don't know who you are, but you're not a priest. You'd better get the hell out of here before the Gestapo grabs you."

A look of concern spread across the face of the man in black with the backward white collar. Indeed he was a bogus priest dressed for a mission, a member of Centurie whose assigned perilous task had been to get a closeup look at the German gun position and report on the caliber of the weapon and its firing direction.

Before rapidly departing, the "priest" was curious. "Tell me, how did you *know* I'm not a priest?" he inquired.

Pointing toward his feet, one of the men replied, "Because those bright red socks of yours stick out like two beacons!"

Late in May, the gargantuan Anglo-American operation known as Overlord was activated. All over southern England, the dusty roads and narrow-gauge railroads heaved and groaned under the mighty army edging southward to the coastal ports. Seaborne assault troops, grim and tight-lipped, marched into assembly areas called *sausages* because of their oval shapes on high-level military maps.

Neptune, the assault phase of Overlord, was an enormous operation, unmatched in the annals of warfare. The printed plan was nearly five inches thick. Even the typed list of American units—fourteen hundred of them—came to thirty-one pages, from two-man photo teams to entire divisions. On D-Day alone the equivalent of two hundred trainloads of American troops—fifty-five thousand fighting men—would be put ashore at Utah and Omaha.

Troops of the U.S. 82nd and 101st Airborne divisions took up residence in long rows of pyramidal tents at scattered airfields in southern England. There they feasted on such luxuries as fried chicken, fruit cocktail, and white bread with butter.

"Fattening the lambs for the slaughter!" exclaimed teenaged Private Don Lassen, expressing the sentiment of all airborne men. Lassen would soon make his first combat jump, into Normandy with the 82nd Airborne.

One who took the possible "slaughter" of American airborne troops seriously was the air commander in chief for Overlord, British Air Marshal Trafford Leigh-Mallory. Twice in recent weeks he had been overruled while trying to have the American airborne assault behind Utah Beach cancelled, despite the bitter objections of the American ground commander, General Omar Bradley. Leigh-Mallory apparently had dedicated himself to preventing the Americans from inflicting a catastrophe upon themselves. Furious American generals declared the British air marshal was merely laying the foundation to prove himself "right" if U.S. airborne troops became casualties in wholesale numbers among the tangled hedgerows and apple orchards of Normandy.

On May 30, with D-Day at hand and assault troops briefed and sealed into their sausages, Leigh-Mallory paid a call on General Eisenhower to protest one final time the "futile slaughter of two fine American airborne divisions." The tune was the same; only the words were different.

Previously Leigh-Mallory had couched his protests in such phrases as "excessive losses." Now the term "futile slaughter" was hurled at the beleaguered supreme commander. "You can expect seventy percent casualties among American glider troops and fifty percent among parachute troops," the air marshal insisted. It was a frightening prediction to be dumped onto Eisenhower's already sagging shoulders at virtually the final minute.

The implication to be drawn from Leigh-Mallory's contention was chilling. If the air marshal, billed as SHAEF's expert on such matters, turned out to be accurate and Eisenhower permitted the American airborne assault to proceed as planned, then the slaughter of the 82nd and 101st would result in disaster for the Utah seaborne landings. And that would mean that the seizure of the invasion's primary objective, the crucial port of Cherbourg, would be impossible.

Without the major port to bring in reinforcements and supplies, the two American, one Canadian, and two British divisions landing on the Calvados coast west of Utah would be cut off from the large harbor and left to flounder on the shore like a huge beached whale. There would be a monumental Allied debacle possibly leading to the loss of the war against Nazi Germany.

Grim-faced and worried, the supreme commander retired to his tent to ponder. It was his decision to make, and his alone. Eisenhower anguished for more than an hour, reviewing over and over each step in the Allied plan of attack.

From a personal point of view, if he knowingly disregarded the recommendation of his air expert and the American airborne divisions were slaughtered, Eisenhower would carry to his grave a conscience weighted down with the knowledge that he had foolhardily sacrificed thousands of the flower of American youth. From a professional soldier's perspective, if he cancelled the airborne attack the Utah seaborne assault would fail, Cherbourg would not be captured, and the entire invasion would be in the most serious peril.

The supreme commander rose from his chair, smothered the tenth cigarette he had smoked during the past hour, returned to his headquarters and placed a call to Air Marshal Leigh-Mallory: The American airborne attack was on as planned.

As Eisenhower's mighty force was marshalling in southern England, General of Panzer Troops Hans Cramer, the last commander of the vaunted Afrika Korps, was closeted with high-ranking members of the Oberkommando der Wehrmacht in Berlin. Through the intervention of Providence, General Cramer had obtained startling intelligence information that delighted the OKW. He had just seen with his own eyes the powerful Army Group Patton, which was poised across the Strait of Dover to strike at the Pas-de-Calais.

Cramer's "coup" was precisely what the OKW had been urgently seeking: eyewitness corroboration from an authoritive source that Army Group Patton indeed was massing.

Hans Cramer had been the unwitting dupe of a devious Allied plot by officials of Quicksilver to indelibly imprint on OKW the bogus fact that the phantom million-man Army Group Patton would launch the Allies' main effort after a diversionary attack in Normandy.

Cramer, who had been captured in Tunisia in May 1943, was being held in Wales. He had become ill and a decision was made to repatriate him to Germany through the Swedish Red Cross. Making this decision, on virtually the eve of D-Day, were the officers who ran Quicksilver.

Cramer was driven from Wales to London, and the route took him directly through the bustling American and British marshalling areas of southern England, where he was deliberately allowed to view the immense buildup of troops, armor, shipping, and aircraft. Cramer was astonished at this awesome display of raw military power.

Allied escort officers, accompanying the former Afrika Korps commander in his motor tour from Wales to London, carelessly let slip that they were driving through southeastern England, across from the Pas-de-Calais (actually they were far to the west). The troops he had viewed were members of the U.S. First Army getting ready to assault Normandy. Cramer could not tell where he had been because when England expected a German invasion in 1940, all signposts and other indications of town names had been removed.

General Cramer sailed on the Swedish ship *Gripsholm*, landing in Germany shortly before D-Day. Apparently he had not been very ill. He promptly rushed to the OKW to breathlessly report the espionage bonanza that had miraculously dropped into his lap: Army Group Patton was preparing to assault the Pas-de-Calais.

5

Bitter
Quarrel
Among Weathermen

Emile Antoine, a husky, gray-haired greengrocer, was huddled in the semidarkness of the cellar of his home in the heart of Cherbourg the night of May 29. Only a block down the street stood the stark outline of the Gare Maritime, the hulking structure where, in peacetime, carefree tourists had disembarked from huge luxury liners and caught trains for Paris. To most of those travelers, Cherbourg had been of little interest. It was merely a place one had to pass through to get somewhere else.

But to thirty-seven-year-old Antoine and his petite, black-haired wife Claudette, Cherbourg had always been home. Both were born and reared there, as were their two children, aged eleven and thirteen.

Now, by flickering candlelight, Antoine was fiddling with the dial on a worn old radio, trying desperately to tune in the BBC from London. The receiver crackled, whined, and roared with static as the grocer listened for the radio voice from across the Channel with one ear while the other was cocked for the footsteps of a German police patrol—or worse, the Gestapo. In Nazi-occupied France, the mere possession of a radio was a serious offense. One could be punished by deportation to a labor camp in Germany or even executed as a spy. And Antoine was a spy—a member of the Cherbourg cell of Centurie.

As Claudette busied herself upstairs with household chores, Antoine was trying to pick up the 9 P.M. news in French for clues to the date and place of the looming invasion. It was near at hand, of that he was certain.

In recent days and nights, a thunderous crescendo of Allied bombs had rocked the Cotentin Peninsula. As mighty as this barrage was, Antoine and others in Centurie had no way of knowing that it was only a portion of a gargantuan Allied bombing campaign to soften up the invasion area and isolate it from the rest of France. For each bomb dropped by Allied air forces in Normandy, two bombs were released elsewhere along the French coast and in the Low Countries to befuddle the enemy.

Down the peninsula from Cherbourg Allied bombers pounded rail centers, bridges, and suspected German headquarters and troop concentrations. Radar sites on either side of the port of Cherbourg, one three miles northeast of Saint-Lô, at the base of the peninsula, and another on the cliffs overlooking the harbor at Arromanches, were blown to bits. All had been pinpointed by the amateur agents of Centurie.

Antoine, admittedly no expert on aerial bombardment, was puzzled: Why hadn't the bombers attacked the Cherbourg docks, which were being used nightly by the Kriegsmarine to bring in supplies and troops? The harbor had been left untouched.

Now in the cellar of his modest stone house, the Centurie agent peeked at his watch. It was 9:15 P.M. and he knew that his cantankerous radio had forced him to miss the nightly BBC news. Prepared to abandon his effort for the night, Antoine heard the old receiver crackle once more and a solemn British voice intone: "French residents living along the coast. You are urged to abandon your homes temporarily and move far inland to a safe place. Repeat, you are urged . . ."

Antoine's heart skipped a beat. Surely the Big Day was fast approaching. But which day? And where would the Allies strike? Belgium? Holland? Pas-de-Calais? Brittany? Or . . . *Normandy*?

He flipped off the radio, buried it deep in a mountain of dirty clothes, and scrambled upstairs to tell wife Claudette of the development.

Meanwhile that same day, 100 miles north of Emile Antoine's cellar in the port of Cherbourg, General Eisenhower moved from Bushy Park outside London to his invasion headquarters at Southwick House, a stately and commodious mansion perched on a wooded hill overlooking the coastal city of Portsmouth. Eisenhower, the Kansas farm boy who made good, had still another momentous decision facing him—selection of the day and precise hour to smash into the Atlantic Wall.

Neptune, the massive assault on Normandy, had originally been set for "the favorable period of the May moon" by the Joint Chiefs of Staff but had been moved ahead to a "favorable period in June" on the supreme commander's recommendation.

In recent weeks, as planning for Overlord became steadily more hectic, demanding, and nerve-wracking, Eisenhower, the man with the ultimate burden on his shoulders, was beginning to develop symptoms of the enormous strain. Yet, outwardly, he had to continually project a relaxed attitude of self-assurance and confidence, even bouyancy.

Only Eisenhower's intimates knew that he had been undergoing secret medical treatment for an eye that was inflammed and sore and that resulted in blurred vision on occasion. He was also being treated for a ringing in the ears. Most nights, as only his long-time friend and naval aide, Commander Harry C. Butcher knew, the supreme commander was so exhausted he could hardly undress and get into bed. Even then he was wracked with visions of seemingly unsolvable problems, knowing as he fitfully drifted into slumber that his ordeal would resume with the arrival of dawn.

Along with his man-killing, mind-numbing duties as supreme commander, Eisenhower had to tend to family and social requirements. He tried to write wife Mamie as often as possible during his crucial period in history, but he sometimes could not remember if he had written her that morning or several days previously. In the midst of his nerve-wracking duties in these late days in May, Eisenhower was forced by the niceties of inter-Allied relations to accept an invitation to lunch at Buckingham Palace with gracious, vivacious Queen Elizabeth and retiring, pleasant King George, who remained silent during lunch except to shyly point out to the general that he had dropped his napkin. Patton, also a guest at the affair, later observed in his diary: "The King is a nice little fellow . . . and one rung above a moron."

No detail in the Overlord planning had been too small to find its way to the supreme commander. In recent days he had been forced to settle a lower-level dispute over the amount of toilet tissue to be taken ashore in the first week of the invasion. Buck-passing halted at his desk.

Now, on his arrival at Southwick House, Ike, as he had been known to friends since boyhood, promptly discovered that the tension that had become increasingly thick at SHAEF had spread across the Atlantic. He was handed a top-secret telegram from U.S. Army Chief of Staff George Marshall in Washington: the American Chiefs of Staff (army, navy, and air) would arrive in London on June 7. The purpose of the trip by America's highest military brass, Marshall explained, was to be on hand "in the event major decisions by the Combined Chiefs of Staff are necessary" with regard to Neptune, the combined assault on Normandy. It was hardly the kind of thinly veiled "encouragement" a harrassed Eisenhower needed at this point. It told him that his own superiors were wracked with doubt.

One source of encouragement to the supreme commander on this May 29 was the spring weather: for the entire month the sun had shone brightly, only gentle breezes blew, and the English Channel had remained calm. Even more heartening was the report given him that evening by his chief meteorologist, Group Captain John Stagg of the Royal Air Force. Readings indicated, Stagg assured Eisenhower, that the weather would remain placid for the next several days.

That evening Eisenhower called in his right-hand man and alter ego, Beetle Smith. The SHAEF chief of staff bustled importantly into Eisenhower's office. "Okay, Beetle, send it out!"

"It" was the code-phrase *Exercise Hornpipe Plus Six,* which was flashed to all top commanders. This told them that D-Day had been set for six days hence: June 5.

Despite the most intense and painstaking planning and projections, in selecting D-Day and H-Hour General Eisenhower was at the mercy of a master he could not influence—the English Channel tides. Only twice each month did tidal conditions meet the requirements of a massive combined operation against continental Europe. The first acceptable period was June 5–7. If bad weather forced a postponement the assault would have to be put off for two weeks. If it then became necessary to move D-Day ahead again, the invasion would have to be delayed until July.

Prospects for a delayed July landing on the Far Shore would be frightening. More than one hundred and fifty thousand Allied assault troops had detailed knowledge of Neptune. They would have to laboriously disembark and be locked up incommunicado for nearly a month—if such a feat were possible. Another monumental factor would be even more frightening. A month's postponement in the invasion would mean one-third less time on the continent for Lightning Joe Collins' corps to seize the crucial port of Cherbourg. And it would give Erwin Rommel four additional weeks to bolster the port's defenses.

After September 1, beach unloadings in the capricious English Channel would be dangerous, jeopardized by gale-force winds and 20-foot waves. If the Germans could hold on to heavily fortified Cherbourg for six or seven weeks after a July landing—a distinct possibility—the Allied force in Normandy would be without a major port and in serious danger of being stranded. A second, even more gigantic Dunkirk might be in the making.

Now, with the launching of Neptune at hand, Group Captain Stagg, a Scotsman who'd earned a fine reputation in his field, and his Meteorological Committee had suddenly been transformed into the most significant military intelligence detachment in the free world. On the basis of their weather forecasts could rest success or disaster for the invasion.

The Meteorological Committee headed by Stagg included his deputy, U.S. Army Air Corps Colonel D. N. Yates; meteorologists from Allied ground, sea, and air forces; the British weather ministry; and the United States weather service.

A picket line of vessels and aircraft stretching around the North Atlantic—in the Caribbean, near the Canaries and Azores, up through Nova Scotia, Newfoundland, and Greenland, as well as reporting stations along the eastern seaboard of the United States, daily poured weather data in to Group Captain Stagg and his committee associates.

On June 1, the euphoric weather forecast that had buoyed Eisenhower and other Allied commanders since Stagg's May 29 prediction fell apart. Stagg, after consultation with his meteorological associates, hurried to Eisenhower's office to report that the latest forecast for the 4th, 5th, and 6th was "not good."

The following day, June 2, Stagg again consulted by scrambler telephone with outlying weather reporting stations, which agreed that weather disturbances were forming in the Atlantic. Data kept pouring into Stagg's headquarters from reporting stations in the Atlantic, but the information was confused and uncertain.

"The entire North Atlantic appears to be filled with depressions," a worried Captain Stagg observed to his associates. At their daily conference, one heavy with tension, a heated squabble broke out that made it impossible to arrive at a consensus forecast. Stagg made a crucial decision: he would not inform Eisenhower of the bitter disagreement raging among individual members of the Meteorological Committee about the significance of the large number of depressions in the Atlantic. Eisenhower, Stagg concluded, already was burdened with enough problems.

Time was running out for the supreme commander to decide whether to procede with D-Day on the 5th as planned, or to postpone it for twenty-four hours. He called a conference of his top commanders for 9:30 that night, Friday, June 2.

Prior to this crucial meeting, Captain Stagg again met with Meteorological Committee members and wrangling once again erupted. Some members expressed themselves as "positive" that inclement weather would

57

not strike the Channel in the next few days and that cloud cover would be minimal, but Stagg and others thought the weather picture vague and uncertain.

A worried Stagg was skewered on the horns of a dilemma. If at Eisenhower's commanders' conference in one hour he presented the views of those forecasters who predicted that the weather would be calm and cloud cover minimal, the supreme commander might launch the invasion only to meet disaster in a Channel lashed by high, angry waves and an overcast that would ground the Allies' powerful air force.

Long faces were the norm when Allied commanders assembled that night in the austere conference room at Southwick House. Present in addition to Eisenhower were his three commanders-in-chief for ground, sea and, air—Field-Marshal Bernard Montgomery, Admiral Sir Bertram Ramsay, and Air Marshal Sir Trafford Leigh-Mallory—along with their aides and other top officers. Stagg walked into the room. All eyes were upon him. Eisenhower snapped, "Well, Stagg, what have you got for us this time?"

Captain Stagg replied that the weather situation for the next few days was "potentially full of menace," and he forecast heavy cloud cover and strong westerly winds over the Channel until at least June 6 or 7. Eisenhower, after deliberation with his 15 commanders, decided to postpone his go or no-go decision for at least another 24 hours.

Saturday, June 3, was the most nerve-wracking day of John Stagg's life. He had pitched and turned in his sleep throughout the night, only to arise to find that the weather pattern in the Atlantic was more complex and confusing than ever. His spirits were not materially raised when he passed a well-meaning friend who called out, "They'll string you up from the nearest lamppost if you don't read the omens right!"

Stagg already felt as though he were swinging by the neck from a lamppost—and the noose was getting tighter each minute.

This day, June 3, was the day of decision. Thousands of tense Allied assault troops and their guns, tanks, trucks, and an infinite variety of the sinews of violence were loaded and ready to sail for the Far Shore. Some Allied flotillas were so far from the landing beaches that they would have to shove off that night to reach Normandy in time for the June 5 assault.

At Eisenhower's conference with his top commanders that night, the beleaguered John Stagg had nothing to comfort the eager, worried listeners. He predicted that the weather over the Channel from June 4 through June 7 would be windy, cloudy and stormy, but cautiously expressed the "possibility" that the cloud cover might break. A grim-faced supreme commander then made a tentative decision to delay D-Day for twenty-four hours.

Another meeting was scheduled for 4:15 A.M., Sunday, June 4, at which time Eisenhower would make his final decision on the twenty-four-hour postponement. In the meantime, Group Captain Stagg and his warring associates on the Meteorological Committee were to continue to review the weather situation and report back.

A solemn-faced, sleepy-eyed group of Allied commanders assembled at 4:15. Apprehension hovered like a thick blanket over the conference table. Eisenhower, grim and unsmiling, merely nodded at Stagg to present his forecast. It was unchanged from six hours before. After discussion with his commanders, Eisenhower ordered his chief of staff, General "Beetle" Smith, to flash the code-phrase—*Ripcord 24*. D-Day had been postponed for twenty-four hours.

A worried and exhausted Dwight Eisenhower walked out of the conference room, rubbing the lucky coins he had long carried in his pocket for just such dire situations.

As anxiety increased at Southwick House, thousands of American and British assault troops, solemn, quiet, burdened with weapons and equipment, began filing out of their sausages at Torquay, Plymouth, Portland, Dartmouth, Portsmouth, and nineteen other ports, bound for the docks. There they climbed aboard squat, gray transports that would carry them to France.

On his command ship, the cruiser USS *Augusta*, on June 3, General Omar Bradley, the home-spun, bespectacled leader of American ground forces in Neptune, was meeting with reporters. A large map of Normandy hung on a wall of the cabin with the words *Festung Cherbourg* prominently written in with red crayon and circled. Pointing toward the map, a newsman asked, "General, how soon do you expect to take Cherbourg?"

Bradley, in his high-pitched voice, replied, "I'm going to stick my neck out. But at this moment I'll gladly sell out for D plus fifteen—even D plus twenty."

"Then why is it marked for capture on the map for D plus eight?" the reporter pursued.

"That estimate was reached before Rommel started pouring troops into the Cotentin Peninsula recently," the First Army commander responded.

One quality American correspondents liked about the man they called Omar the Tentmaker, in addition to his modesty and willingness to heap credit on others, was his unfailingly candid replies to their questions. If the Tentmaker said it was going to be tough to take Cherbourg, then it was going to be tough. The projection was not being made to enhance Omar Bradley's and Lightning Joe Collins' reputations in the unlikely event Cherbourg fell like an overripe apple.

General Bradley had no way of knowing while talking to reporters that his able opponent across the Channel, Field Marshal Rommel, would have been "pouring" even more troops into Normandy had he not run up against opposition he could not overcome: Hitler's fears of concentrating too much power in the hands of any one person and the jealousies and monumental egoism infecting other military leaders of the Third Reich.

Rommel believed that there would be two landings, of which Normandy would be the first. He was determined that the second would never take place. The first would be smashed on the beaches of Normandy through fierce counterattacks by German reserves held only a short distance behind the shoreline.

Convinced that the Allies would strike at the Cotentin Peninsula and the Calvados coast, Rommel urgently submitted his shopping list to the Oberkommando der Wehrmacht in Berlin. He asked for twenty-four additional antiaircraft batteries to be positioned between the Vire and Orne rivers (the precise sector of one American and three British beaches for D-Day), for the crack 12th SS Panzer Division to be moved up from far inland to the Cotentin Peninsula south of Cherbourg, for a brigade of *Nebelwerfer* (large six-barrelled mortars) near Carentan, for the battle-tested Panzer Lehr Division to the base of the Cotentin Peninsula near Avranches, and for the Kriegsmarine, at this late date, to start mining the Bay of the Seine through which thousands of Allied vessels soon would be plowing.

What Rommel wanted for the Atlantic Wall in Normandy and what he got were entirely different. Now the green monster of envy at high levels of the divided German command in the West reared its ugly head. Erwin Rommel, the Boy Marshal of homefront legend, had gained far too large a share of the limelight in the Fatherland. Few were the men and women of the Third Reich who did not daily see Rommel's determined face in their newspapers, a commander working feverishly to strengthen the Atlantic Wall and ultimately destined to smash the great invasion. The field marshal's popularity on the homefront rivaled that of Adolf Hitler himself.

The 24 antiaircraft batteries on Rommel's shopping list were controlled by Reich Marshal Hermann Göring, obese, flabby jowled, vain, and now addicted to wearing rouge and lipstick on occasion. Göring, Number 2 man in the Reich and commander of the Luftwaffe, promptly turned thumbs down on the request, even though the batteries were not then being utilized.

Admiral Theodor Krancke, Navy Commander-West, refused to mine the Bay of the Seine. The previous year, before the arrival of the energetic Rommel on the scene, Krancke had concluded that the Normandy coast was too rocky for an amphibious invasion, and so had left the Bay of the Seine unmined. Now he was not about to admit by implication that he had been wrong. Krancke also declined Rommel's request for five thousand marines who were posted in Paris and largely involved in ceremonial activities.

Hitler, in his capacity of army commander, bluntly declined to allow the two crack panzer divisions to move up near the Normandy coast. The Führer also refused the *Nebelwerfer* brigade that Rommel wanted.

Rommel would have to make do with the resources available to him. His urgent requests had been summarily denied by commanders of lesser foresight.

As the commander of German Army Group B choked with rage and frustration, General Eisenhower and his subordinate commanders across the Channel were nearly frantic. One Allied convoy had failed to receive the Ripcord 24 signal and was steaming directly toward its assigned position off Normandy—a sure tipoff to the Germans of Allied intentions.

Many Allied vessels were already at sea, headed for Utah and Omaha beaches, when Ripcord was flashed at approximately 5 A.M. Sunday, June 4, postponing D-Day for 24 hours. Most major units turned around in the storm-pitched waves and inky blackness and headed back to port, while others much farther away halted in place. A convoy of more than one hundred and twenty-five vessels, carrying troops of the assaulting U.S. 4th Infantry Division and other personnel, failed to receive the urgent message. It sailed on toward Normandy.

Efforts to reach the imperiled convoy by radio were fruitless. Airplanes were dispatched to search out the errant flotilla; they flew through rain squalls and limited visibility through much of the day before the quarry was spotted. A plane swooped down below one hundred feet over the command ship to drop a cannister with an official message in code. The container missed its target, and plunged into the angry waters. The convoy steamed onward.

Frantic, the pilot scratched out his own note, put it in another cannister, zoomed in over the command ship once again, and released the message container. This time the aim was true—the cannister landed right on deck and was taken to the convoy's commander. For thirty minutes the flotilla steamed on toward France, now only some 30 miles away, as the British naval officer pondered the authenticity of this curious message from an unidentified pilot of an airplane with Royal Air Force markings. Surely, he thought, the Luftwaffe would have a captured aircraft of this type in its possession. This could be a diabolical German trick to disrupt the invasion.

Finally a worried convoy commander reached Allied authorities by radio at a port in southern England. Barely in the nick of time the convoy reversed course and returned to its base. Now yet another nagging question beset Allied commanders: Had Luftwaffe search planes spotted that large convoy, crammed with assault troops, steaming hell-bent for the shores of Normandy?

There was little time to ponder the question. The following day, Sunday, June 4, would be one of the most significant dates of the war. Eisenhower and his advisors would be forced to decide if the pentup man-made hurricane that was the Allied war machine would be unleashed against the Atlantic Wall on June 6, or the dangerous alternative of a postponement of two weeks or more put into effect. The supreme commander and his chief meteorologist, Captain Stagg, awoke that morning to a foreboding weather picture—an intense storm was raging in the Channel, clouds were thick, and winds were howling violently.

Hurrying from his tent at Southwick House to the weather center early that morning, Stagg felt a tinge of optimism. The weather charts indicated to him that Tuesday, June 6, could allow the assault on Normandy. That afternoon Stagg met with his weather committee. He expected the proceedings to run smoothly; instead, an even more violent disagreement than before erupted, lasting for nearly three hours.

At 9:30 P.M., Captain Stagg was on his feet before a solemn group of top Allied commanders. What was decided in that room at that time could well alter the future course of the war in Europe. The Scot weighed his words carefully, but told the intently listening group that he believed that cloud conditions on June 6 would allow the Allied air force to strike with accuracy and that naval bombardment ships could fire with accuracy.

Stagg also predicted that the wind around midnight of June 5 would not be strong enough to interfere with the delivery of paratroopers. He stressed that these weather conditions, while not ideal, would at least permit the invasion to be launched.

As the meteorologist concluded, the crowded room was hushed in utter silence. Then an intense discussion followed, with each commander asked to comment. Beetle Smith was for launching the attack on June 6. General Montgomery was decisive—*Go!* Air Marshal Arthur Tedder, Deputy Supreme Commander, was cautious, settling for pronouncing a Tuesday attack as "chancy." Air Marshal Leigh-Mallory doubted that the air force could operate effectively in the cloud cover Stagg had predicted.

Deliberations were over. Others could, and did, equivocate. Eisenhower would have the burden of saying yes or no. A silence again blanketed the room as he pondered the issue one last time. Outside, nature was playing an eerie, soul-wracking background overture—howling winds that rattled the shutters on Southwick House and torrential rains that splattered against the windows of the conference room.

Finally, Eisenhower spoke, softly but firmly: "I am quite positive that we must give the order . . . I don't like it, but there it is. The question is, how long can we hang this thing out on the end of a stick and let it hang there? . . . I don't see how we can do anything else."

D-Day was set: Tuesday, June 6, at 6:30 A.M. In the event of a sudden turn for the worse in the weather, there would be one final meeting at 4:15 the following morning, June 5.

At that time Captain Stagg told the commanders that there was little change in the forecast, if anything "a slight change toward optimism."

Now, as if a magic wand had swept away the pall of gloom and despair that had clogged the conference room for three days and nights, a bold sense of optimism gripped the commanders. For the first time since June 1 a broad smile spread across Dwight Eisenhower's face. One hour later an historic code phrase was flashed to all Allied commanders and the Combined Chiefs of Staff: "Halcyon plus 5 definitely confirmed."

Minutes later the many-armed invasion juggernaut, its tentacles extended into scores of crowded transports, airfields, harbors, estuaries, encampments, and towns, began slowly to unwind and edge inexorably toward the Far Shore. Of such magnitude was this immense war machine that it was now beyond the capability of mere mortals to postpone or cancel Neptune. Now the Plan had taken over.

6

A Dynamite
Keg
Ready to Explode

A husky, black-haired major, a helmet clamped on his head, wearing olive drab shirt and trousers and a .45 Colt revolver strapped to a hip, edged halfway down the perpendicular steel ladder leading from above into a stifling hold of a hulking transport ship anchored in Torquay harbor. Shoehorned inside the enclosure were grim-faced men who would be the "point" of the entire Allied invasion apparatus stretching all the way back to the United States—the men with the rifles, machine guns, and mortars.

Hearing the clatter of footsteps on the metal ladder, the assault troops of the 4th Infantry Division braced for what was expected to be a certain, yet dreaded announcement. These men would be the first to hit the Atlantic Wall at a hostile strip of sand they had been told was code-named Utah Beach. Now each stared for an instant at the major hanging on the steel ladder, much as a condemned man would react as the warden entered his cell to announce the result of the convict's appeal to the governor for clemency.

"H-hour six-thirty in the morning!" the major called out.

That was all. The final piece of the gigantic jigsaw puzzle that was Operation Overlord had been fitted into place.

The message sent chills racing up and down the spines of the green young fighting men. Many a soldier felt a sharp blow at the pit of his stomach, as though some monstrous gladiator had struck him with a mailed fist. An eerie silence fell over the hold packed with olive-drab humanity. The condemned had had their execution time set—6:30 A.M.

Most felt a massive blood bath was about to engulf them on the shores of something named the Cotentin Peninsula.

Perhaps they would not even make it to shore before suffering a hideous death, many believed. In recent days a rumor had swept through the 4th Division assault troops that Hitler had been saving a diabolical secret weapon to thwart the Allied invasion. As assault troops approached the beaches, the rumor went, the English Channel would be turned into a roaring inferno of fire for two miles out to sea, incinerating all those trapped in the cauldron.

Late that afternoon of June 5, the decks of a transport in the harbor at Torquay were packed with men of the assault battalion. Suddenly, a voice called out over the ship's loudspeaker: "Stand by for a word from the general." The speaker was not further identified.

"Men," a voice rasped out over the amplifier, "there's so many generals running around England, I'd better tell you which one this is—I'm Teddy Roosevelt."

A ripple of subdued laughter floated across the decks. Ears perked up. Soldiers nudged each other with elbows.

Brigadier General Theodore Roosevelt, Jr., son of a former president of the United States, was short in physical stature, extremely long in heart. He had fought the Germans in North Africa as assistant commander of the 1st Infantry Division, where he gained wide fame as a fearless combat leader who disdained enemy fire. The perquisites of rank meant nothing to Teddy Roosevelt, and he often had not bothered to put on his general's star when on field or combat duty.

Roosevelt was casual about his personal dress; he usually wore a wool knit cap and left a pant leg flopping over his leggings. Such lack of self-discipline was viewed with a jaundiced eye by some high-ranking staff officers far removed from the clash of combat. "Roosevelt's got to go!" was the rear-area battlecry.

The spunky little one-star general was summarily relieved from his post, and for months was shuttled about from one inconsequential job to another. Roosevelt pined for a combat assignment. "Hell, if they want me to, I'll lead a squad of infantrymen!" he told friends repeatedly. With one of history's most monumental military operations looming, Roosevelt intensified his badgering of SHAEF leaders and finally was assigned to the 4th Infantry Division as a spare brigadier.

His relaxed ways, coupled with his reputation as a fearless battle leader, soon won the hearts of the men of the division.

As D-Day moved inexorably closer, Teddy Roosevelt, who as a spare general had no troops to command nor any specific assignment, cornered his immediate boss, Major General Raymond O. Barton, commander of the 4th Division. "Tubby, our boys are green as the growing grass," Roosevelt began. "They've never heard a shot fired in anger. The first men to hit Utah are going to be scared as hell and confused. They need someone like me with them."

As Barton digested these words, Roosevelt continued on the attack: "Let me go in with the first wave. If the boys see an old son of a bitch like me standing up under it, they'll feel that they can, too."

Rubbing his arthritic shoulder, Roosevelt had a twinkle in his eye as he added, "Besides, if the boys see a general on the beach, they'll think it's a safe place to be."

Barton summarily turned down the eloquent plea. Utah Beach was no place for an American general, he thought. But the fifty-seven-year-old Roosevelt was persistent. He put his request in writing and this time, against his better judgment, General Barton reluctantly agreed. Teddy Roosevelt, son of the man whose motto was "speak softly and carry a big stick," would be among the first American seaborne soldiers to set foot on Fortress Europe.

Now, talking over the ship's loudspeaker to the men he would lead ashore, General Roosevelt continued: "Most of you are going into combat for the first time in the morning—and you're probably scared. That's normal. I'm going with you in the first wave and I'll be scared too. Some of you have heard about the invincibility of the German soldier. But let me tell you this: I fought the Kraut for months in North Africa. He's disciplined. Many are tough. But he *ain't* a superman!"

Jammed on deck shoulder to shoulder, the assault troops listened intently. Here was a man speaking their language, telling them what they wanted to hear.

"I'll tell you what I think of the Kraut," the raspy voice over the amplifier continued. "When we hit the beach in the morning, I'm going to be armed only with a .45 Colt and a walking cane. And I'm going to grab the first goddamned armed Kraut I see and ram the cane three feet up the part of his anatomy where it will do the most good."

A resounding chorus of laughter rang out across the water. Men slapped their thighs in glee and nudged comrades. Tears rolled down cheeks. The terrible, suffocating pall of fear and despair had been partially lifted. "If this little, fifty-seven-year-old, arthritic guy is not afraid of the Krauts, then

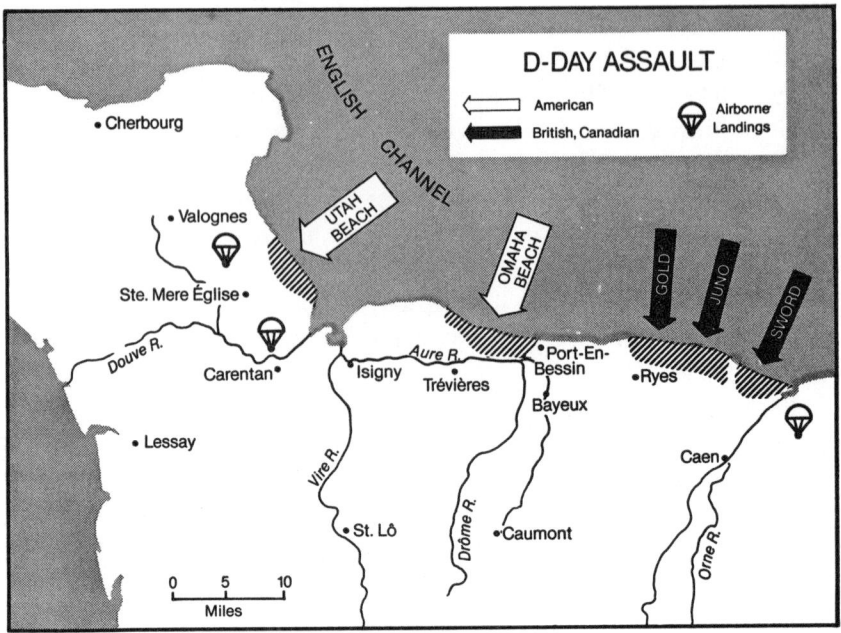

maybe things won't be as bad as we thought," many told themselves.

"Good luck, men," Roosevelt concluded. "Get in there and give the bastards hell. I'll see you on the beach at six-thirty!"

No one knew at the time that Teddy Roosevelt, he of the fighting heart, would be dead in six weeks—not through enemy action but of a heart attack.

A short distance along the coast from where General Roosevelt was addressing the shipboard troops at Torquay, Major General J. Lawton "Lightning Joe" Collins, directly responsible for Utah Beach and the early seizure of crucial Cherbourg, was on his command ship, the USS *Bayfield*, anchored in Plymouth harbor. Also on board the attack transport was Major General Raymond O. "Tubby" Barton, a friend of Collins' going back two decades, along with a battalion of the 8th Infantry Regiment that would assault Utah.

Commanded by Colonel James M. Van Fleet, another good friend of Collins' from their days at West Point, the men of the 8th Infantry liked to boast to follow-up troops, "When we hit the beach there'll be nothing between us and the Krauts except the buttons on our shirts!"

As the *Bayfield* edged out of Plymouth harbor late on the afternoon of the 5th, Lightning Joe Collins, having done all that he could to prepare for the clash now only fifteen hours away, retired to the solitude of his cabin. He took pen in hand and wrote Gladys, his wife of twenty-three years:

> I thought of you all most keenly yesterday morning, as I do each Sunday, as mass was celebrated in the main mess hall aboard ship. The hall was packed with soldiers, sailors, officers and men alike. I am sure the thoughts of everyone were more on our families at home than they were on the services.

Collins told Gladys that the "seriousness of the project on which we are now embarked came home to me for the first time," as he believed it did to others in the mess hall:

> This feeling was reflected in the frank whole-heartedness with which the men joined in the singing of the hymns that most of them had rarely sung since they were boys.

> As I offered a soldier next to me one of the hymn books being passed about, he answered me almost scornfully, "I know them hymns!" And he did, from "Holy God We Praise Thy Name" to "God Bless America."

Finishing his letter, General Collins walked outside for a stroll around the deck, weaving his way through the throng of troops. It was still daylight as the corps commander glanced skyward, puzzled by the tranquility that continued to reign over the English Channel. Where was the Luftwaffe? Around him, as far as the eye could see and beyond, were vessels of every size and type. It was inconceivable that the German air force would fail to discover this colossal Allied fleet steaming out of scores of ports in southern England and from as far away as Scotland and Northern Ireland.

Joe Collins would have breathed easier had he known that the Luftwaffe that June 5 had sent out only one reconnaissance aircraft to probe Allied activity—with orders to scour the sea off the coast of Holland.

As the Allied armada made its way through the Channel, General Eisenhower was having dinner with Major General Maxwell Taylor at an airfield at Greenham Common. Taylor commanded the untested but tough and eager 101st Airborne Division, and in a few hours he would be making his first combat jump, into Normandy. The 42-year-old Taylor had replaced Major General William H. Lee, an airborne pioneer, as commander of the Screaming Eagles after Lee suffered a massive heart attack in February.

Eisenhower, outwardly buoyant and confident, drove after dinner with Taylor to several nearby airfields where hundreds of paratroopers were donning their heavy burden of combat gear. Many of Taylor's parachutists were wearing Indian warpaint and had cropped their hair into freakish "warpath" designs.

Grinning, Eisenhower whispered to Max Taylor, "I don't know if your boys will scare the Germans, but they sure as hell would scare me!"

Circulating among the paratroopers, Eisenhower was tormented by a continuing echo racing through his mind: Air Marshal Leigh-Mallory's frightening warning: "Your American airborne divisions will be slaughtered." Was he stupidly sending these cheerful, bright-faced youths to their deaths in wholesale numbers?

As he went from plane to plane talking with troopers in his friendly man-to-man style, his inner spirits soared. "Now don't you worry about a goddamned thing, general," the men told him repeatedly. "The 101st Airborne is on the job!"

It was still daylight of English double summer time at shortly after 9 P.M. when Eisenhower, his round of visits to the paratroopers completed, shook hands with General Taylor. "Well, good luck, Max," he said softly to the airborne commander. As Eisenhower walked to his waiting staff limousine to return to invasion headquarters at Portsmouth, an aide cast a furtive glance at the supreme commander. There was a tear in the general's eye.

At one of the nearby airfields from which elements of the 101st Airborne would soon take off, Colonel Howard R. Johnson, the firebrand leader of the 501st Parachute Infantry Regiment, was standing on the hood of a jeep, his men assembled around him. Johnson had commanded the 501st Infantry since its formation and had always seemed to be consumed with an apparently insatiable need to demonstrate that he was the toughest, most daring man in his outfit. Many thought he was.

Now, in the gloaming on the hood of his jeep, Colonel Johnson had lashed his men into a frenzy with a spirited pep talk. He reached down to his jump boot, whipped out his trench knife, brandished it overhead and shouted, "I swear to you that before the sun rises I'll plunge this dagger into the blackest-hearted Kraut in Normandy!" Cheers and screams of frenzy saturated the air.

At an airfield in the area of the 82nd Airborne Division, veterans of savage fighting in Sicily and Italy, Lieutenant Colonel Edward R. "Cannonball" Krause, leader of the 3rd Battalion of the 505th Parachute Infantry, was also atop the hood of a jeep exhorting his men. Holding Old Glory above his head, Krause shouted, "This was the first flag to fly over Naples when we captured it. Tonight we're going to march on Sainte-Mère-Église in Normandy, liberate its people, and fly this flag from the tallest building in town!" A chorus of cheers rocked the airfield.

Soon there were shouts of "Load 'em up!" at scores of scattered airfields in central and southern England. General Taylor of the 101st, burdened with heavy combat gear, made a hurried final inspection of his equipment before boarding a C-47. He felt his leg bag. Yes, it was there—a bottle of Irish whisky he prudently stored.

In the 82nd Airborne area, Brigadier General James Gavin was giving a last-minute check to his equipment and the M-1 rifle he habitually carried in combat. Gavin, despite his relative youth, had been given command of Task Force A, consisting of all three of the division's parachute regiments in the assault—the 505th, 507th, and 508th. To control this sizeable force, Gavin would have at his disposal only an aide, a radio operator, an orderly, and one staff officer, Captain Willard E. Harrison.

The orderly was, in fact, a bodyguard, who Colonel Reuben H. Tucker, commander of the 504th Parachute Infantry Regiment, insisted accompany his friend, Jim Gavin. Tucker's regiment had only recently come to England from extensive fighting in Italy, and would not be ready for the Normandy jump.

"He's the toughest man in my regiment," Tucker had told Gavin. That's saying a lot, the young one-star general thought to himself. The bodyguard wore a gold earring in one ear and talked hardly at all. He would later bail out on Jim Gavin's heels, never to be heard from again.

At 11 P.M. more than 800 squat, low-winged C-47s, crammed with nearly thirteen thousand paratroopers of the 82nd and 101st Airborne Divisions, began lifting off in the dusk from airfields scattered about the southern half of England. The skies above the lush green fields and rows of neat, thatch-roofed houses throbbed with the ear-splitting roar of mighty aircraft engines. Squadrons circled, formed into Vs of Vs, and under the benign gaze of a faint moon comfortably perched in the heavens far removed from the madness of man down below, set a course for the Cotentin Peninsula.

In Normandy, June 5 had been just an ordinary day of watching and waiting by German soldiers and French civilians alike. The evening promised to be equally routine. The weather was hot and sultry.

Just after 10:30 P.M. a flight of Allied bombers flew over Cherbourg and dropped its lethal cargo on German gun batteries along the Atlantic Wall. Natives took the nightly appearance of the bombers for granted. More often than not, the local residents knew, the bombs missed the targets.

Although German weather reports assured commanders that the *Gross-invasion* could not come on June 6, some Wehrmacht officers and soldiers who would have to repel an Allied onslaught seemed to sense that the great event was about to be launched. Lieutenant Colonel Friedrich August von der Heydte, commander of the elite 6th Parachute Regiment, stationed in the Périers–Saint-Lô–Carentan triangle behind Utah Beach, was one of those.

During the afternoon of June 5, while General Collins' assault troops were sailing out of Torquay and other ports in southern England to smash at Utah at dawn, von der Heydte learned of the mysterious desertion of twenty Alsatian soldiers conscripted into his unit by force to perform logistical duties. Since it would be difficult for the twenty French deserters to hide in a region packed with German troops, von der Heydte concluded that the local underground had tipped them off that the Wehrmacht would soon be too occupied to search for them.

Concerned by the implications he'd drawn from the event, von der Heydte recalled several of his units that were on maneuvers inland. He had an uneasy feeling, the parachute commander confided to aides.

A cook in a German battery located a mile from Second Lieutenant Arthur Jahnke's Strongpoint W-5, was another who had an intuitive feeling that "something big" was about to strike the area. As had been his practice, just after 5 P.M. on June 5 the cook walked to the nearby farm owned by the Lavelle family to get a drink of fresh water. He puzzled the farm residents by saying, "This is certainly the last time I'll come. There is very bad news in store for us."

The German cook was prophetic—he never returned. His corpse, mutilated by grenade fragments, would be found the next morning sprawled by his mobile kitchen.

These were the exceptions. Most Germans along the Atlantic Wall, and those in the rarified atmosphere of the Oberkommando der Wehrmacht, relaxed the evening of June 5, confident that the turbulent English Channel, and the heavy winds and overcast skies predicted for the morrow would keep tethered the Allied war machine straining at its leash in the British Isles.

In the French village of La Madeleine, close to what the invaders called Utah Beach, the *Feldgrau* (field gray, after their uniforms), the average German soldiers were feasting, drinking, and singing raucously. They whooped and applauded a visiting troupe of actors.

The master of ceremonies had burst onto the stage and called out, "How much longer are we going to sit on this keg of dynamite?" The rafters rocked with laughter. Humor, dry "inside" humor, was not limited to the Allied armies.

In a few hours they would learn that the joke was on them: indeed the powder keg would soon explode, and there would be nothing funny about it.

As the last faint rays of daylight prepared to vanish, three-17-year-old *Fallschirmjaeger* (paratroopers) of the German 6th Parachute Regiment were perspiring after several hours of carefree volleyball. Wolfgang Geritzlehner, Egon Rohrs, and Josef Kiessel were quite worried. None had ever been under fire. Their unit had been sitting idly in place for many weeks.

"You know, I'm afraid this damned war might end before I get into it," Geritzlehner fretted to his comrades. In less than twelve hours all three would be pressed to the ground near Sainte-Mère-Église under a frightening hail of Allied bombs and naval artillery rounds. One would vanish— the victim of a direct hit by a huge shell.

On the June 5 eve of a world-shaking event, pessimism and gloom hung like a choking pall over the highest councils of military and government in England and the United States. In the White House in Washington, D.C., President Franklin D. Roosevelt, whose cousin Brigadier General Teddy Roosevelt at that moment was sailing for an appointment on the northern coast of France, spent a quiet evening with First Lady Eleanor. At last the President was able to tell her the momentous secret he had shared with few others in America—D-Day would be at dawn in Normandy. Apprehensive and restless, Franklin and Eleanor prayed.

In London, Prime Minister Winston Churchill, nearly seventy, but keen and energetic spent the evening quietly drinking brandy with his long-time male secretary. The British Bulldog was uncommonly silent. Even brooding. More than most, Churchill realized that all the cards were on the table.

In keeping with his low-key personality, General George Marshall, the U.S. Army's senior soldier, who was responsible more than anyone else for raising, training, and sending Eisenhower's force overseas, declined to inform others of his whereabouts on the eve of momentous events. He was thought to be in the War Department, on hand to receive the earliest news flashes from Normandy.

Marshall's opposite number in the British Army, Field-Marshal Alan Brooke, poured out his deep inner concerns to his diary: "I am very uneasy. At the worst it may well be the most ghastly disaster of the whole war. I wish to God it were safely over."

Dwight Eisenhower by midnight had returned to invasion headquarters at Southwick House, Portsmouth, after a two-hour ride with his driver Kay Summersby and naval aide Commander Harry C. Butcher. Summersby and Butcher had been with the supreme commander for two years and were quick to sense his moods. The long drive from the airfields was made in almost total silence. Eisenhower, his brow furrowed much of the time, was deep in thought and worry.

In the remaining hours until reports filtered in from Normandy, the supreme commander nervously paced the floor; he chain-smoked, gulped down cup after cup of coffee, and tried to relax by engaging in his favorite diversion—reading Western pulp magazines.

Nearby, the one man in the Allied camp who was impervious to the electric tension had been sound asleep since 10 P.M. Field-Marshal Bernard Montgomery, commander of ground forces for Neptune, without fail crawled into bed each night at that time, regardless of the battle situation. Montgomery knew that he had done all he could do. Neptune's implementation now was out of his hands, so he saw no reason to sit up late and worry about it.

Across the Channel in France and in Germany, the turbulent weather that had so recently tried the judgment and emotions of the Allied supreme commander and his battle leaders soothed the German commanders. It had been one of the hottest, driest spring seasons in the memory of oldtimers in France. But early on the morning of June 4 a raging storm broke out over Normandy and throughout central France, deluging the landscape with sheets of rain and rattling windows with gale-force winds.

Later that day at his Paris office, Professor Walther Stroebe, the Luftwaffe colonel who was chief meteorologist for German forces in the West, forecast disturbed weather over the Channel for the next several days. He predicted winds of Force 7 at Cherbourg and Force 6 at the Pas-de-Calais, with a cloud base of 900 to 1,800 feet—conditions that ruled out Allied aerial bombardment or paratroop operations. The current storm had lashed the Channel into a frothy frenzy with waves of seven to nine feet, making an amphibious assault impossible.

During this period the tide and moon would be right for an Allied landing, but the turbulent weather would rule out combined amphibious operations along the French coast for two weeks, the German navy assured Rommel.

So certain was Professor Stroebe and his top aide, Major Ludwig Lettau, that an Allied landing would be impossible for at least two weeks that they gave officers the day off on June 5 to take in the sights and fleshpots of Paris.

Neither Stroebe nor Lettau had the means to spot an alarming danger signal: conditions in the Atlantic had abruptly changed and a new front bringing improved weather was heading toward the Channel—the front detected by Group Captain John Stagg and his meteorological associates in England. Unlike Stagg, Stroebe had no far-reaching network of weather stations, well-equipped weather ships, and aircraft in the Atlantic.

With these certain omens of treacherous weather on June 5 the Wehrmacht relaxed. Field Marshal von Rundstedt had a long, enjoyable luncheon with his son, a young lieutenant, at his favorite dining spot outside Paris. Von Rundstedt was looking forward to driving to the coast the following morning, June 6, to show his son the Atlantic Wall. The Commander in Chief, West, retired early at his comfortable chateau at Saint-Germain, since there was no reason to alter his routine. Earlier that day he had sent off a situation report to OKW in Berlin: "As yet there is no immediate prospect for the Grossinvasion."

Erwin Rommel was dining in casual clothes with his wife Lucie Maria and son Manfred at the family's modest frame home in the hillside village of Herrlingen, outside Ulm in southern Germany. With his chauffeur Daniel at the wheel, Rommel had left his headquarters at the Chateau de la Roche at 6 A.M. the morning of June 5 for the long drive to Herrlingen.

Rommel had an urgent personal reason for wanting to get home, so he was thankful for the raging storm that was lashing the Channel. June 6 was Lucie Maria's birthday. Officially, the Desert Fox was en route to *Adlerhorst* (Eagle's Nest), Hitler's retreat on towering Obersalzburg near Berchtesgaden, to make one final appeal to the Führer to turn over to his control the armored divisions being held in reserve far behind the coast.

"I can smash the enemy at the beaches if I have those panzers and move them up closer to the shoreline where they can counterattack the first day!" a frustrated Rommel had often exploded to his aides.

While a mighty armada of 6,939 Allied vessels was plowing through the heavy swells of the Channel, Hitler was relaxing with his mistress Eva Braun and absorbing the melodic strains of Wagner at the Eagle's Nest. A night person, the Führer idled away the hours at the plush Bavarian chalet until 4 A.M. on June 6, when he gulped several barbiturate pills and climbed into bed.

Admiral Walther Hennecke, the naval commander at Cherbourg, was entertaining guests in a lavish affair at his villa atop his underground command post. Lieutenant General Dr. Hans Speidel, Rommel's intellectual chief of staff who had been left behind to mind the store, was hosting a small dinner party at the Chateau de la Roche the evening of June 5, sure in the knowledge that the Allies could not strike that night.

In Caen, Major General Josef Richter, concluding a staff conference that night at the headquarters of his 716th Infantry Division, solemnly told the gathering that he had learned from a "high authority" that the invasion would take place between June 6 and 10. As his colonels stared at him, Richter added, "Of course I've been receiving the same warning at every new and full moon since April 1." A chorus of laughter rocked the room.

Colonel General Friedrich Dollmann, the silver-haired commander of Seventh Army, which was responsible for defending Normandy and Brittany, was away from his headquarters in Le Mans this night of June 5. He was in Rennes to which he had summoned his corps and division commanders for a paper *kriegspiel,* war game. One of those driving through the dark, rain-swept night for Rennes for the next day's meeting was Lieutenant General Karl von Schlieben, the commander of the 709th Coastal Division whose mission it was to defend the port of Cherbourg.

As Wehrmacht commanders relaxed or slept, secure in the knowledge that the invasion was impossible for the present, minutes after midnight on June 6 more than eighteen thousand American and British paratroopers began bailing out of aircraft into the dark unknown of a hostile Normandy, their billowing white parachutes resplendent as they swayed gently in the breeze. It was a fascinating sight—an awe-inspiring one to the German grenadiers below who were soon to feel the wrath of these warriors from the sky.

It was 12 minutes into D-Day when Lieutenant Noel Poole, a member of Great Britain's elite Special Air Service, leaped from a Royal Air Force Stirling flying 3,000 feet above the Cotentin Peninsula. Poole was in charge of a three-member detachment known as a Titanic party, and he became the first Allied paratrooper to touch down on Fortress Europe.

Lieutenant Poole struck the tail of the aircraft he bailed out; he was stunned, but landed safely in a daze in a wet meadow some five miles west of Saint-Lô. A few minutes later a second Titanic party, commanded by Captain Harry Fowles, jumped into the same general area.

As Lieutenant Poole and Captain Fowles and their men reached ground, a formation of Stirlings flew overhead and dropped more than two hundred half-size dummy paratroopers. When they hit the ground, the dummies emitted the strident sounds of battle—simulated rifle and machine-gun fire and all the pyrotechnics of a fierce firefight. The Special Air Service men on the ground then turned on loudspeakers and recordings of mortar shells exploding, officers' shouted commands, cries of the wounded; all rang out across the dark landscape.

Similar deception operations took place at numerous other points all the way to the outskirts of Paris, more than 100 miles from the Normandy landing beaches. The purpose of this ingenious strategem was to send mobile German reserves out into the countryside chasing these "airborne attacks" while the U.S. 82nd and 101st Airborne Divisions landed in the Cotentin Peninsula and the Red Devils of the British 6th Airborne Division touched down in the vicinity of Caen.

As German night fighter-planes in northern France scrambled into the air to pursue 31 British and American bombers heading toward Germany—the bombers were dropping *Window,* metal foil strips to make it appear to German radar that the small force was a huge Allied bomber stream—hundreds of C-47s carrying American paratroopers knifed in over Normandy without losing a single aircraft to the Luftwaffe. Although the sky train carrying the 82nd and 101st was unmolested by German fighters, the parachute force began running into unforeseen difficulties.

Heavy flak, a strong wind, darkness, and pathfinder detachments dropped far from the true landing zones, all contributed to a chaotic situation for American paratroop formations. Maxwell Taylor's 101st Airborne was scattered over an area some 28 by 17 miles. Within two hours nearly fifteen hundred of its sixty-six hundred parachutists were dead, captured, drowned, or seriously crippled by injuries received when they crashed into the ground.

Resourceful by nature and trained to function in unfavorable situations behind enemy lines, the Screaming Eagles assembled into small parties in the darkness and promptly attacked the primary division objectives, the five causeways leading inland from Utah. As anti-invasion measures, Rommel's engineers had manipulated the century-old La Barquette locks near Carentan to cause the Douve River and its tributary, the Merderet, to spill over and flood the lowlands behind Utah Beach.

The only way a seaborne landing force could drive inland to the high ground was by using the five causeways to cross the inundated regions. A couple of machine guns and two or three mortars positioned at each end of a causeway could hold up Allied invaders indefinitely until German reinforcements could rush to the area from around Cherbourg to drive the attackers into the Channel.

Seizing those five causeways was crucial to the Utah assault. By dawn of D-Day the crossings were in the hands of baggy-pantsed paratroopers wearing Screaming Eagle shoulder patches.

Major General Matthew Ridgway's 82nd Airborne Division encountered similar difficulties. Dropped at 2:30 A.M., one hour after the 101st Airborne had jumped, its three parachute regiments under Brigadier General James Gavin were scattered from the Carentan region, at the base of the Cotentin Peninsula, all the way north to Valognes, 10 miles south of Cherbourg. Drownings took a particularly heavy toll among the 82nd parachutists, who plunged into swamps and flooded areas and were dragged under as they struggled to free themselves from chutes and heavy equipment.

As with the 101st, Ridgway's men up and down the peninsula gathered into small groups, headed toward drop zones, and before dawn were fighting for their objectives—holding crossings over the Douve and Merderet, capturing Sainte-Mère-Église and defending positions north of that once-quiet little town to prevent German troops around Cherbourg from smashing into the right flank of the bridgehead.

True to his promise of the previous night, two hours before Colonel Jim Van Fleet's 8th Infantry Regiment stormed ashore at Utah, 82nd Airborne battalion commander, Lieutenant Colonel Ed Krause, proudly raised the American flag that had flown over Naples the previous September from "the tallest building in Sainte-Mère-Église"—a three-story structure. The first Nazi-occupied town in France had been liberated.

Major-General Richard Gale's British 6th Airborne Division was more fortunate in its drop in the vicinity of Caen, in front of the British and

Canadian landing beaches. The Red Devils came down more or less on their assigned drop zones and quickly seized objectives. The battle-tested and fully equipped 21st Panzer Division was only a few miles away from the Red Devils' landing, but its commander, Major General Edgar Feuchtinger, did nothing, although he had alerted his command to strike. Feuchtinger had been sternly warned not to make any move until ordered to do so by Field Marshal Rommel.

Rommel could not give the order. He was relaxing with Frau Rommel at the family home in Herrlingen, hundreds of miles away.

BLOODY JOURNEY TO A PORT

7

Thunder Over the English Channel

A t 2:29 A.M. on June 6, the USS *Bayfield,* carrying the Navy task force commander for Utah, Rear Admiral Donald Moon, and the ground commander, Major General J. Lawton Collins, slipped silently into its assigned position off the landing beaches. Around the *Bayfield,* their silhouettes ghost-like in the darkness, were other troop transports, large landing craft jammed with infantrymen, warships, and communications vessels. It was eerie there in the silence and grotesque shadows of the night.

Less than a dozen miles away, thousands of German defenders of the vaunted Atlantic Wall were in position. Were they alert and ready? Or asleep? Until this moment, the mammoth fleet had apparently gone undetected by German radar, the Kriegsmarine or the Luftwaffe. Inland behind Utah thousands of American paratroopers were engaging in countless scattered and confused firefights with a surprised enemy force, but here off the beach tranquility reigned.

Suddenly the quiet on the *Bayfield* and surrounding vessels was shattered. Chains rattled and scores of heavy iron anchors plunged into the dark waters of the Channel, sending tingles of concern up the spines of countless fighting men. An anguished voice called out in the darkness of a *Bayfield* deck, "For Chrissake, why in the hell don't we send the Krauts a telegram and let them know we're here?"

Everyone was edgy. The anonymous call expressed the sentiments of all, including Admiral Moon and General Collins, who stood side by side on the dark bridge, peering intently through the night toward Utah, unseen in the blackness just over the horizon. Both commanders were deeply perplexed: how could they have anchored under the noses of a customarily vigilant Wehrmacht totally undiscovered?

As Collins conferred quietly with his friend Don Moon, the corps commander was once more gripped with a deep concern he had felt for several weeks—the admiral's health and emotional outlook. Collins, himself a bundle of energy and a hard worker, had noticed that all through Neptune planning Moon habitually labored long, tedious hours without respite, and had brought an even heavier burden upon himself by insisting on handling routine details instead of delegating them to his staff. Admiral Moon was incredibly conscientious and dedicated.

Often, back in Plymouth over the weeks, Collins had thrust his head into Moon's office at the end of the day to invite the admiral to join him for tennis or a relaxing walk. Invariably, Moon would politely decline with, "I'll take a rain check." The "rain" never arrived.

Collins had discerned another trait in Admiral Moon in recent weeks, one that concerned him still more: Moon, obviously near exhaustion from his ceaseless back-breaking, mind-numbing workload, combined with previous harrowing experiences escorting convoys to Russia, had grown fearful, given to exaggerated concerns—a dangerous frame of mind for a battle commander.

General Collins, there in the darkness of the *Bayfield,* quickly dismissed these fleeting thoughts from his mind. There were far more significant immediate concerns. But Collins' worry over his friend's health proved valid. A few weeks after D-Day, gentle, pleasant, capable Don Moon would take his own life, an invasion casualty as surely as if he had been struck down by enemy action.

Suddenly there was a roar of aircraft engines. Collins and Moon looked up and saw that the low-flying silhouettes were not Luftwaffe bombers but American C-47s heading back to England after dropping the 82nd Airborne Division inland. As the oncoming transport planes approached from the west at nearly masthead level, a chill surged through General Collins. He recalled that in a similar situation off landing beaches in Sicily the previous July, 23 C-47s loaded with paratroopers of the 82nd Airborne were mistaken for enemy aircraft and shot down by nervous, trigger-happy "friendly" gunners on ships and ashore. Was this tragedy about to be repeated? The C-47s definitely were off course. They were supposed to avoid the heavy concentration of Allied vessels off Utah.

Collins held his breath and offered up a brief, silent prayer as the lumbering C-47s flew low over the vast assemblage of shipping. Later he was able to breathe a sigh of relief—not a shot had been fired by the hundreds of guns in the fleet.

Just as had the *Bayfield,* up and down a 60-mile stretch of Normandy coast several thousand vessels were steathily edging into position, 11 to 12 miles from the shoreline. Everywhere there were disconcerting thoughts. Where was the Luftwaffe? The fast, deadly E-boats? The artillery fire from the massive German coastal guns? All was quiet—and sinister.

Was one of the most monumental traps in military history about ready to be sprung? Had the Wehrmacht known for hours that some fifty-six Allied convoys were on the way and were they stealthily lying in wait? Perhaps at that point, when the amphibious attack was at its most vulnerable, Hitler would unveil his long-promised secret weapons.

And what was the significance of the Germans leaving the tall, brilliant light at Barfleur, one of the brightest beacons in the world, burning all night? Was the Barfleur light to be suddenly extinguished at the proper time as a signal to German units up and down the vast sweep of the Normandy coastline to spring the diabolical trap on the unsuspecting invaders? Perhaps the beacon would signal the incendiary blaze that would engulf the shoreline far out to sea and burn to a black crisp every Allied soldier caught in the devil's cauldron. That was the rumor that had spread through the 4th Infantry Division transports the day before.

At 3:35 A.M., General Omar Bradley, commander of the assaulting U.S. First Army, was in restless slumber below deck on the nine thousand-ton American cruiser *Augusta,* anchored 11 miles off Omaha Beach and some 20 miles east of the USS *Bayfield.* Bradley had gone below at 11 P.M., removed his life preserver and with boots still on climbed into bed. It would be a hectic nerve-wracking time for Bradley in the days and nights ahead, and he would need what little sleep he could steal.

Suddenly there was a loud clanging from a bell just outside his quarters. The crew were being summoned to battle stations. Bradley grabbed his helmet and preserver (which all troops were required to wear) and rushed to the bridge. Neptune had been launched.

There was a throbbing roar of powerful aircraft engines overhead as 1,327 Royal Air Force bombers began pounding fortifications and installations up and down the coast of Normandy, between Cherbourg and the mouth of the Seine. There was a steady ker-thump, ker-thump as tens of thousands of heavy bombs exploded. Much of the sky along the coast reflected an eerie orange glow as countless fires raged out of control.

As RAF bombers were dropping their lethal burdens along the Atlantic

Wall and farther inland, below deck on the *Bayfield* assault troops of Colonel Van Fleet's 8th Infantry Regiment were sitting silently around long tables in the mess hall. They had been served a sumptuous meal of T-bone steaks and all the trimmings, plus ice cream and other delicacies they had all but forgotten existed. Few had an appetite; most simply picked at their food.

"This is the United States Army's version of the Last Supper," a voice called out. No one laughed. Somehow humor had gone out of their lives, left behind days before in the Pink Ox, the Queen's Carriage, the Boar's Head, and other friendly, cozy little pubs of southern England when the impending clash on the Far Shore was still an abstract exercise to be implemented at some future date. Now the ominous steel-and-concrete Atlantic Wall, with its ponderous guns, forests of minefields, and spitting machine guns was suddenly real—and immediate.

It was 4:05 A.M. Below deck in the cramped, dingy holds of the *Bayfield,* the *Barnet* and other attack transports off Utah, assault troops of Van Fleet's 8th Infantry waited nervously. Many were struck with sudden or recurring attacks of religion, pulling out miniature Bibles and prayer books to read a few last-minute verses. Some felt in pockets to make sure their crucifixes were in place. Here and there lips moved imperceptibly in silent prayer.

Moments later intercom systems in the holds called out a chilling message: "Assault troops to your boarding stations!"

With a rustling of gear, the infantrymen scrambled up steel ladders and onto the decks, then to assigned positions just above the tiny LCVPs (landing craft, vehicular-personnel) that would carry them onto the hostile beaches. The LCVPs were pitching and heaving about in the seven foot swells, clanging and banging against the iron sides of the transports. The din reverberated long distances over the sea, and nervous assault troops cursed and ranted over this "announcement that we're on the way."

Despite the loud clatter of the 30-foot LCVPs striking repeatedly against the hulls of the larger vessels, Van Fleet's men talked in whispers as though the enemy, 11½ miles away, might overhear them. Muted loudspeakers rasped out an occasional message. "Why doesn't someone shut that son of a bitch up?" a nervous voice called out in the darkness on the *Barnet.*

The moon darted in and out of the clouds, occasionally outlining the sleek configurations of command ships bristling with a forest of antennae, control vessels, destroyers, and attack transports. All were dark. Everything around was dark and eerie. Ears were cocked for the distinctive throb of airplane motors that would herald the arrival of the Luftwaffe. Where was the Luftwaffe? Even the most myopic German bombardier could hardly have missed the juicy target of hundreds of Allied ships anchored off Normandy.

Nervous, faces grim or contorted from strain, men of the 8th Infantry stood by on deck as the seconds ticked away. Stomachs knotted and churned. Perspiration dotted foreheads. Palms perspired. Knees felt weak, even jelly-like. Old friends solemnly shook hands. There were whispers of "Good luck!" and "See you on the beach!" What else was there to say at a time like that? Some men vomited.

As the infantrymen stood along railings in silence, another call, this one frightening and with a tone of finality, rang out over the decks: "Now hear this—board your landing boats!"

It was the dreaded order most did not want to hear. Yet each knew it had to come.

"Okay, let's go men," young lieutenants and captains called out, as legs were thrown over railings and, with a heavy rustle of equipment, Colonel Van Fleet's boys began the hazardous descent down slippery rope ladders and into the LCVPs.

Curses rang out as men lost their footing and dangled from the ladders by their arms alone, often kicking the man below in the face. Rifle barrels were inadvertently swung against the head or body of other men slithering down the slippery rope. A few feet below, the LCVPs heaved upward in the violent swells of the Channel, and it was a perilous task to time the final leap into the bucking little boats. Many crashed onto the unyielding steel bottoms in tangled heaps.

Inching his way methodically down the rope ladder of the *Barnet* was the imperturbable mortar-squad sergeant, Karl Kaupert. As he always did in training, Kaupert carried out the transfer to his LCVP in routine fashion. "Just another monumental military operation," he was thinking. He felt to see if his comic book, stashed in a musette bag strapped to his back, was in place. It was a new one and he hadn't had a chance to read it yet.

Scrambling down the rope net of the *Bayfield* with no apparent difficulty was a fighting man nearly three times Sergeant Kaupert's age. Clutching his main weapon—a wooden cane—Brigadier General Teddy Roosevelt negotiated the arduous descent and dropped into the pitching LCVP. His assault boat would be one of the twenty carrying the six hundred men of the 2nd Battalion who would be the first Americans to storm ashore on Fortress Europe, at Utah Beach. The 1st Battalion would come in right on the heels of Teddy Roosevelt's spearheading force.

Once all the LCVPs were loaded, they began to circle endlessly around the mother ships, waiting for the long, cold, wet run. Already men were violently ill, from tension and the pitching and lurching of the tiny LCVPs tossed about like matchsticks in the heavy swells. It was much like riding a bucking bronco. As each powerful wave crest replaced another every few seconds, the LCVPs and their cargoes of fighting men would nearly rise off the water and the wave would strike the little craft with a tremendous impact. Soon a rhythm had been established by the angry waves—slap, slap, slap, slap.

Each time a new wave would smash into an LCVP it would give the miserable assault troops a sensation of being punched in the stomach by a giant fist. With each new wave, a shower of English Channel water would pour over the huddled men of the 8th Infantry, inundating them and their already sagging spirits. In minutes each man had been soaked to the skin. The wind was howling and cold, and the relentless pattern of dousings with sea water and chilling blasts of air caused even the heartiest to shiver uncontrollably.

It was nearly 4:45 A.M., 105 minutes until H-hour, when the naval assault-controller boomed out the final instructions—Teddy Roosevelt and his six hundred men, crammed thirty to a boat, were to start the run to the beaches. The twenty lurching LCVPs maneuvered abreast and, with a loud revving of engines the boats roared off toward Utah, 11.5 miles away and unseen in the inky blackness over the horizon.

The drive to capture the port of Cherbourg had been launched.

Huddled in their bucking assault craft, fearful and miserable, the men in the first wave periodically shouted to be heard above the rumble of motors and the roaring of waves, "Why in hell haven't the Krauts opened up?" Out in front of them in the darkness were twenty-eight German gun batteries in the network of coastal fortifications defending the sector that included Utah. These batteries were composed of 110 guns ranging from mammoth 210-millimeter guns at Saint-Marcouf and 170-millimeter guns at Cap Barfleur, at the northeast tip of the peninsula, to 75- and 88-millimeter field pieces.

Causing General Joe Collins, commander of the assaulting U.S. VII Corps, and his battle leaders the most worry were the heavy naval guns at Saint-Marcouf, seven miles north of Utah and four miles inland. Besides four of the long-barreled 210-millimeter guns, the position sprouted six 75 millimeter antiaircraft guns and one 150-millimeter gun—all under thick concrete casements.

Collins had no way of knowing that his deep concern about Saint-Marcouf was unwarranted; the four big guns were not yet fully installed. And because the Channel weather was so turbulent, making *der Grossinvasion* impossible for at least two weeks, most of the four hundred gunners, a hodgepodge group of men over thirty-eight, were in more comfortable quarters in the nearby villages of Saint-Marcouf and Crisbecq as the U.S. 8th Infantry Regiment moved toward the Cotentin beaches.

Meanwhile, the twenty spearheading LCVPs carrying Roosevelt's men, many of them now covered with their own vomit and furiously bailing out water to keep from being swamped, burrowed on through the heaving swells. At H-hour minus 40 minutes, a mighty roar, a cacophony of sound, suddenly erupted, piercing the ears of the assaulting troops and echoing for miles across the turbulent sea. It was music to the ears of these infantrymen, upon whom the success of the entire Utah operation depended.

Seventeen gray-colored, powerful warships of Navy Task Force 129, under U.S. Rear Admiral Morton L. Deyo, had opened fire over the heads of the advancing LCVPs and were pounding known German gun batteries and strongpoints. Battleships anchored 11,000 yards offshore and cruisers in place only 5,000 yards from the sandy beaches sent salvo after salvo of huge shells hurtling toward enemy positions. Deyo's guns, belching orange flame and thick black clouds of smoke, lifted their fire when company commanders in Teddy Roosevelt's first wave fired flares into the air, signalling that the LCVPs were nearing the shoreline. Naval gunfire was then shifted to inland targets.

At 5:52 A.M. two hundred and seventy-six Marauders of Major General Hoyt S. Vandenberg's U.S. Ninth Air Force winged overhead in precise formation and cascaded 4,400 tons of bombs onto the Utah Beach sector, a deluge that caused the ground to tremble and sent gushers of earth and pieces of concrete and debris hurtling skyward. Due to the overcast and the fear of hitting assault troops, many bombs exploded harmlessly a mile or two inland, but most found their targets.

Hardly had the last American Marauder droned off in the distance than twelve ships mounted with 4.7-inch guns let loose with a continuing barrage that raked the shoreline and points just behind it. Moments later, with Teddy Roosevelt's assault wave only 700 yards from the beach, eerie screeches suddenly rent the air. Thousands of rockets, fired from eighteen specially equipped vessels, shot high into the dismal sky and crashed down onto German bunkers, batteries, and strongpoints.

In the concrete bunkers the heavy naval and air bombardment was ceaseless, uninterrupted hell for the cringing German defenders. Shells and bombs fell upon the entire sweep of the coastline. Inside a thick-walled position known as W-5, located directly in the path of General Roosevelt's oncoming assault wave, Lieutenant Jahnke, the bespectacled veteran of the Russian front, tried to calm his terrified men. Jahnke, who had been seriously wounded on the Eastern Front and medically downgraded to duty on an inactive sector, had himself been under heavy fire many times—but never anything like this.

All around W-5, trenches were leveled. Barbed-wire entanglements were ripped to shreds and scattered to the winds. Painstakingly prepared minefields were blown up, shaking Jahnke's bunker as they exploded. Blockhouses were caved in and sand sent gushing into the air by bombs poured in on the terrified defenders. A nearby stone building used by Jahnke as a telephone communications center was blown from the face of the earth.

Many of the German soldiers went berserk under the horrible man-made rain of steel and explosives. They screamed and shouted, thrashed around on the bunker floors, pressed hands over terrified eyes and ears as if to shut off the nightmare that had suddenly and without warning been unleashed upon them. Other Germans merely lay still in the sand or in bunkers, staring sightlessly into space as bombs and shells exploded around them. Only the periodic blinking of their eyes distinguished them from the dead. These had taken total leave of their senses.

Bits and pieces of what had once been human bodies were hurled into the air by explosive blasts—arms, legs, mangled heads. Screams of the mutilated wounded rang out above the din. And still the blows continued to strike the German defenders along the shoreline.

The terrific pounding by sea and by air had raised a thick, choking pall for long stretches up and down the sandy shores, where only the day before carefree members of the Wehrmacht had been frolicking, secure in the knowledge that the Allies would not strike for many days. Smoke, dust, and haze now obscured the coast.

Now, with the 20 LCVPs carrying American assault troops only 300 yards from Utah, and wave after wave of follow-up echelons behind them, an eerie blanket of silence had fallen over the beach. American naval gunfire had been lifted, but the Germans were too stunned and confused to rake the targets approaching from the sea.

In his little assault boat at the center of the line of LCVPs, General Roosevelt, clutching his walking cane in one hand and a commander's inevitable map case in the other, was peering intently ahead through the narrow vision slot in the ramp. He was perplexed by what he saw—or did not see. The pall of smoke and dust clinging to the beach had drawn a curtain over the few terrain features that were to guide in the first wave. For countless hours he had studied photographs of the beach; now there was no landmark he recognized. Something definitely had gone wrong, Roosevelt knew. Always imperturbable, he kept his apprehensions to himself for the moment.

The spunky little general took a hurried peek at his wristwatch. It was precisely H-hour—6:30 A.M. That's a good omen, he thought, the first wave hitting the beach right on time. Moments later Roosevelt's LCVP scraped bottom, still 200 yards from his force's immediate goal, the seawall that ran for 10,000 yards along the edge of the sand dunes. There the assaulting battalion could gain cover behind the masonry barricade, which was four to five feet high, and hurriedly organize for the push inland.

The young Navy coxswain, steering the craft from his exposed position at the rear of the LCVP, lowered the large, heavy ramp at the bow, which groaned and creaked in protest. Roosevelt and others in his boat leaped down into the thigh-high water. Those in the remaining 19 LCVPs in the first wave also were scrambling off ramps into the surf, and the six hundred men of the 8th Infantry, tense, wary, rifles at the ready, began slogging ashore.

Now Roosevelt and his relatively few men were at their most vulnerable, wading ashore with no cover or concealment. Eyes peered intently ahead, seeking to part the thick pall of smoke, dust, and haze, which, they were convinced, concealed unknown terrors about to engulf them.

Inside his concrete bunker in W-5, the German strongpoint along the shore in front of Roosevelt's assault wave, Lieutenant Jahnke was trying to rally his dazed men. The massive bombardment had lifted, and Jahnke, gazing out through vision apertures, could see the long line of American soldiers advancing through the surf toward him. Behind the first wave of invaders Jahnke detected another group of LCVPs heading for the beach—the second wave, consisting of the 1st Battalion of the 8th Infantry.

There was no time to lose. "Open fire!" he shouted. "Open fire!" He called out the order to his left and to his right where machine-gun crews and 88-millimeter gunners were to be in place. The order was passed along to several positions, but there were few machine guns or 88s still operable after the bombardment.

As the American first wave scrambled across the wide beach toward the seawall, a few 80-millimeter mortar rounds began to explode around the advancing soldiers, and here and there an isolated German machine gun loosed short, sporadic bursts. An 88 gun, placed in the turret of a buried French tank, began to rake the beach, but in minutes it was taken under fire by vessels offshore and put out of action.

Lieutenant Jahnke was near despair. "It looks as though God and the entire world have foresaken us," he mused resignedly to one of his men, whose nose and ears were oozing blood from the concussion of naval shells that had struck their bunker. "Where's the Luftwaffe? Where's the Kriegsmarine? What happened to our artillery? Where's the artillery observer in the church tower at Sainte-Marie-du-Mont—asleep?"

The observer had not fallen asleep. Shortly after dawn an American fighter-bomber had swooped in low over Sainte-Marie-du-Mont and blasted the observer out of the spire. His presence in the vantage point would have achieved nothing—at the same time he was taken under attack American Marauders had bombed his gun battery into twisted chunks of metal.

Only a few 88-millimeter shells, fired from mobile batteries concealed far off in the distance, joined in protesting the invaders' arrival. Here and there one of Roosevelt's men went down from enemy action as the first assault wave trotted up to the protective embrace of the seawall. "What the hell's going on?" a soldier called out in disbelief. He and his comrades were amazed at the lightness of the fire they met as they waded ashore.

Minutes later twenty-three LCVPs carrying the second wave scrunched to a halt offshore, and 605 members of the 1st Battalion, crouching over by instinct, hurriedly moved across the great open beaches and joined their comrades along the seawall.

Hunkered down behind the concrete barricade, General Roosevelt was intently studying his map. He concluded that the entire first and second waves had landed some 2,000 yards south of the intended beach.

"I'm going to have a look around," Roosevelt told a young second lieutenant. With that the son of a president got to his feet, his walking cane in hand, and moved up over the seawall and onto the dunes ahead.

Strolling nonchalantly along he would have made a fine target for any German sniper. Roosevelt continued on to the head of the causeways that would be used for the 4th Division to advance inland, then returned to his former position along the seawall.

"I'm convinced we're about a mile and a quarter south of where we're supposed to be," General Roosevelt told the two 8th Infantry battalion commanders, lieutenant colonels Conrad C. Simmons and Carlton O. MacNeely. "I think we ought to push on inland, anyhow. There don't seem to be too many live Germans around."

A cool, veteran campaigner who realized there was not a moment to be lost, Teddy Roosevelt quickly improvised an attack to seize a causeway and push inland across the inundated area. "Okay, let's move out!" the brigadier rasped to Simmons and MacNeely. "If those German bastards want war, this is a good enough place to start it!"

In minutes shouted commands rang out along the seawall, and with a rustling of equipment being adjusted, hundreds of 8th Infantry assault troops climbed to their feet and moved out across the sand dunes toward the nearest causeway. Without pause the men of the 4th Infantry Division assault waves pushed on across the flooded area toward the main lateral road three miles inland. Their progress was impeded only by an occasional sniper and sporadic eighty-eight sky bursts.

General Roosevelt, trudging along the causeway, had no way of knowing it at the time, but God had apparently taken a hand in the Utah assault—on the American side. A combination of tides and the obliteration of terrain features by the heavy bombing and naval barrage caused the first waves to come ashore more than a mile off-target, and that resulted in far fewer difficulties for them than had they arrived where planned. Underwater obstacles were much less thickly planted and fortifications less formidable than they were on the designated strip of beach to the north.

This act of Providence, together with those of Admiral Mort Deyo's naval gunners, the airmen of General Vandenberg's Ninth Air Force, and the paratroopers of the 82nd and 101st Airborne Divisions, provided the Utah assault troops with a far less costly path than even the most optimistic SHAEF planner had dreamed possible.

Meanwhile, back on the *Bayfield* about 11 miles from the clouds of smoke and dust clinging to the sandy shores, General Collins was undergoing the inner torment of a high commander who has trained and launched his troops into the assault, and then must bide his time, helpless to

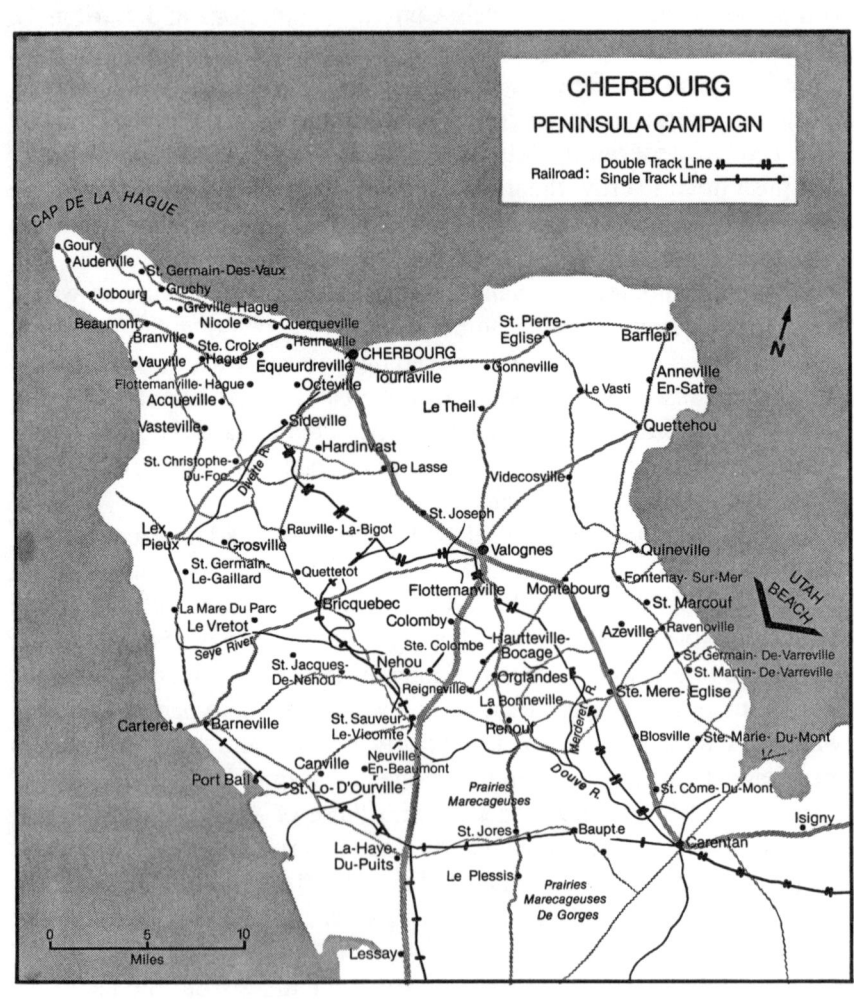

CHERBOURG
PENINSULA CAMPAIGN

Railroad: Double Track Line
Single Track Line

intervene, as the Plan takes over. Collins had had little to do since the first wave sped off in the darkness; now he stood on the bridge and peered intently through his binoculars toward Utah.

There was little of significance the VII Corps commander could see. He had received no reports from the beach. The clock ticked on—6:30 A.M. . . . 7 A.M. . . . 7:15 . . . 8 . . . 8:37 . . . still no word from General Roosevelt, Colonel Van Fleet (who had landed with E Company shortly after the first wave), or anyone else in the assault.

At 9:40 A.M. the radio crackled on the *Bayfield*. A message was coming in from the beach: "I am ashore with Colonel Simmons and General Roosevelt, advancing steadily." It was from Colonel Van Fleet. General Collins breathed a sigh of relief and wide smiles broke out on the command ship.

At 11:45 A.M. Admiral Moon met with reporters on the *Bayfield*. Favorable reports of progress and sporadic resistance continued to pour in, and follow-up troops, weapons, guns, and tanks were moving across Utah.

"The assault has gone essentially according to plan," Moon told the eager-eared newsmen. "The initial build-up has been won. Next phase will be a race between build-up of the Allied forces and movement by the enemy reserves."

Lightning Joe Collins by now was straining at the leash to get ashore and direct the action from his customary vantage point—up close to the fighting. But he knew that in the existing situation he had to remain aboard the *Bayfield*. The ship had been specially equipped with radio communications to keep him in contact with V Corps at Omaha Beach, with General Bradley, with the 4th Infantry Division moving over the beaches, and with the 82nd and 101st Airborne Divisions fighting for their lives a few miles inland. Collins' decision to remain aboard the *Bayfield* proved to be a fortunate one.

Later in the afternoon, Admiral Moon had become deeply disturbed over the loss of several of his vessels to German gunfire and mines. A short time later, Navy Lieutenant Mark Dalton, who had been sent ashore by Moon's intelligence officer to assess and report back on beach conditions, returned and relayed to the admiral the situation as he had found it. He mentioned that the beach was under periodic shellfire.

In the middle of Lieutenant Dalton's presentation, Moon suddenly proposed halting further landing operations. General Collins, who was present, was shocked at the suggestion and its far-reaching implications. It would be disastrous. Though equal in rank to the Navy Task Force commander, Collins knew that Moon was in charge of the operation until VII Corps was firmly established ashore.

Now was the time for a combination of diplomacy and firmness; Lightning Joe Collins adamantly opposed such a drastic proposal and came down hard on his friend, Don Moon. This was the precise situation that Collins had been worried about for several weeks; he'd observed close-up how the admiral had grown fearful as a consequence of intense strain from relentless hours of painstaking, detailed planning for Neptune. As the result of Collins' vehement protest, Moon changed his mind. Landing operations proceeded as planned.

At 6 P.M. on D-Day 21,328 American troops, 1,742 vehicles, and 1,695 tons of supplies had poured over Utah. The initial assault by General Barton's green 4th Infantry Division had been carried out with astonishingly low casualties—12 dead and 106 wounded.

Meanwhile that day, British and Canadian forces had stormed ashore at Gold, Juno, and Sword beaches, along the Calvados coast between Port-en-Bessin and Ouistreham. They then had rapidly dashed inland for a penetration of seven miles at Bayeux, famous for its association with William the Conqueror in the 11th Century. But the primary D-Day objective, the key road junction of Caen, eluded the assault forces.

At Gold, the British 50th Infantry Division, veterans of Sicily and the African desert, encountered stubborn resistance, and the Canadian 3rd Infantry Division at Juno was raked by automatic-weapons fire from bunkers that had survived an aerial saturation bombing. Elements of the 50th Division stormed ashore at Sword and promptly ran into heavy fire and could not link up with the hard-pressed and isolated British 6th Airborne Division for 18 hours.

But it was at Omaha, between the U.S. 4th Infantry Division assault at Utah and the British attack at Gold, that the D-Day situation was the most precarious. At Omaha the invasion nearly met with disaster, due to a combination of faulty intelligence, a turbulent English Channel, and inadequate bombardment.

Allied intelligence had reported that one regiment of the "static" and low-grade German 716th Infantry Division was strung out along the Omaha beaches, but in recent days two regiments of the first-class, veteran 352nd Infantry Division had moved into commanding positions on the bluffs looking down upon the shoreline. Somehow both Ultra and the Centurie spy network had missed this crucial redeployment.

Commanded by Major General Helmuth Kraiss, who was at his command post and ready for action at 2 A.M. following initial reports of Allied paratrooper landings, the men of the 352nd Division had been alerted and calmly lay in wait on the high ground as the American LCVPs churned through the pitching surf toward the beach.

Overhead, Allied medium bombers dropped 1,285 tons of bombs in support of the approaching assault waves of the veteran U.S. 1st Infantry Division and an attached regiment of the 29th Infantry Division. Fearful of striking the assault troops, most bombardiers overshot their targets, and thousands of bombs fell between one and three miles inland.

Virtually untouched by the aerial bombardment or naval gunfire, the experienced grenadiers on the bluff held their fire until the troop-laden LCVPs reached shore and began disgorging their passengers. And then the Germans opened up with every weapon in their arsenal, raking the helpless Americans with rifle, machine-gun, mortar, and artillery fire.

Within minutes, chaos reigned along the strip of beach called Omaha. Many assault troops had leaped from LCVPs into neck-deep water, and were pulled under by the strong current. Others, burdened with heavy weapons and equipment, slogged through the surf and were cut down by automatic-weapons fire. Screams and cries for medics rang out over the din of battle.

Hundreds of dead Americans, bodies mutilated and grotesque, washed back and forth in the heavy surf. Soon the white froth on the water was mixed with the red of blood. Succeeding waves continued to pile up on the beach. A few vehicles got ashore, and now thick black clouds of smoke spiraled into the air where jeeps, trucks, and two or three tanks had been struck by artillery and mortar fire. A debacle was in the making.

Twelve miles offshore on the *Augusta,* General Omar Bradley was facing a momentous decision: should Omaha be written off as a bloody failure and succeeding waves be diverted to Utah or the British beaches?

Once more, Providence took a hand. The sun came out and the winds blew, clearing away the haze, smoke, and dust from the scene of the carnage. Allied fighter-bombers swooped down on German positions on the bluff and on artillery positions to the rear, bombing and strafing. Allied warships, now able to clearly see the targets, moved in perilously close to shore and fired flat-trajectory salvos into the grenadiers along the high ground.

There was a noticeable slackening of fire from the bluff overlooking Omaha. One by one, in tiny groups and even by squads, fighting men of the Big Red One and the 29th Infantry Division began edging up the lower slopes of the bluff. Inspired by their example, others followed, first in driblets, then by the hundreds.

Perched on Pointe et Raz de la Percée, looking down on the swarms of humanity thrashing about on the beaches and now edging up the bluff toward them, German commanders hurriedly put in a call to higher headquarters: the American assault had not been smashed at the waterline as previously reported. In fact, the shaken Wehrmacht leaders on Pointe et Raz de la Percée reported, the invaders were now clambering up the bluff like swarms of locusts.

On the *Augusta,* General Bradley exuded a confident manner; inside he was wracked with worry. The most excruciating ordeal for a top commander, knowing his troops are engaged in a crucial and bloody struggle, is an almost total absence of news. Bradley was undergoing torment as the minutes and the hours ticked by.

At 1:30 P.M., seven hours after the initial assault, a junior officer dashed up to Bradley with a message from Major General Leonard T. Gerow, commander of V Corps: "Troops formerly pinned down on beaches . . . advancing up heights beyond beaches."

Audible sighs of relief and beaming faces erupted on the *Augusta.* But the jubilation was subdued. Although a crisis had been overcome, the hard-pressed fighting men now on the bluff at Omaha were hanging on by their fingertips to a sliver of the bridgehead, without artillery or tanks—and the Germans continued to resist with their customary tenacity.

As follow-up regiments steadily poured over Omaha and moved inland late that afternoon and into the evening, General Bradley, taking advantage of the long daylight, was aboard an American PT boat bound for the USS *Bayfield* off Utah Beach. The skipper was barreling along through the heavy spray with the throttle wide open.

Bradley at first was curious about why two sailors were hugging the bow of the speeding boat, and he asked a junior officer. "Oh, they're watching for floating mines, general," was the reply.

Easily locating the *Bayfield* by its forest of antennae from among the swarm of vessels off Utah, Bradley scrambled up the rope ladder to be greeted by an elated General Joe Collins, who quickly gave him a rundown on the situation in his area. Collins said that he had established contact with Maxwell Taylor's 101st Airborne Division on the southern end of his beachhead, near the village of Pouppeville, shortly after noon. But the fate of Matthew Ridgway's 82nd Airborne, which was to have jumped farther inland, remained unknown.

"No word from Ridgway at all?" Bradley pursued.

"Nope, none at all," Collins replied matter of factly. "But I'm not worried. The 82nd can take care of itself."

General Collins then told the First Army commander of Admiral Moon's proposal that afternoon that landing operations be halted after several vessels had been lost to enemy gunfire and mines.

"Let the Navy expend its ships, if that's what it takes," the tough-minded and realistic Bradley responded. "But we've got to get the build-up ashore even if it means paving the whole damned Channel bottom with ships."

A gloaming was starting to settle in over the embattled Cotentin and Calvados coasts as General Bradley took his leave of General Collins, slithered back down the rope net over the *Bayfield's* side and into his pitching PT boat for the return trip to the *Augusta*. It was nearly dark when the sleek motor craft carrying the First Army commander neared his headquarters ship.

Suddenly antiaircraft guns on scores of nearby vessels opened fire and brilliant streams of tracers crisscrossed the sky. The mysteriously absent Luftwaffe had made its appearance. The PT boat skipper hailed the *Augusta* through a megaphone. "Lie off!" came the stern reply. "Lie off until we get an all-clear!"

For twenty minutes the PT boat and its high brass idly circled the warship, as Bradley became increasingly uneasy. If he had to be caught in the middle of an air attack offshore, he would rather take his chances in the heavy-plated cruiser rather than on a little PT boat with a paper-thin skin.

Again the PT boat edged up to the *Augusta*. "Ahoy—can we come on board now?"

Again came back the call from the darkness above: "Lie off! Lie off!"

"But we've got passengers aboard," the PT skipper shouted.

"*Prisoners?* You've got prisoners?" came back the curious voice in the dark. "Stand by to bring the prisoners aboard."

Hearing the shout concerning German prisoners about to climb aboard, men rushed for the railing. Many sailors had never seen real live German soldiers.

As the army commander wearily pulled his way up the slippery rope ladder and threw a long leg over the rail, a disgusted sailor nearby called out, "Oh, hell, it's *only* General Bradley."

Exhausted, hungry, his head spinning from the deep emotion of the monumental day, Bradley was satisfied with the progress. Hitler's "impregnable" Atlantic Wall had been breached, 57,506 American and

75,215 British and Canadian soldiers had established themselves ashore, and 15,500 American and 7,900 British airborne men were engaging the enemy inland.

Without removing his boots, General Bradley flopped onto a cot and in moments was deep in fitful sleep.

8

Bloodbath
on the
La Fière Causeway

M ajor Friedrich Hayn, intelligence officer of the German
LXXXIV Corps, was at work in the bunker at his headquarters
in Saint-Lô, some 25 miles southwest of Utah Beach at the base
of the Cotentin Peninsula. It was late in the morning of June 8. A liaison
officer from the 352nd Infantry Division, the battle-tested outfit that had
nearly thrown the Americans back into the sea at Omaha Beach two days
previously, burst into Hayn's office.

Begrimed and weary from numerous dashes for the ditches under attack
from strafing American *jabos* (fighter planes) in his perilous drive to
Saint-Lô, the officer tossed a large sack onto Major Hayn's desk.

"What is all that?" Hayn asked, half in curiosity, half in displeasure as
the sack spread a layer of dust across his desk.

"Captured American documents."

"How did you get hold of them?"

The liaison officer said that a smashed landing craft, riddled by gunfire,
had washed up onto land near the point where the Vire River emptied into
the English Channel. On board were five dead American naval officers,
one a beachmaster responsible for directing landing traffic on shore. The
beachmaster had in his dead hands a case containing maps and documents,
apparently of a secret nature.

Major Hayn reached into the water-logged, mud-stained sack and
pulled out a handful of the material, much of it stuck together by the salt
water of the Channel. Hayn's eyes lit up. He knew this was a highly
significant haul. Code words he did not fully understand were stamped in
large letters all over the documents. He recognized timetables and the
names of many French towns, some circled in red crayon.

Hayn immediately sent for interpreters and analysts and excitedly turned over the documents to them, requesting an early report on the contents. In less than a half-hour, one of the analysts rushed back into the intelligence officer's room: "Good news, *Herr Major.* This is the entire operations plan of the Allied forces in the invasion!"

Providence now seemed to have joined the ranks of the Wehrmacht.

Minutes later, General of Artillery Erich Marcks, the astute commander of LXXXIV Corps who had left a leg on a Russian battlefield two years previously, was staring at the captured operations plan laid out before him on a large desk. Marcks could not believe his good luck. Here was a detailed compilation of Allied plans, not only for General Collins's VII Corps on the Cotentin Peninsula but also for the U.S. V Corps at Omaha and the British XXX Corps at the three other beaches.

Peering through his rimless glasses, the laconic General Marcks noted that the first planned step for the Allies, now that they were ashore, was to link up Utah and Omaha beaches at Carentan to establish a continuous beachhead. Suddenly the little town of Carentan, a rail center through which passed Route Nationale 13, the major highway running from Cherbourg to Paris, became of utmost significance.

Marcks promptly ordered copies of the documents made and rushed to all division commanders. Major Hasso Viebig, the corps chief of operations, was designated to hurry the originals to Field Marshal Rommel at Army Group B headquarters at La Roche-Guyon, northwest of Paris. It was not a coveted assignment. Viebig was chased by low-flying fighters virtually all the way to the Chateau de La Roche.

Reflecting on the intelligence coup, General Marcks, though elated, had one gnawing thought: what good was it to have the enemy operational plans in detail if he did not have the resources to thwart those plans?

The commander of LXXXIV Corps had no way of knowing he had no reason to be unduly concerned over the answer to this question. Four days later he would die in a roadside ditch near his headquarters after leaping out of his camouflaged staff car, riddled by the bullets of a strafing fighter plane.

As indicated by the captured plans, the town of Carentan had indeed become a significant locale. General Eisenhower himself had only the day before asked General Bradley why Carentan had not been seized on D plus 1 as called for by the plan.

"You've got to join up with Gerow [V Corps] just as quickly as possible," Bradley told Collins at First Army headquarters in an orchard behind Point du Hoc, near Omaha. Bradley expected the looming attack on Carentan to be a bloody one because the Germans had flooded vast areas of marshland leading to the town.

"If it becomes necessary to save time, put five hundred or even one thousand tons of air on Carentan and take the town apart," Bradley ordered. "Then rush it and you'll get in."

"Rushing" Carentan would be elements of the 101st Airborne Division, which the day before (June 8) had seized the town of Saint-Côme-du-Mont four miles northwest of Carentan and now had established a defensive arc facing southward. Collins told Bradley that he had great confidence that General Taylor's men would soon close the gap between the two American beachheads.

Eisenhower and other Allied leaders had good reason for deep concern over the failure of Utah and Omaha forces to link up rapidly. They feared the wily Erwin Rommel would spot this yawning gap and rush an armored division through it to the coast. Rommel did spot the wide gap—but was helpless to take advantage of it. As the field marshal had constantly warned Hitler, the German armored reserves in France were held back so far from the beaches that it would take many days for them to reach the front under the suffocating blanket of overwhelming Allied air power.

Along with stressing the immediate urgency of seizing Carentan, General Bradley instructed General Collins to drive his VII Corps westward to cut off the Cotentin Peninsula before launching a main effort to capture the port of Cherbourg. Bradley and Collins had hoped that battlefield conditions would be such after the Utah assault that the 4th Infantry Division could turn north and race for Cherbourg. But as the Ivy Division attacked northward along the coast it ran into stubborn opposition from German strongpoints, and enemy reserves rushed down from Cherbourg, many on bicycles.

In order to launch a full-scale attack westward to reach the sea and prevent the Germans from reinforcing Fortress Cherbourg from the south, General Collins would need a secure jumping-off point from which his assaulting forces could move ahead at a steady pace. That launching locale would be a bridgehead on the west bank of the Merderet River, five miles west of Sainte-Mère-Église—an area fiercely defended by the reinforced 1057th Grenadier Regiment, a component of the first-rate 91st *Luftlande* (Air Landing) Division. Here American paratroopers had been fighting for three days.

Some 82nd Airborne DZs (drop zones) had been west of the Merderet and on June 8 scattered packets of American paratroopers were known to be isolated there behind German lines. Now the tactical situation facing 82nd Airborne leaders was how to get across the Merderet in the face of savage opposition by entrenched grenadiers to establish a firm bridgehead on the far bank.

The terrain was ideal for the defending Germans. Between the grenadiers and the American paratroopers on the east bank was a flooded area several miles long and some 500 yards across. Stretching over this inundated region was the La Fière causeway, which had a bridge in the center.

On June 8, the newly arrived 325th Glider Infantry Regiment, commanded by Colonel Harry L. Lewis and seeing its first combat, was given the mission of forcing a crossing. A paratrooper patrol had discovered a ford, submerged at high water, a few hundred yards north of the La Fière bridge, and under cover of darkness the 1st Battalion of the glider regiment, under Major Terry Sanford, was sent across.

Moving in a column of companies, Sanford's battalion reached the far bank with little difficulty and was moving ahead against sporadic resistance when the Germans struck. Raked with artillery, mortar, and machine-gun fire, the inexperienced glidermen faltered, became confused, and were driven back across the Merderet. Left behind on the west bank were scores of dead, wounded, and captured men of the 325th Regiment.

At dawn on June 9, Brigadier General James Gavin, who had been directing operations along the Merderet for three days, received details of the bloody rout of the inexperienced glider force. He was alarmed. There were indications that the already strong German force on the far bank was steadily being reinforced. Gavin was determined to force a crossing that day to rescue the isolated 82nd Division paratroopers. There was only one course of action: a rush across the exposed La Fière causeway.

It was now evident to the higher command that Jim Gavin and his airborne men had a tough nut to crack on the Merderet. That morning he received 12 Sherman tanks and the use of the 155-millimeter guns of the just-landed 90th Infantry Division to support the attack across the La Fière causeway and drive the Germans back.

Gavin set jump-off for 10:45 A.M., with a 15-minute artillery bombardment of the far bank to begin at 10:30. Brigadier General John M. Devine, the 90th Division artillery commander, had come forward to coordinate the barrage with Gavin.

"Let's go up there a little way and I'll point out to you precisely what I want you to hit," the airborne commander told Devine.

104

Crouching low to present a smaller target, the two generals moved ahead until they reached a point only 75 yards from the La Fière bridge—in No-Man's Land. There they got down on all fours and crawled to a slight rise that gave them a clear view of the causeway and German positions 500 yards away on the far bank. Lying flat on their stomachs, Gavin and Devine could see several ancient stone houses and a few wooden barns clustered around the far exit of the causeway, which were known to be occupied by enemy grenadiers. Not a German could be seen, although Gavin knew that they were there in force. He pointed out to General Devine the locales from which the Americans had been receiving fire, and the two men crawled back from their exposed observation post.

Moving hurriedly as time for the assault crossing of the causeway was steadily growing closer, General Gavin sent for Captain Hugo Olson. "Hugo, have those Shermans line up about 10 yards apart a couple of hundred yards back," Gavin instructed. "Tell them to open direct fire on the Germans when the artillery barrage begins at ten thirty."

General Gavin kept his immediate concerns to himself, but he was skeptical about the ability of the glidermen to successfully make the assault. He knew that the regiment had only the experience of yesterday's combat and might break and run in the face of the certain heavy German fire that would greet them.

The attack plan was quite simple—and perilous. The flooded terrain would canalize the assault along the narrow causeway and the Germans on the far end could be counted upon to cluster their heaviest firepower along this sole avenue of approach. At the same time the American artillery was pounding the west bank, smoke shells would be fired along the causeway to cloak the charge by the glidermen, who would be forced by necessity to dash at full speed the entire 500 yards to the far bank, a considerable task, and close with the enemy as soon as the barrage lifted. There could be no pause along the way, for there was no place to take cover or concealment.

At about 9:30 A.M., one hour prior to jump-off, the 3rd Battalion of the 325th Glider Infantry, which had been designated by the regimental commander to make the causeway assault, approached from its reserve positions to the line of departure. General Gavin sent word for the battalion commander to report to him for last-minute instructions.

When the battalion commander moved forward to Gavin's front-line command post, he said that he would not be able to lead the causeway attack.

"Why not?" a stern-faced Gavin demanded.

"Because I'm ill," was the reply.

General Gavin promptly relieved the glider battalion commander, sent him to the rear, and put another officer in charge of the assaulting force.

This latest development did nothing to relieve Gavin's apprehension about how the glidermen might react to their first taste of combat—a baptism of fire that would have sorely tested an experienced force. He sought out Captain R. D. Rae, who commanded the one company of paratroopers available on the site.

The general discussed the situation with Rae, a combat veteran who was noted for his battlefield courage. "I want every weapon your company has to fire at the far bank once the crossing begins," Gavin ordered. "I'm afraid the 325th might break under the hail of fire they'll receive."

If that were to happen and the glidermen began to straggle back across the causeway, Gavin said he would signal to Captain Rae to lead his paratroopers in a charge across the runway, an example that might cause withdrawing glidermen to turn around and join the attack against the German positions.

As the tense glidermen of the assaulting battalion crouched in ditches along the side of the road, at 10:30 a terrific roar erupted along the Merderet and echoed over the flooded landscape as 90th Division artillery, a dozen Sherman tanks, a few mortars, automatic weapons, and rifles—everything the airborne force at La Fière had in its arsenal—opened up on the far bank. Shells screamed into German positions and the impact area ignited in sheets of flame. A thick pall of smoke and dust enveloped the target as the drumfire of explosives continued for fifteen minutes.

Just before the artillery lifted, General Gavin, from his exposed CP near the entrance to the causeway, signaled the crouched glidermen to start the 500-yard dash across the flooded marshland. Captain John B. Sauls, a company commander of the glidermen, leaped to his feet, made a forward motion with his arm and shouted, "Okay, let's go!" His men behind him started scrambling out of ditches and, with Captain Sauls in the lead, began running at full speed across the thin strip of causeway.

Heavy boots clomping on the macadam surface, personal weapons flopping about from the bouncing gait, Sauls and his men, wheezing and grunting from the exertion, had nearly reached the bridge at the half-way mark when the Germans at the far end of the causeway opened fire. Bullets, heavy and hissing, flew past the running men's heads like swarms of angry bees. Now mortar shells began to plop down along the causeway, exploding in sharp blasts and sending shrapnel into the bodies of the exposed men, many of whom staggered and fell wounded into the ugly brown marsh water and drowned.

Captain Sauls and a handful of his men continued to move forward in the face of the withering fire. There was no place to hide, no place to take cover. The glidermen were naked in the gunsights of the enemy. Men continued to go down like flies showered with a killing chemical, and soon bodies, dead and wounded, were sprawled about on the causeway.

Behind Sauls and his men other glidermen had started the dash over the elevated road. Bullets were beating on the bridge like hail, and other pellets ricocheted off the hard surface, casting gigantic firefly-like sparks into the air. Now there were screams from the mutilated and the dying. A few men faltered, then more halted, confused, terrified, uncertain. A jam developed along the causeway as more glidermen joining in the dash piled up behind. Into this mass of helmeted humanity milling about on the narrow elevated road, the Germans on the far bank poured increasingly heavy fusillades of automatic-weapons fire and mortar shells.

The chaos mounted as a Sherman sent across the causeway to support the beleaguered glider infantrymen struck a mine and slewed sideways, grinding to a halt along the bullet- and shell-swept passage. Machine-gun crews were launched into the attack and after edging part-way across could not get through the congestion. They set up their weapons alongside the causeway, adding to the chaos and confusion. All along the lengthy elevated road, the exposed glidermen continued to fall.

Now General Gavin became deeply concerned about the mass chaos on the causeway, as he saw that stragglers were beginning to filter back to the jump-off point. Fearing that the withdrawal by some could quickly become panic on the causeway, the airborne general signaled to Captain Rae and his reinforced company of paratroopers in foxholes behind a stone wall.

Rae jumped to his feet and waved his men forward. Yelling at the top of their voices the entire company set out in a run across the causeway, weaving in and out of sprawled bodies, discarded equipment and weapons, the disabled tank, as well as hesitant and reluctant glidermen who were dazed and confused by the inferno of death and mutilation into which they had been suddenly immersed.

The far bank was shrouded in a pall of smoke and dust and from his vantage point General Gavin looked on anxiously as Rae's men, somehow finding the reserve of energy to yell battle cries as they picked their way through bodies, disappeared into the man-made fog. Gavin had no way of knowing that Captain Sauls, the glider officer who was the first man to dash out onto the causeway at the head of his company, had raced through the hailstorm of fire and reached the far bank—but with only a handful of his company.

Now Captain Sauls, the gliderman, and Captain Rae, the paratrooper, and their men were fighting it out with the tough grenadiers of the German 1057th *Luftlande* Regiment along the western side of the flooded area. Other members of the 325th had been thrown into the attack, and moving ahead by leaps and bounds had reached the far bank and were soon absorbed into the close-quarters combat.

About noon, an hour and a quarter after Captain Sauls had begun his dash into the cannon's mouth, a heavy weapons platoon reached the far bank and three Sherman tanks clanked over the causeway and rumbled up onto dry land in support of the hard-pressed infantrymen. Other parachute and glider formations were shoved over the elevated road and the attack continued, hampered by faulty communications among infantry, tanks, and headquarters. Captain Rae and his parachute company had fought their way for about a mile and on into the hamlet of Le Motey. There they were heavily pounded by artillery—American guns unaware that friendly troops were in the village.

Hard on the heels of the first 82nd Airborne men to reach the far bank, General Gavin made the crossing. There he witnessed the tremendous German firepower that had been marshaled against his men. Out in a field, less than 100 yards from the causeway, were 12 heavy mortars, dug into pits some eight-feet square. Sprawled about the positions were the bodies of several gray-clad grenadiers, their sightless eyes staring intently skyward.

As Gavin continued to move about the far bank he saw many mobile artillery pieces, half-tracks, and self-propelled guns, their crews either lying dead beside the weapons or having fled on the approach of the airborne men across the causeway. He started down a road to the left and found it cluttered with litter, abandoned and destroyed vehicles, and other debris.

Shortly Gavin came upon a German mortar crew, all dead or wounded, sprawled in a ditch where they had fallen after being surprised and gunned down by an American armored car that had come this way just ahead of General Gavin. A German lieutenant in the ditch, dead but still limp, was lying face down and clutching a map of the La Fière region. Gavin took it from him, hoping it would reveal German troop dispositions. It did not.

Disappointed, the airborne general turned the map over. There, to his amazement, was a map of England with the region clearly marked from which the 82nd Airborne had taken off for the D-Day drop. Gavin was puzzled. At first he thought the Germans had ferreted out top-secret pre-invasion information, but on reflection decided that the map had been prepared for Operation Sea Lion, Hitler's planned assault on England nearly four years previously. It was not the 82nd Airborne region that had been marked on the map, but by coincidence a Wehrmacht objective for *Sea Lion.*

The dead Wehrmacht lieutenant did serve one useful purpose. General Gavin had lost his wristwatch on a jolting parachute landing a few nights before. He removed the German's watch, strapped it to his own wrist, and moved off down the road.

A short distance ahead he came upon a sight that revolted and angered him. Near an abandoned German CP a dead paratrooper hung limply in his harness where he had been shot after his parachute caught in a large apple tree. "The bastards could have taken him prisoner," Gavin said to himself.

As the afternoon wore on the 82nd Airborne men battled through the hedgerows, and by 3:45 P.M. had reached two large isolated pockets of comrades who had been behind German lines since bailing out days earlier. The bridgehead over the Merderet had been carved out to a depth of three-quarters of a mile along a two-mile stretch of the river, and German resistance was slackening. It appeared obvious that the situation was well in hand, so General Gavin hopped into a jeep and drove back to the division CP near Sainte-Mère-Église to confer with his boss, General Ridgway, and to learn how the division as a whole was progressing.

At the same time Gavin was making his favorable report to the division commander on the assault across the La Fière causeway and the solidifying of a bridgehead on the far bank, the acting commander of the 91st *Luftlande* Division, Colonel Eugen Koenig, was hurriedly issuing orders for a counterattack to wipe out the 82nd Airborne enclave on the west bank of the Merderet. Koenig found himself in command of the 91st Division early in the morning of D-Day when its leader, Major General Wilhelm Falley, was ambushed and killed by American paratroopers.

Koenig was fully aware that the American VII Corps' plan was to attack westward and cut off the Cotentin Peninsula before turning north to drive on Cherbourg. The colonel only the day before had received copies of the entire Allied operational plan for Neptune.

Despite the fact that the 1057th Grenadier Regiment had been badly chewed up in the terrific artillery bombardment earlier in the day and in subsequent fighting in the tangled *bocage* (hedgerow) countryside west of the Merderet, Colonel Koenig sent the unit back into the attack. At shortly after 6 P.M. the Germans struck.

The heaviest blows in the fierce counterattack fell upon elements of the 325th Glider Infantry Regiment, which had seen action that day for the first time and whose ranks had been riddled in the dash across the causeway. In less than a half-hour after the German counterattack was launched, the 1st Battalion of the glider regiment was cut off, and other elements began to show signs of disintegrating under the sledgehammer attack of the veteran grenadiers.

Back at the 82nd Airborne Division CP near Sainte-Mère-Église, General Gavin, who thought the Merederet bridgehead was secure, received an urgent message: American positions on the west bank were breaking up under heavy enemy assault and stragglers were starting to pull back over the causeway. The young general was alarmed. The report indicated that a smashing German battlefield triumph was in the making.

Gavin promptly collared Captain Willard Harrison and Lieutenant Colonel Arthur A. Maloney, executive officer of the 507th Parachute Infantry Regiment, and hurriedly explained the situation to them. The three leaped into a jeep and, like cavalry commanders of the previous century when a battlefield crisis developed, "galloped" to the danger point in great haste.

Gavin's jeep screeched to a halt in front of an old stone farmhouse on the far bank of the causeway which was the CP of the 325th Glider Infantry Regiment. There he quickly learned that the situation was even worse than he had feared, and it was deteriorating rapidly. The regimental commander late that afternoon had been evacuated with combat fatigue and his executive officer and the rest of the staff were now hastily making preparations to abandon the command post and pull back over the causeway.

Angry, General Gavin barked to the executive officer in command, "What in the hell do you think you are doing?"

"The Germans are attacking," was the reply. "We can't hold."

With that, Gavin became even more furious. Elements of the 82nd Airborne had been battling furiously for three days to establish a bridgehead on the far bank and had paid a heavy price in blood. He had no intention of giving up the causeway.

"We're going to counterattack with every resource we have," the young general told the glider force commander. "That includes clerks, headquarters people, jeep drivers, anyone with a weapon we can get our hands on—including yourself!"

The acting 325th commander turned ashen for a few moments and looked startled. Then he replied simply, "Yes, sir."

Gavin then motioned Lieutenant Colonel Maloney and Captain Harrison outside the farmhouse and told them, "I want you both to take up positions at the head of the causeway. Stop any of our men who try to recross it."

How they would be stopped was left up to the two parachute officers. Gavin knew that he couldn't find a pair of men better suited for the task. Maloney was big, tough, and impressive looking. Adding to his fierce appearance was a three days' growth of red beard that was streaked with blood after he had been hit earlier in the day but refused evacuation. Harrison was the officer whom Colonel Rueben Tucker, the pugnacious leader of the battle-tested 504th Parachute Infantry Regiment, had insisted go along on the Normandy mission with Gavin. Harrison, in savage fighting in Sicily and Italy, had gained a reputation, in Colonel Tucker's words, as "one tough cookie."

With these two redoubtable paratroop officers standing guard at the head of the causeway, much like Horatius at Rome's Tiber River bridge in 508 B.C. to thwart the invading Etruscan army, General Gavin knew that no one was going to get past them and recross the flooded Merderet to the east side.

There was no doubt in Gavin's mind that the Germans were making an all-out effort to crush the American bridgehead. All around him he could hear the fierce fire of enemy automatic weapons, the crash of mortar shells and grenade explosions. The situation appeared to be nearly out of control.

He sent a parachute officer in an armored car southward with instructions to "tell any men you run into that we're not withdrawing, we're attacking." Gavin then went forward on foot toward the hamlet of Le Motey where Captain Rae and his parachute force had been heavily pounded by "friendly" artillery that afternoon. Le Motey was a key crossroads and a likely objective in the enemy counterattack.

Along the way Gavin periodically encountered airborne men, many confused and uncertain what action to take. To each group, the general's message was the same: "We're not withdrawing, we're counterattacking! We're keeping this bridgehead!"

The angular general was hunched over and picking his way through a golden field of grain when he abruptly noticed that stalks were being hacked off all around him, as if by a huge scythe. Gavin flopped to the ground as torrents of enemy bullets hissed just over his head, and crawled forward on hands and knees for several hundred yards. There he reached

Captain Rae and his parachute company, which had withdrawn from Le Motey a few hours before when American artillery shells began screaming into the village.

Above the din of enemy smallarms fire, Gavin shouted instructions to Rae: "Go in and take Le Motey—and hold it!"

Less than a half-hour later Captain Rae and his paratroopers were entrenched in the key hamlet.

As small groups of paratroopers and glidermen battled the 1057th Grenadier Regiment among the hedgerows, there was a gradual reduction in firing, and by 8:45 it had dwindled away altogether. The German effort to wipe out the bridgehead on the west bank of the Merderet had itself been smashed. Now the stage was set for the VII Corps drive westward to cut the Cotentin peninsula and snap the trap shut on German forces defending Cherbourg.

A heavy price in blood had been paid for the important victory. In its first day of battle, nearly 50 percent of the two participating battalions of the 325th Glider Infantry Regiment became casualties, many of them in the sprint across the causeway. Sixty glidermen had been killed during the day, 283 seriously wounded, and 246 were missing, presumably captured or drowned.

As dusk began to settle over the Merderet River crossing that evening of the ninth, an eerie silence had fallen over the corpse-strewn battleground. Only an occasional mortar shell explosion or the isolated crack of a rifle dented the ghostly tranquility. Into this setting forward elements of the green 90th Infantry Division were approaching the causeway. Having landed just that afternoon, the men of the 90th had marched from Sainte-Mère-Église and were to pass through the 82nd Airborne bridgehead on the west bank of the Merderet the following morning and attack westward.

Few in the 90th Infantry Division had ever heard a shot fired in anger or seen a corpse dead of violence. On the march from Sainte-Mère-Église the soldiers had become increasingly nervous and apprehensive as they passed scattered German and American bodies, the charred, twisted remains of knocked-out vehicles and other ominous signs of the conflagration that had engulfed the area during the previous four days.

Rounding a turn in the road just before reaching the La Fière causeway, the leading troops were suddenly confronted by a terrifying sight—a large number of German soldiers were moving across the elevated road directly toward them, less than 100 yards away. The startled 90th Division troops opened fire at the oncoming enemy troops with every weapon available to them, and for several minutes the flooded landscape echoed with the din of American automatic weapons and smallarms fire.

When the fusillade of fire had run its course, the eerie lull again settled. Sprawled about grotesquely in death were the bodies of many German soldiers. Muted moans wafted over the causeway from other enemy soldiers, shot and writhing in agony but still alive. Every German had been killed or wounded.

Only then was it realized that a tragic mistake had occurred. The Germans were prisoners, captured in the fighting on the west bank, and being escorted back over the causeway by a few airborne men.

That evening of June 9, nearly 100 miles to the east of the Merderet River, Field Marshal Rommel was strolling in the park of his headquarters castle at La Roche-Guyon with his naval advisor and confidant, Rear Admiral Friedrich Ruge. Since rushing back from his home in Herrlingen in southern Germany, early on D-Day morning, the commander of Army Group B had been racing up and down the front like a man possessed. Outwardly exuding confidence, the field marshal became increasingly despondent.

The suffocating Allied air superiority made it impossible to tactically deploy troops; supplies were slow in arriving; and artillery could not move into firing position. To add to Rommel's burden, the Oberkommando der Wehrmacht—meaning Hitler's orders translated through Field Marshal Keitel—had overruled the Desert Fox's plan to group his forces for an all-out attack on the U.S. VII Corps in the Cotentin Peninsula. Hitler was convinced that heavily fortified Fortress Cherbourg could hold out indefinitely with the troops in that vicinity.

Now, in the pristine tranquility of the gardens of the Ducs de la Roche, Rommel was baring his soul and inner torment to Admiral Ruge. His was now an especially heavy emotional burden; he felt an enormous responsibility not only for the Normandy front but for the ultimate destiny of the Fatherland. Rommel had predicted to Ruge and to his other confidant at Army Group B headquarters, his chief of staff, General Hans Speidel, that a successful invasion of northern France would mean the war was lost. Now he felt a need to talk about the situation.

Ruge felt deep sorrow for the tormented Rommel. On one hand the field marshal was utilizing all the exceptional military skills he possessed to halt the Allied avalanche, while at the same time seeking out the propituous time and method for overthrowing the man he thought was taking Germany down the road to destruction—Adolf Hitler.

Rommel and Ruge, later joined by Dr. Speidel, talked far into the starry night.

At the same time, Field Marshal von Rundstedt, at his castle at Saint-Germain outside Paris, was growing increasingly nervous about a quick breakthrough to Cherbourg by the U.S. VII Corps. "I cannot believe that tired men and a few Luftwaffe airplanes can save the town," von Rundstedt observed resignedly to his staff. Mindful of Hitler's stern admonition that no major port was to fall into Allied hands intact, and although Carentan was still in German hands and a wide gap existed between American forces at Utah and Omaha, just before midnight on June 9 von Rundstedt issued a fateful order: "Begin at once to destroy Cherbourg harbor."

9

"Death Alley" at Carentan

Lieutenant Colonel August Frieherr von der Heydte, commander of the tough German 6th Parachute Regiment, hopped out of his camouflaged Volkswagen at a road intersection just north of the outskirts of Carentan. It was the afternoon of June 9 and von der Heydte was inspecting defensive positions of his paratroopers who, he knew from the captured Allied operational plan, were about to be struck by the U.S. 101st Airborne Division.

A classic confrontation was shaping up—one of America's finest, toughest fighting formations, the Screaming Eagles, versus one of the Third Reich's best, the 6th Parachute Regiment.

Von der Heydte's force was composed of youths who, in normal times, would just be graduating from high school; the average age was 17.5 years. But the youthful German parachutists were keenly trained, had exceptional esprit, and were deeply devoted to Hitler and Nazism.

In recent days, Colonel von der Heydte's paratroopers had proven their mettle. When the Allies landed on June 6, the 6th Parachute Regiment was based at Carentan and Périers, at the base of the Cotentin Peninsula. Early that morning, the regiment had rapidly marched northward and, without armor, air or artillery support, forced its way into the key road junction of Sainte-Mère-Église, which had been captured during the night by elements of the U.S. 82nd Airborne Division.

Attacked by American paratroopers and strong armored forces from Utah, and with its ammunition nearly depleted, the 6th Parachute Regiment had been ordered to withdraw toward Carentan, abandoning heavy vehicles and equipment in order to save the superb troops to fight another day.

General Marcks, commander of LXXXIV Corps, headquartered in Saint-Lô, ordered von der Heydte to dig in just north of Carentan to block an American attack down Route Nationale 13 and also to dig in east of the key traffic center in order to halt an approach from the direction of the British sector.

Lieutenant Colonel von der Heydte was not the stereotype of a tough paratroop commander, although he had distinguished himself in the Wehrmacht's spectacular airborne seizure of the large Mediterranean island of Crete from the British in 1941, and prior to that in the parachute and glider assaults in Belgium and Holland to spearhead the German army's invasion of France.

Von der Heydte had several strikes against him in Nazi Germany. He was born of the nobility, and bore the title of baron. He was also an intellectual and had been a professor of law at a leading German university. Despite these "obstacles" to military advancement, von der Heydte retained his command of an elite force for one reason—he produced on the field of battle.

Von der Heydte had been a thorn in the side of stiff-necked staff officers at the Oberkommando der Wehrmacht in Berlin for many months. He was expected to keep his mouth shut and somehow help repulse the Allied avalanche when it struck. Instead he had ceaselessly pestered OKW for better armament and equipment for his teenage paratroopers. In exasperation, an OKW general turned down a request with the curt comment: "Parachutists need only knives."

Furious at this observation by a staff officer who had not been closer than 500 miles to the threatened French beaches, von der Heydte snapped back, "Parachutists are only human."

The professor/paratrooper was held in deep affection by the young men in his regiment, who regarded him as something of a father as well as commander. After all, the colonel was "old"—all of 34. He had an engaging sense of humor, and his calmness under fire in tense situations had a soothing effect on his men.

Despite the fact that his parachute regiment was short of weapons and equipment and had suffered many casualties during the previous three days in the bitter fighting among the hedgerows outside Sainte-Mère-Église, Colonel von der Heydte felt confident that his men would give a good account of themselves in the impending showdown for Carentan. His troops, he knew, would never break and run, but would stick to their shallow foxholes until each was routed out at bayonet point.

Von der Heydte was aware that his troopers would be on their own, without tank or air support and with only a few pieces of artillery, but he was encouraged by the difficult terrain over which attacking Americans would have to cross to get to his men at their barriers north and east of Carentan. For nearly two miles to the north of the town, the ground was a marshland, impassable to American tanks and vehicles, and American infantrymen would soon be exhausted if they tried to cross it.

The asphalt Route Nationale 13 from Saint-Côme-du-Mont ran southward straight as an arrow over the swamps and flooded areas, its crown some six to nine feet above the dingy brown water and clusters of ugly reeds protruding upward. To come to grips with von der Heydte's defenders, assault forces of General Maxwell Taylor's 101st Airborne Division would have to dash for long distances across this exposed causeway. There the Screaming Eagles would be naked targets, with nowhere to dig in, take cover, or pause to regroup.

The 101st Airborne's plan of attack called for two crossings of the flooded Douve River to close in on Carentan from the north and east. One force would, of necessity, make a frontal rush down the 30-foot-wide elevated causeway from the north, bypass Carentan, and seize Hill 30, southwest of the town. Possession of Hill 30 would put the Americans astride the principal escape route from Carentan, as a German withdrawal would be canalized by heavy swamps to either side of Hill 30.

While a frontal assault against Carentan was being launched along the causeway, the 327th Glider Infantry Regiment was to cross the Douve three miles northeast of Carentan, then drive southwest to seize the town.

General Taylor's instructions from VII Corps had been terse and to the point. When Taylor on June 8 reported to General Collins that Saint-Côme-du-Mont, four miles north of Carentan, had been captured, the corps commander replied, "Fine, Max. Now take Carentan."

On the afternoon of June 9, Colonel Robert F. Sink, commander of the 506th Parachute Infantry Regiment, which was in position astride Route Nationale 13, took nine men and moved south along the causeway toward Carentan to reconnoiter the situation. The patrol moved forward for several hundred yards without being fired upon, crossed over a short bridge and advanced about a quarter-mile farther where they came upon another bridge. This one had been blown up by the Germans as they pulled back to positions around Carentan, and there was a 12-foot gap in the structure.

Locating a leaking old boat, Colonel Sink and his men rowed across the narrow stream. As the troopers in the patrol became increasingly apprehensive, Sink pushed on down the exposed causeway, the men's figures forming stark silhouettes against the sky. The only sound to be heard was the footsteps of the parachutists. Presently the patrol reached a third bridge, and minutes after passing over it the tranquility was shattered as machine-gun bursts began raking the Americans.

Hitting the ground, Sink and his men clung to the hard asphalt surface until firing ceased, then withdrew back down the causeway. The colonel promptly reported to 101st Airborne headquarters that his patrol had not been fired on until it had crossed Bridge 3. Sink's report became garbled while being passed upward through channels and gave the higher levels of command the impression that Carentan was defended only by a small delaying force.

At the same time Colonel Sink and his patrol were being fired on along the causeway, Lieutenant Ralph B. Gehauf, intelligence officer of the 3rd Battalion of the 502nd Parachute Infantry, was flying over the causeway and Carantan in a light reconnaissance plane. Winging in low to seek out enemy troop dispositions, Gehauf's craft was not fired on, nor did the lieutenant spot a single German soldier. His report to higher headquarters reinforced the prevailing opinion that the key traffic center of Carentan was only lightly held.

Lieutenant Colonel von der Heydte and his young troopers were there all right. They weren't about ready to reveal their presence until the moment was right—when attacking Americans were moving across the exposed elevated causeway with nowhere to take cover.

About 9:30 P.M. that same evening, Captain Henry C. Plitt, intelligence officer of Lieutenant Colonel John H. Michaelis' 502nd Parachute Infantry, was undergoing an experience similar to Gehauf's. Lifting off from a strip at Houesville in a Piper Cub, with the purple shadows of dusk starting to enfold the countryside, Plitt's aircraft flew back and forth over Carentan for half an hour at a height of 1,500 feet. The recon plane was not fired on, nor did Plitt see any indication of a German presence in or around the town.

When he landed, Captain Plitt reported to regimental headquarters: Carentan had been evacuated by the Germans. This optimistic report was relayed to General Taylor at division headquarters, who promptly ordered the 502nd Parachute Infantry Regiment to attack over the causeway before dawn and occupy Carentan. The 3rd Battalion, commanded by

Lieutenant Colonel Robert G. Cole, was chosen to spearhead the assault, which was to jump off at 12:15 A.M.

Fifteen minutes before the paratroop battalion was to start forward, Colonel Cole's energetic intelligence officer, Lieutenant Gehauf, who that afternoon had flown over and around Carentan in a recon plane, was moving toward the enemy once again—this time on foot. At the head of a 10-man patrol, Gehauf wanted to reconnoiter the route over the causeway before the battalion marched along it. He especially wanted to make certain that the work party of the 326th Airborne Engineer Battalion, which had been sent out to repair the gap in Bridge 2, had completed the job.

As Gehauf and his men marched along the causeway, the moon darted in and out of puffs of rapidly moving clouds, causing the troopers to be alternately illuminated and plunged into dark shadow. A thick mist hung over the swamps to either side of the elevated road. All was silent—even eerie, sinister. The marching men winced at the dull thumping of their heavy jump boots against the asphalt.

"For Chrissake, don't walk so goddamned loud!" a trooper hissed in a stage whisper to a comrade.

The steady clonking of the boots seemed to the patrol to carry for miles across the desolate swamps, a certain signal to the Germans that Americans were approaching down the causeway.

It was nearly 1:30 A.M. when Gehauf and his men, armed only with rifles and pistols, cautiously edged up to the damaged bridge which, by now, should have been repaired. To Gehauf's dismay, for the entire 3rd Battalion was to reach this point shortly, the yawning gap in the span glared mockingly at him in the muted moonlight. It had not been fixed.

Moving about the bridge, Lieutenant Gehauf discovered ropes, wooden beams, and other repair material piled around the span, but no sign of the airborne engineers who should have been working there. Finally Gehauf located the missing workmen; they had taken cover in a water-filled trench a short distance from the bridge. They told Gehauf that a German 88-millimeter gun had been firing shells at the damaged bridge and that they had been forced to quit work and seek cover.

Was this an isolated gun placed to cover the German withdrawal from Carentan? Lieutenant Gehauf asked himself. Or did it have a more ominous meaning—that the enemy was present in force at the end of the causeway?

Locating a small boat, Gehauf and his men, three at a time, rowed over the stream and as they reached the far bank the night air was fractured: eeeekkk—CCRRAAACCKK! A high-velocity 88-millimeter shell, fired directly down the long straight causeway, had exploded nearby. Dropping to the hard asphalt, the troopers waited for more rounds to pound them, but none came. They got to their feet, now more tense and wary than ever, and continued forward along the elevated road.

Led by Sergeant Robert P. O'Reilly, the patrol, in single file, pushed on past Bridge 3, where Colonel Sink and his men had come under fire the previous afternoon, and reached Bridge 4, which ran over a canal only 600 yards from the outskirts of Carentan. Now, with tension growing with each step, the Five-O-Deuces edged onward with Private First Class James R. Pace and Private First Class James Roach at the point. Fifty yards past the canal bridge, Lieutenant Gehauf called out softly to the pair of scouts, "Let's hold up here and give the rest of the battalion a chance to catch up with us."

Hardly had the words left the lieutenant's mouth than a mortar shell exploded near the patrol. The men flattened on the ground. A split-second later flares shot into the air from in front, bathing the causeway and the troopers in brilliant light. As if on cue, enemy machine guns located on higher dry ground to the front and to one side began to rake the little band of exposed paratroopers. Now clusters of mortar shells began bursting around the prostrate Americans. Shrapnel hissed and fluttered just over their heads.

Baron von der Heydte's resolute teenagers of the 6th Parachute Regiment had opened up with all their weapons on the American patrol.

Above the raucous din, Lieutenant Gehauf shouted at a trooper, "Get on back to the battalion and tell them to hurry some mortars up here to knock out these goddamned machine guns!" The messenger took off and soon was swallowed up by darkness.

Trotting along the asphalt causeway toward the rear, the courier came upon Lieutenant Colonel Cole at the head of his marching battalion just as it was approaching the damaged bridge. Excited and new to combat, the trooper blurted out, "Lieutenant Gehauf said not to bring the battalion up, the fire's too heavy!"

That was precisely the opposite of what the urgent message was to convey—a plea for help in dealing with the German automatic weapons that were raking the patrol on the causeway outside Carentan.

In any event, Cole's strung-out battalion was blocked by the failure of the engineers to repair the gap in Bridge 2, so the regimental commander,

Colonel Michaelis, radioed to call off the attack for the night and for the battalion to return to its jumping off spot. No one thought to inform Lieutenant Gehauf's isolated patrol of the change in plans.

Worried that help had not arrived, Gehauf sent Private First Class Allen W. Bryant back along the causeway to find out what had become of the 3rd Battalion, and his first messenger. Bryant returned to the patrol just as dawn was breaking. He had trekked the entire length of the causeway without finding Colonel Cole's battalion. Even the engineers were gone from their cover at the demolished bridge.

Puzzled about what had happened to the 3rd Battalion, Gehauf and his men returned to the village of Les Quesnils near the head of the causeway. There they located Colonel Cole—just ready to send out an officer with a small patrol to bring them back.

While the attack by a battalion of the 502nd Parachute Infantry was being aborted the night of June 9, the 327th Glider Regiment, commanded by Colonel George S. Wear, had launched an amphibious assault across the Douve toward Carentan. As darkness fell, men of the 327th carried rubber boats nearly a mile to the river where the glidermen prepared to cross after a heavy artillery and mortar barrage of the far bank.

As the preparatory fire lifted, a company of glidermen of the 1st Battalion shoved off from shore and paddled the rubber boats across the stream, touching down minutes later on the far bank, at 1:45 A.M. Casualties from enemy fire were minor, but on reaching the other side of the stream a series of explosions caused about twenty glidermen to go down. In the dark the glidermen had stumbled into an extensive mine field.

Colonel Wear hurried the remaining elements across, and by 6 A.M. all of the 327th Glider Infantry was on the enemy side of the Douve, three miles northeast of the Carentan causeway, and preparing to attack along the south side of the river to fight its way into the town from the east.

Meanwhile that night, inside Carentan at his basement command post, Lieutenant Colonel von der Heydte was becoming worried. His men were running low on ammunition just as it became apparent that the Americans were in the process of attacking the town. He had large stores of artillery ammunition—but no guns to fire it. His most pressing need now was for automatic weapons ammo and mortar rounds. He sent an urgent plea for help to LXXXIV Corps in Saint-Lô.

Much to von der Heydte's surprise, several truckloads of ammunition reached Carentan under cover of night. The cargo was mainly French mortar shells—of the wrong caliber for his mortars.

Early on the morning of June 10, Lieutenant Colonel Robert Cole was advised at Les Quesnils that his 3rd Battalion was to attack once more across the causeway, that same afternoon. This assault would be even more perilous, for the paratroopers would not be shrouded in a cloak of darkness. Cole, concerned that the 12-foot gap in Bridge 2 still might not have been repaired, took the peripatetic Lieutenant Gehauf, Captain Robert L. Clements, and two troopers to the span. Cole's fears were justified—nothing had been done to repair the bridge and there were no engineers in sight.

Taking the problem into his own hands, Colonel Cole told the others to pitch in and lug to the bridge the planking and other materials left by the engineers. Together the five men constructed a foot bridge over the stream—wobbly, but passable.

At about 3 P.M. the battalion, with Lieutenant Gehauf and Private First Class Bryant in the lead, reached and crossed the rickety improvised foot bridge in single file and continued to march forward along the causeway. A lone German .88-millimeter gun far to the front sent an occasional shell screaming into the causeway, but no one was hit.

With each forward step Colonel Cole's men became increasingly hopeful that the Germans had indeed pulled out of Carentan and that they would be able to stroll into town. Leading elements of the battalion reached Bridge 4, where Lieutenant Gehauf and his patrol had been pinned down during the night, and they were forced to halt by a Belgian Gate the Germans had dragged across the road. A Belgian Gate was a heavy iron fence, about 30 feet long, with a gate in the center, which the Germans used as a roadblock or for other defensive purposes. The point of the parachute battalion was now only some 600 yards from the northern outskirts of Carentan and still not a shot had been fired.

Troopers could muscle open the ponderous gate only 18 inches and through this narrow gap the lead scouts began squeezing, one at a time. This slow process caused the remainder of the battalion, strung out for a mile all the way back to the damaged Bridge 2, to stop on the causeway as each man waited his turn to squeeze through the obstacle.

Suddenly, all thought of a peaceful walk into Carentan vanished. From higher ground to the front and a large farmhouse surrounded by thick hedgerows to the right, German paratroopers began pouring withering bursts of machine gun and rifle fire into the exposed Americans on the causeway. The troopers, with nowhere to take cover, flattened themselves

122

on the asphalt surface as swarms of bullets buzzed past them. Here and there was a sickening thud as a bullet found its mark.

Now above the grinding chatter of German machine guns a series of sharp cracks engulfed the American parachutists who were on the enemy side of Bridge 4 as mortar shells exploded, sending white-hot chunks of metal whizzing over the causeway. Troopers at the point of the attack could see enemy machine guns spitting at them from 100 yards ahead, but could do nothing but cling to the asphalt or press up against the wet mud of the embankments.

Private James E. White, a scout who had just squeezed through the Belgian Gate, felt a burning sensation on top of his head as he hugged the hard surface. Removing his helmet, he saw a gaping hole in the headgear where a bullet had entered before grazing his scalp. A nearby comrade, Private Carl Deyak, screamed. A mortar shell had burst beside him, leaving his face a gusher of blood.

Another trooper at the point, Private Tony De Leon, felt a sharp pain as though a red-hot poker had been thrust into his arm. Frightened, he called out over the din, "Hurry! I'm hit! I'm hit! I'm going to bleed to death!" A soldier crawled through a hail of bullets and put a tourniquet on the arm. De Leon passed out.

The German 6th Parachute Regiment had sprung its death trap. The American parachute battalion, spaced out for great distances on the barren elevated road, could not charge forward because of the Belgian Gate, and withdrawal was hampered by the 12-foot gap in Bridge 2. Swamps to each side of the causeway made maneuver there impossible. Colonel Cole's battalion was being raked with automatic-weapons fire and pounded with heavy mortar barrages, and was unable to move forward, backward or to either flank.

For the next two hours, the American parachutists wiggled around on their bellies atop the causeway as the young *Fallschirmjaeger,* dug in and concealed, were reinforced and their withering automatic weapons and mortar fire ripped deeper along the prostrate American column. Meanwhile, six or seven more paratroopers had squeezed through the obstacle.

It was about 6 P.M., three hours after the causeway attack had jumped off, that Lieutenant Colonel Cole left his CP at Bridge 2 and began working his way forward along the columns of sprawled paratroopers. Ignoring enemy fire, Cole reached one of his companies that was clinging to the side of an embankment, doing nothing.

Cole stood over them and shouted, "Goddamn it, start firing and keep firing."

Cole's shouted exhortations achieved nothing. For two hours the exposed Company I, with no cover or concealment, had tried to edge forward. All during that time it had been raked incessantly by enemy automatic weapons from one side across the swamp. Lieutenant George A. Larish, leader of the 1st platoon, was shot through the heart. Lieutenant John P. Painschab and Corporal Earl Butz were killed instantly. Medic Private First Class Stanley W. Tkaczyk was hit in the head and died on the spot. After 15 of Company I troopers were cut down, a sort of stupor infected the remainder in the alley of death. They resignedly waited for the bullets that would rip into them.

Here and there up and down the long strung-out American column machine guns were set up and fired at the unseen enemy on the flanks. But the men of the German 6th Parachute Regiment, scenting total annihilation of the 101st Airborne Division battalion, kept pouring mortar and automatic-weapons fire along the entire length of the causeway. Cries and screams regularly pierced the air as Americans were struck by the hail of flying lead. The causeway to Carentan was slippery with blood.

Now dusk was gathering and German fire dwindled. The enemy parachutists could no longer see the wriggling American targets in their gunsights.

Suddenly the American parachutists heard the roar of a motor and looked forward in the twilight to see the outline of an airplane coming directly toward them, flying at about 150 yards up directly along the causeway. The men recognized the craft as a dive bomber, but no one shouted warnings because the troopers had become accustomed to seeing only Allied fighter-bombers. Directly above I Company, the unit Colonel Cole had been unable to energize and which had been so hard hit during the day, the German airplane let loose a cluster of anti-personnel bombs. They exploded along the causeway where the company was lying.

After dropping its cargo, the enemy aircraft continued on down the elevated road, heavily machine gunning Colonel Cole's trapped battalion. After the smoke had cleared, about 30 dead or wounded Company I troopers were strewn about the causeway and down the muddy embankments.

In their shallow foxholes and machine-gun posts on the outskirts of Carentan and on either side of the marsh, the German paratroopers stood and rousingly cheered the unexpected and timely arrival of a lone Luftwaffe dive-bomber. It was the first friendly aircraft they had seen since the Allied landing five days before.

German cheers would have been even louder had the defenders of Carentan known the devastating accuracy of its pilot. The solo air attack had virtually completed the destruction of Company I.

Private Glenn A. Moe of I Company had been hugging the surface as the enemy aircraft zoomed in. A blinding orange flash and ear-splitting roar erupted nearby and Moe winced as glowing bomb fragments tore into his shoulder and hand. Two other troopers lying alongside were also wounded by the same bomb. Despite his extreme pain, Moe lifted one of the wounded men off the ground and carried him the entire length of the causeway to an aide station.

There Private Moe's wounds were dressed. He made the long perilous trek back to the point along the causeway where he had been struck by bomb fragments and, with the help of a stretcher bearer, brought out the other wounded comrade. It was 4 A.M. by the time Moe, his white bandages glowing like beacons in the darkness, had completed his second rescue mission of the night.

Only minutes after the dive bomber disappeared from view, the handful of surviving troopers of Company I fell victim to a curious phenomenon that often is a shock by-product of sudden disaster. The men, showing no interest in their predicament nor curiosity about which of their comrades had been hit, began falling asleep on the causeway. A platoon leader, Lieutenant Robert G. Burns, tried desperately to awaken his men, but with darkness at hand his task became most difficult—he could not tell who was asleep and who was dead.

Burns saw bodies roll off the causeway and tumble partly submerged into the swamp. The lieutenant scrambled down the embankment to check on these men and heard loud snoring from each helmeted figure. Efforts to rouse the sleepers, who were in danger of drowning, were to no avail.

American paratroopers, clad in jump suits and with helmets still clamped on heads, lay exposed on the causeway deep in sleep through the remaining hours of darkness. But the enemy also gave indications that they, too, were near exhaustion. The sky was clear, visibility excellent, and the Germans knew that the Americans were still on the elevated road. Yet not another mortar shell or automatic weapons bullet shattered the moonlit quietude over the Carentan swampland.

Only a mile from where the Screaming Eagles were lying sprawled about—in a stuporous sleep or dead—the German commander was reading a message he had just received in a dimly lit cellar that served as his command post. It was from the Führer himself: "You are to defend Carentan to the last man and the last bullet."

Elsewhere in the town and around its outskirts, Baron von der Heydte's stubborn paratroopers that night had occasion to let loose with another round of cheers. The Luftwaffe had made its second appearance over Carentan in the past few hours; JU-52 transports parachuted in scores of containers with ammunition for automatic weapons and mortars.

About 4 A.M. Captain Cecil L. Simmons, commander of H Company, had taken advantage of the lull to squeeze his men, one at a time, through the Belgian Gate at Bridge 4, only a stone's throw from German positions. Simmons crawled forward on reconnaissance until he heard German voices talking near the ditch he was in. He turned around and edged backward to his radio, called the fire-control center and asked for a salvo on the spot he had heard the Germans talking. The reply: "The guns can't fire at night."

Simmons' anger over this response was deepened when, a few minutes later, he heard the creeking of wagons out to his front. Then he knew what the Germans he had heard were doing—laying mines.

In the meantime, Lieutenant Colonel Cole had gone back to the 502nd Regiment's command post to brief Colonel Michaelis on the perilous situation his battalion would face with the imminent arrival of dawn. Michaelis listened then issued an order: "Continue the attack."

On returning to the causeway, Cole was encouraged to learn that Captain Simmons had pushed his H Company on through the tiny opening in the Belgian Gate and that Company G had followed. Now half of the battalion was on the enemy side of the road block.

By dawn's early light, H and G companies, followed by Headquarters Company, were off the causeway, had reached solid ground, and were advancing. The cost of traversing the elevated road had been heavy: H Company had dwindled to 84 men, G Company to sixty men, and Headquarters Company to one hundred and twenty-one. Hard-luck I Company, in the forefront of the causeway assault, had been cut to twenty-one men and two officers.

But whatever destiny Fate held in store for Colonel Cole's 3rd Battalion, the paratroopers were out of the horrors of Carentan's "Death Alley."

10

Bayonet Charge on a Farmhouse

Lieutenant Colonel Cole was crawling along a ditch toward the front of the bloody causeway his men had just navigated. Whistling just over Cole's head were swarms of automatic weapons' rounds that were being fired from the vicinity of a group of farm buildings just west of the causeway. Colonel Cole had been advancing with H Company minutes before when young *Fallschirmjaeger* of the 6th Parachute Regiment suddenly unleashed a withering fusillade of smallarms fire from the farmhouse complex at the American paratroopers advancing across an open field.

Private Albert W. Dieter, H Company's lead scout, was the first to be cut down, his left arm shredded. Other troopers near the front collapsed in bloody heaps, and in seconds the entire company column, strung out in single file for 200 yards, was raked with intense mortar and automatic-weapons fire.

As bullets whistled by just over his head, Colonel Cole looked behind him and spotted the artillery observer, Captain Rosemond, edging forward in the ditch. Cole shouted above the din of the angry gunfire, "Get some goddamned rounds on that farmhouse and the hedgerows around it!"

Rosemond called back, "I can't. The artillery commander is not with the guns to okay it."

Cole was furious. "Goddamn it, we need artillery fire and we can't wait for some goddamned general!"

Less than fifteen minutes later Rosemond's batteries began shelling the farmhouses.

It was now 5:30 A.M. For nearly a half-hour the American artillery pounded the targeted area. Yet there was no slackening of the heavy bursts of smallarms fire. The young German paratroopers of Baron von der Heydte did not give up. Bullets continued to whiz past Colonel Cole and other Screaming Eagles pinned down in ditches and behind trees and other cover.

At this point, the battalion commander had to make a crucial decision. He could either order his men to start crawling toward the rear and, in effect, abandon much of the ground purchased with huge quantities of paratrooper blood, or he could charge the farmhouse complex and risk getting the entire H Company wiped out in the process.

Cole shouted to Major John P. Stopka, his second in command, who was pinned down to Cole's left a short distance across a narrow dirt road: "We're going to get some artillery smoke on that goddamned farmhouse. Then we're going to make a bayonet charge!"

Stopka was startled. He thought bayonet charges had gone out with the First World War. But he shouted back, "Okay."

On the other side of the dirt road from Cole were the remnants of G Company and Headquarters Company. The battalion commander thought that word had been passed to H, G, and Headquarters to fix bayonets and reload with full clips, then wait for the signal to charge.

Minutes later smoke shells began dropping around the German-held farmhouse and adjacent out buildings and soon the enemy's defensive positions were shrouded. At 6:15 A.M. the artillery lifted its fire. Cole leaped to his feet, pulled out his .45 Colt and brandished it defiantly overhead. He blew his whistle, waved his arm forward, and dashed ahead. Twenty men followed.

Across the road, Major Stopka shouted, "Let's go!" and some fifty troopers took out after him.

Halfway along the 200-yard distance to the enemy-held farmhouse strongpoint, a huffing Colonel Cole dropped to one knee and looked back over his shoulder to see if his three companies of paratroopers were keeping close behind him. He was shocked by what he saw: only a trickle of his men had joined in the bayonet charge. The thought flashed through Cole's mind: "My men have let me down!"

The fog of war had interceded. Cole's troopers had been scattered over a wide expanse of meadowland. In the cacophony of battlefield noise, some did not get the order to charge. Others had vaguely heard something about "bayonets."

But the die had been cast. Colonel Cole, waving his men onward, was firing with his .45 Colt in the direction of the farmhouse. "Goddamn, I don't know what in hell I'm shooting at, but I've got to keep shooting!" he roared.

A few men nearby, despite the peril of their situation, laughed at the remark. "The colonel is really gung-ho!" they thought.

Dashing onward, Cole leaped a hedgerow—and landed in a ditch with water almost up to his neck. Major Stopka, shouting to his men relentlessly, "Let's go! Let's go!" jumped over the same hedgerow but missed the water-filled ditch. He saw Bob Cole, his jump suit soaking wet, clambering out.

Now the artillery-laid smokescreen began to dissolve and the charging Americans were visible to German defenders. A few troopers reached and passed Major Stopka. One of them, Private Edwin S. Pastouris, was cut down by a machine-gun burst. As blood gushed from the trooper's chest and stomach, he heard a faint voice: "How are you, Pastouris?" It was Major Stopka hovering over him.

"I'm okay," the seriously wounded young trooper replied weakly. "Keep going. Keep going."

Stopka patted the youth on the shoulder, then resumed the run for the farmhouse.

Private Bernard Sterno was dashing across a field when he felt a dull thump in one hand. But his gloves were on, so he saw nothing amiss and kept going as bullets hissed past his head. He did not realize that a finger had been shot off.

Sterno ran on and came to a medic who told him that his hand was bloody. The aid man took off Sterno's glove, and the young rifleman looked in astonishment at where his finger had been only minutes before. The finger stump was bandaged and Sterno resumed the attack.

Moving past a hedgerow, Private Sterno heard a plaintive call, "Help me. Help me." It was a sergeant from his company who had been shot in the stomach and leg. Blood had saturated his jump suit and his face was ashen. Next to him was the medic who had just treated Sterno's finger stump—dead with a bullet through the head.

Sterno took the aid man's kit and treated the grievously wounded sergeant, although he knew it was hopeless. The young rifleman patted the injured man on the shoulder, told him he would be in good shape as soon as he was evacuated to the rear, picked up his rifle, and ran forward.

Private Sterno reached the farmhouse from which the German parachutists, strongly entrenched, had raked the Screaming Eagles on the causeway for two days and nights. There he saw Colonel Cole and Major Stopka. Cole was waving troopers forward with the .45 Colt he was brandishing in one hand. "Keep going!" the colonel shouted. "The bastards are on the run! Get after their asses!"

First Sergeant Kenneth M. Sprecker shot the lock off the farmhouse door and, Tommy gun at the ready, dashed inside along with another trooper. The building was empty except for the dead bodies of several Germans, clad in their round bowl-like paratrooper helmets and camouflage smocks. Glassy eyes peered mockingly. These were some of the young paratroopers who only a few days previously had been engaging in carefree volleyball games, singing and laughing and worrying if the war would end before they had a chance to get into it.

Those German machine gunners and riflemen who could pulled back along the adjacent hedgerows as the American paratroopers charged the farmhouse and foxholes. Not all were able to withdraw. Scores of young *Feldgrau* lay sprawled grotesquely in death around the hedgerows, foxholes, and buildings.

Private Sterno, whose shot-off finger stub was now starting to give him intense pain, ran on past the farmhouse for some 30 yards, leaped into a ditch filled with water, and began firing in the direction of the enemy, using a rifle he had picked up from a dead trooper.

Sterno's bandage, once white but now caked with a mixture of blood and ugly brown mud, had worked itself loose. Another medic spotted the blood spurting from the hand and ordered Sterno to return to the rear for treatment. Sterno refused.

Around the young private in the ditch were several badly wounded troopers who had been hit in the bayonet charge. The road along which the ditch ran was being raked regularly by high-velocity 88-millimeter fire from the direction of Carentan. At irregular intervals there would be the frightening sound of sswwiiissshhh-CRACK! as a shell exploded nearby.

Next to Sterno was a trooper whose bloody eye had been gouged out by shrapnel. Frightened, near unconsciousness from shock, pain, and loss of blood, the youth weakly asked Sterno, "Is my eye gone?"

Sterno didn't want to answer. "Well, even if it is, you ought to be glad you've got the other one."

Private Sterno then began crawling up and down the water-filled ditch and tried to pour sulfa into ugly wounds of the others. He heard the ssswwwiiissshhh. There was a blinding flash nearby and an earth-shaking explosion. Sterno felt something strike him in the back as like a giant sledgehammer. Although he thought he had merely been rocked by the explosion, a shell fragment had ripped into his body.

In a dazed condition, Sterno was aware of a man screaming. It was the youth whose eye had been gouged out by a shell fragment. "My arm . . . oohhh . . . my arm!" the trooper was shouting. "Please, please . . . somebody help me . . . oh, my arm!"

Through hazy eyes Sterno saw that the youth's arm had been riddled by the explosion and was hanging in shreds, blood pouring out of the hideous wounds. Next to him another trooper was silent—the blast had torn off half of his head.

Only a few feet down the ditch another Screaming Eagle was muttering unintelligibly. He could not move. Blood was streaming from his ears, nose, and mouth.

Only half-conscious himself, Private Sterno knew that most of these wounded men were beyond help. And he had no means for assisting them. He crawled 50 yards toward the causeway, came upon a foxhole and lowered himself into it. He was still bleeding profusely from his hand and back, from which a large chunk of flesh had been savagely ripped. He was aware of a sharp burning sensation inside his body, but only later would he learn its cause—the white-hot chunk of German shrapnel had lodged near his groin.

He had been in the foxhole only about two minutes when he was rocked by another explosion. A mortar shell had struck just outside his hole, and a piece of the flying metal struck him in the neck.

Meanwhile Lieutenant Edward A. Provost, who had started the bayonet charge with nine men and reached the German-held farmhouse with four, crept up silently to a hedge on the far side of the building where an enemy machine gun was spitting out bullets at Colonel Cole's men. With him was Corporal James O. Brune, who tossed a grenade over the hedgerow.

Five German parachutists were at the gun and in an adjoining trench. The grenade exploded in the middle of them. None of the machine gunners was killed; they lay stunned or stood upright screaming. Provost and Brune, quick to press their advantage, leaped the hedgerow and charged.

Corporal Brune started to fire at the confused Germans. Lieutenant Provost shouted, "Don't waste your bullets—stick the bastards!"

The two troopers bayoneted the five enemy soldiers.

In the meantime, Colonel Bob Cole was in the yard of the farmhouse where he was using a pick handle as a splint on a man's bloody, shredded leg. Seated nearby against the stone house was a young trooper who had taken off his jump boot and was sprinkling sulfa powder on a heel wound.

"Better get the hell out of here right now," Cole urged the youth. "This is a dangerous spot."

"Right away, colonel," the youngster replied. "I want to put some sulfa on this wound so I won't get blood poisoning."

As the boy finished speaking there was the familiar ssswwwiiissshhh-CRACK! A flat-trajectory 88-millimeter shell hit the trooper directly in the chest and thrust him back against the stone farmhouse. His body slid to the ground, a grotesquely shaped bloody pulp.

Minutes later Lieutenant Ralph B. Gehauf, Colonel Cole's energetic intelligence officer, stomped into the farmhouse, now the battalion CP. He was hopping mad and cursing the colonel. Gehauf, who had been near total exhaustion from his efforts over two days and nights, had been asleep in a ditch that morning when the battalion moved out for the attack. Colonel Cole decided to let him sleep.

Other members of the battalion staff, who had been on assorted missions, also arrived at the CP. Gehauf, battalion personnel officer Lieutenant Ralph A. Watson and the rest of the staff were gathered in a room near the front door. Colonel Cole was in an adjoining room tending to the wounded.

Suddenly the sturdy old stone and timber farmhouse was rocked by a blast. A shell had hit on the doorstep outside, sending a torrent of shrapnel through the open doorway. Gehauf, Watson, another staff officer and an enlisted man were hit.

By now Colonel Cole's battalion had so many men wounded that their evacuation became a major problem for the commander. A truck, which had brought up ammunition, was pressed into service as an ambulance. So large was the number of wounded Screaming Eagles that it was necessary to place some of the injured in the bed of the truck and others on stretchers across the top and on the hood. The truck was under fire all the way back along the causeway.

Two jeeps were also commandeered from other duties to help remove the wounded troopers. The GI truck made three trips and on its final journey that day brought up several "straight leg" medics from First Army to help care for the injured.

Intense anger had been aroused on both sides during the struggle for

Carentan's Alley of Death. Colonel Cole sent a ten-man patrol to probe toward the front. As they reached a crossroads four Germans emerged from a thick woods calling *"Kamerad! Kamerad!"* (Literally "comrade," but commonly used for "We surrender!") But the enemy parachutists were holding weapons. Earlier in the day, at almost the precise spot, two Screaming Eagles had been shot down under nearly identical circumstances when the Americans dropped their guard and moved forward to accept the "surrender."

Now, without a word, the American patrol opened fire on the four Germans. Two were cut down, the other two fled back into the nearby thick woods. The Screaming Eagles had entered Normandy green—they were learning fast in the crucible of Carentan.

At noon that day, Colonel Cole took a radio message from regiment: All troops were to cease firing immediately until further notice. The Germans had asked for a truce, presumably to allow medics to haul away the vast numbers of dead and wounded scattered about the swamps, hedgerows, and fields. General Max Taylor, leader of the 101st Airborne, took advantage of the lull to issue a surrender ultimatum to the Wehrmacht commander in besieged Carentan.

Major Douglas T. Davidson, 502nd regimental surgeon, set out down the causeway toward the town, a large Red Cross emblem prominently displayed on an armband. Walking along in front of him were two German prisoners carrying long poles with two white flags.

Davidson moved on into German lines in front of Carentan where he was greeted with sullen stares by the young paratroopers. He told front line officers that he was there as the personal representative of General Taylor and asked for an audience with Lieutenant Colonel von der Heydte to discuss the surrender of Carentan.

As Major Davidson waited, a message was radioed to the parachute regiment leader in his cellar CP in town. Minutes later a response came back: Colonel von der Heydte refused to see the American emissary. With a shrug of his shoulders, the regimental surgeon turned around and headed back down the causeway toward his own lines, the two German prisoners out in front of him.

Davidson had been gone for about an hour, arriving at the American front line at 1 P.M. Almost precisely to the minute that the surgeon reached his unit's forward positions, the German paratroopers dramatically announced a halt to the truce; they drenched American positions with an intense concentration of machine-gun and rifle fire, mortar and artillery shells. Screams of pain and anguished cries for help echoed over American positions as bullets and shrapnel found their marks.

Colonel Cole, at his farmhouse CP, urgently phoned regiment: "The Krauts are giving us hell. Can we return the fire?"

"We have not received word that the truce is officially over," was the response. "Wait."

Colonel Michaelis, the 502nd commander, was concerned for Major Davidson's safety. He was not aware that the surgeon was back in American lines.

Cole waited a few minutes as the heavy concentration of German fire continued to plaster his men. Then he phoned again: "Can we let 'em have it now?"

The voice at regiment was hesitant: "We haven't received word that the truce has ended."

At that moment a shell struck the farmhouse roof right over Colonel Cole's head, showering him with plaster and slivers of wood. The explosion made a terrific noise in the room.

"Listen to that!" Cole shouted into the transmitter. "Does that sound like the Krauts are observing a truce?"

The calm voice at regiment replied: "Wait. Not yet."

But the exchange between battalion commander and regiment was irrelevant. As soon as the Germans had opened fire, the American paratroopers cut loose with every weapon at their disposal. The most intense firefight of the day had been raging for nearly a half-hour.

A few minutes later regiment called Cole: "Your men can open fire now."

Colonel Cole slammed down the receiver without a word.

Having taken advantage of the hour's truce to regroup their forces, the Germans launched a savage counterattack against the scattered and nearly exhausted American paratroopers. Gray-clad enemy parachutists crawled along the hedgerows toward Colonel Cole's men, firing hand-held automatic weapons and rifles and tossing grenades. A steady hail of mortar shells burst around the Americans, the acrid smell of cordite fumes saturating the air.

Von der Heydte's troops knew their business. The Americans seldom saw the advancing Germans until they were but a few yards away. Cole's men could hear the B-r-r-r of burp guns 200 yards away, then 100 yards, and finally only 50 yards ahead. Now they could hear the bolts being worked on enemy rifles and the strident shouts of Wehrmacht officers and non-coms directing their men in the counterattack. It was an all-out German effort to drive the Screaming Eagles back over the bloody causeway.

On came the Germans, hour after hour, sliding along the hedgerows, slipping from tree to tree, pressing ever closer to the beleaguered American parachutists, continually loosing withering fusillades of fire. The German mortar shells never ceased.

Von der Heydte's men reached a point only a hedgerow away from Colonel Cole's men near the American battalion's CP in the embattled farmhouse. German and American paratroopers, the elite of the two armies, were now nearly face to face, tossing hand grenades at each other.

At a defensive position along a hedgerow, 35 Americans were tensely waiting when the Germans launched their heavy counterattack. In only two hours of fighting, the little force had dwindled dramatically. A lieutenant had been hit, fifteen others had been wounded, three killed, and a few had carried the wounded to an aid station. This left only seven men under an acting squad leader, Private Redmond Wells.

The Germans bored in on the seven Americans. Private Wells was firing his Garand rifle when he felt a sharp pain in the shoulder. An enemy bullet had plowed into him. Blood was seeping from the wound. He could barely lift his rifle to fire.

"I think we've had about enough," Wells said matter of factly to the six others as bullets whipped past his head. "I'll stay here, the rest of you drop back to the next hedgerow." Out in front German shouts indicated the enemy was getting ready to charge the position.

Wells' six comrades uttered not a word. They simply looked at him and shook their heads, then resumed firing.

Von der Heydte's paratroopers continued to assault American positions despite heavy losses. Private First Class Charles L. Roderick and Private First Class Franklin E. Cawthon, two young Screaming Eagles, had been firing their machine gun for nearly six hours. The enemy was now having trouble crawling toward them as bodies of their own dead were hampering their advance. Several German bodies lay only 25 feet in front of the American machine gun.

Roderick was firing the automatic weapon when an enemy bullet hit the operating handle of the gun, driving a metal chunk deep into his shoulder. Blood flowed freely down his jacket. Roderick refused to be evacuated, and continued to pull the trigger with his good arm, his other arm hanging limp at his side.

Near the road leading back to the causeway, Sergeant Charles R. Derose fell into a hole and broke his leg. He declined an offer to be evacuated, but continued to stand in the hole for four hours to direct the flow of ammunition from the rear to the front. Derose constantly gritted his teeth. The pain was intense.

A mortar shell burst only 30 feet from Derose as he stood in the hole. "The next one will fall right in here," he called out to some nearby troopers. But he continued to stand and direct the flow of needed ammunition. The next shell landed almost on top of Derose, blowing him into small pieces.

At his farmhouse command post, only a hedgerow or two from the swarms of attacking German paratroopers, Colonel Bob Cole could hear the nearby heavy bursts of enemy fire. He was convinced the remnants of his battalion were about to be overrun and wiped out. There was no longer any question of evacuating his wounded; the battle was too closely joined and there were few medics left to perform the task. The wounded had to lie where they had been hit. Those who were able to crawled away on their own.

Bob Cole, near physical exhaustion after two days and two nights of virtually uninterrupted front-line fighting while directing his battalion, reached an agonizing decision: he would be forced to withdraw his men back over the causeway and leave his scores of wounded behind. There was no alternative, he was convinced; as far as he was concerned, his battalion had fought "to the last man."

At 4:30 P.M. Cole called on the radio to Major Allen W. Ginder, regimental executive officer. "We've had it," the battalion commander stated. "We're going to get out of here—if we can."

Cole stressed that he was giving Major Ginder advance notice of his intentions as dictated by battlefield realities, but that he would not give the withdrawal order pending evidence that the clash now raging around the farmhouse and hedgerows was indeed hopeless.

Major Stopka, who had been moving from window to window in the farmhouse CP, edged up to Cole as he rang off and said, "The bastards are all around us. It's getting goddamned hot!"

Colonel Cole knew there was only one last chance to hold the position—a heavy concentration of American artillery fire almost on top of his CP and his men. But, at this crucial point, Captain Rosemond's radio jammed. The artillery forward observer cursed the radio, striking it with his fist as he manipulated the dials. Outside there was the B-r-r-r of a German

Grim-faced American assault troops head for the Normandy beaches.
(U.S. National Archives)

An allied heavy bomber blasting German positions outside Cherbourg. *(U.S. National Archives)*

Brigadier General Theodore Roosevelt, hero of Utah Beach. (*U.S. Army photo*)

Brigadier General James M. Gavin led the La Fiere Causeway assault. (*U.S. Army photo*)

Lieutenant General Omar N. Bradley, First Army Commander. (*U.S. Army photo*)

Major General J. Lawton Collins, the captor of Cherbourg. (*U.S. Army Military History Institute*)

Lieutenant Colonel Robert H. Cole won the Medal of Honor (posthumously) for Carentan action. (U.S. Army photo)

Brigadier General Anthony Mc Auliffe, a task force commander a Carentan. (U.S. Army photo)

Field Marshal Gerd von Rundstedt, German Commander in Chief, West. (U.S. Army photo)

Major General Elwood R. "Pete Quesada, fighter-bomber chief in th Normandy operation. (U.S. Nationc Archives)

Field Marshall Erwin Rommel, defender of Normandy. *(U.S. Army Military History In-stitute)*

(above) Lieutenant Arthur Jahnke, defender of Block-house W-5

(right) German officers inspect a Goliath pygmy tank (left) that was to have been used against Allied invadors.

(below) A typical concrete gun bunker that protected Utah Beach.

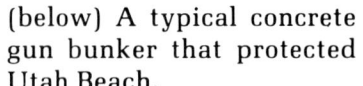

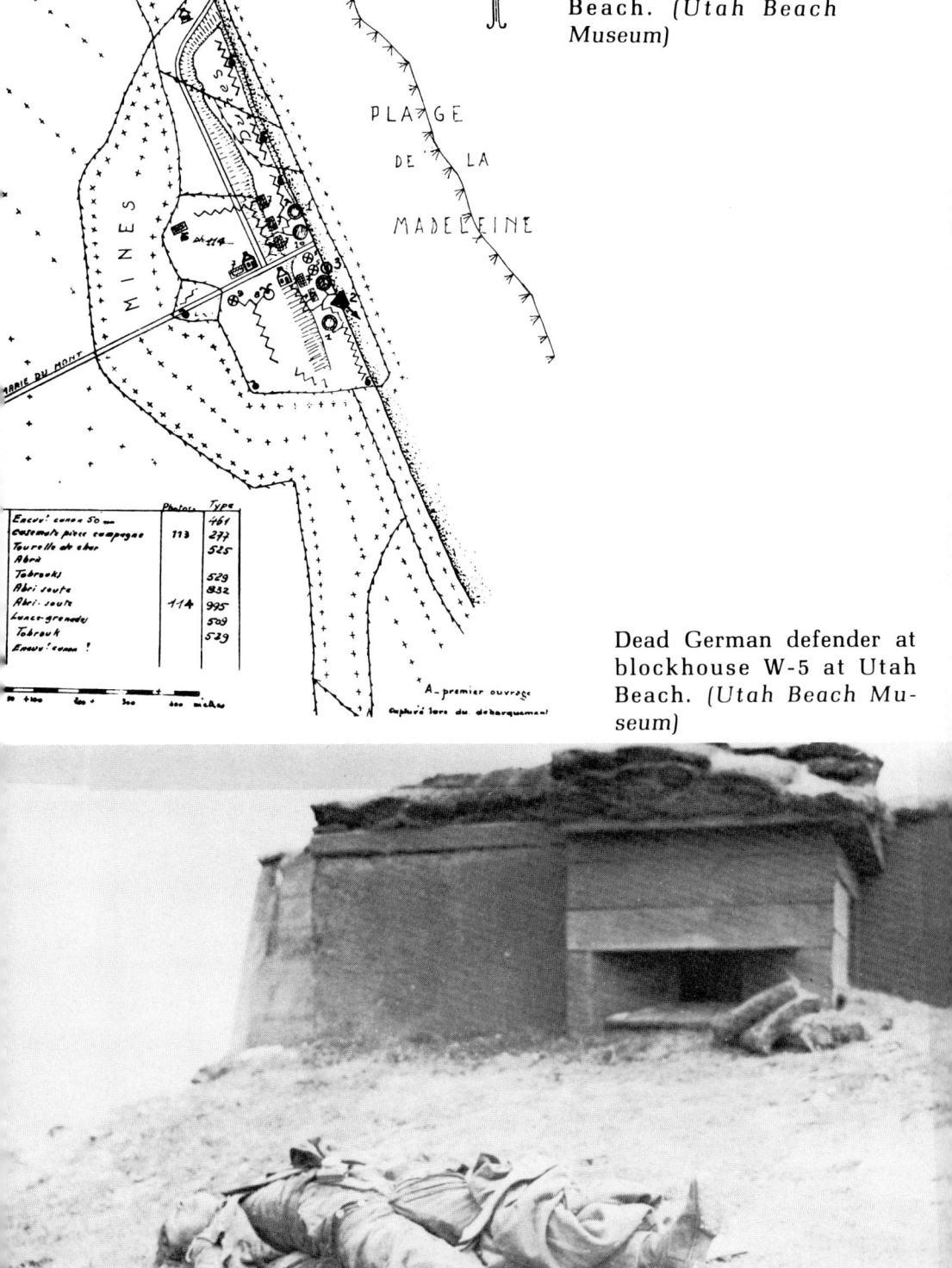

N

PLAGE DE LA MADELEINE

MINES

	Photo:	Type
Encuv.' canon 50 mm		461
Casemate pièce campagne	113	277
Tourelle de char		525
Abri		
Tobrooks		529
Abri soute		832
Abri soute	114	995
Lance-grenades		509
Tobrouk		529
Encuv.' canon !		

A – premier ouvrage
Capturé lors du débarquement

La Fiere causeway. At the time of the fight the lower half of the terrain in the photo was flooded. Elements of the 82nd Airborne Division had to dash across the causeway and the flooded area toward the entrenched Germans, around the buildings at Cauquigny, a distance of 500 yards. *(U.S. Army photo)*

The Carentan causeway. The outskirts of Carentan are in the fore-
ground of this photo, which is looking north. The German position,
the farmhouse, was the target of the bayonet charge. The flatlands to
either side of the causeway were flooded at the time of battle. *(U.S.
Army photo)*

Hitler's Fortress Cherbourg before the Allied invasion.

Cherbourg from the air. (U.S. Army photo)

Lieutenant Colonel August Baron von der Heydte, defender of Carentan.

Men of the 87th Mortar Battalion fire in support of the 101st Airborne Division in the fight at the Carentan causeway.

A German coastal battery outside Cherbourg, smashed by American naval gunfire and bombs. (U.S. Army photo)

American troops move through shell-battered Valonges, a key road center nine miles southeast of Cherbourg. (U.S. Army photo)

American Sherman tanks edged into battered Cherbourg to help mop up final German resistance. *(U.S. Army photo)*

American infantrymen cautiously advance toward the entrance of one of the many underground fortresses in Cherbourg.

American troops stand on Fort du Roule, perched on a cliff 450
high, over smoking Cherbourg. Germans still occupy most of the p
and fire 88-millimeter guns from below up at the fort. At the lov
right of the photo are the two berths where trans-Atlantic luxu
liners tied up in peacetime. *(U.S. Army photo)*

General von Schlieben's force in his underground command post
emerging under the white flag to surrender to the 9th Infantry Division. *(U.S. Army photo)*

(left) A mud-caked and dejected Lieutenant General Karl Dietrich von Schlieben enters VII Corps headquarters outside Cherbourg, after his capture. *(U.S. Army photo)*

(below) Major General J. Lawton "Lightning Joe" Collins (facing camera) confronts the captured commander of Fortress Cherbourg, General von Schlieben, and Admiral Walther Hennecke (left, back to camera), German naval commander for Normandy. *(U.S. Army photo)*

These German troops died for their Führer in the battle for Cherbourg.
(*Courtesy Michel de Vallavielle*)

burp gun and a stream of bullets stitched the wall over Cole's and Redmond's heads.

Finally the radio crackled violently and Captain Charles Aldrich at the artillery fire control center came on the air. Cole and Rosemond sighed with relief. Cole grabbed the transmitter: "Give 'em all you've got—right in front of the farmhouse."

The besieged battalion commander added matter of factly, "If this doesn't work, we'll get the hell out of here right now."

Captain Aldrich's reply sent a mixture of fury and concern racing through Cole's being: "We're almost out of ammunition."

"Then for God's sake, get some!" Colonel Cole roared. "Get it. We've got to have it! Now!"

Less than a quarter-hour later, above the rattle of smallarms fire and the crash of grenades, Cole and Rosemond heard an approaching rustle from behind that brought renewed hopes to their hearts—the sound of American artillery shells, large clusters of them, heading overhead toward the advancing German paratroopers only a hedgerow or two in front.

Dashing to an upstairs window of the farmhouse CP, the parachute officers shouted in glee as they saw the American shells exploding among the hedgerows, giving off geysers of flame and thick black smoke. Every American artillery piece and mortar within range now concentrated fire on the targeted areas. Captain Rosemond, adjusting the guns, pulled back the impact area until American missiles were hissing just above the farmhouse roof.

"Hot damn! They're giving those Krauts holy hell!" a paratrooper at the window called out in glee.

"Listen to it, just listen to it!" Bob Cole shouted at Captain Rosemond.

When the heavy American barrage lifted, the German fire from the front of the farmhouse had diminished to only an occasional rifle shot or burst from a burp gun. Colonel Cole sent patrols forward. The enemy had abandoned the battlefield, leaving behind scores of dead and seriously wounded comrades. The German 6th Parachute Regiment's back had been broken.

At 2 P.M. the following day, another 101st Airborne battalion relieved Bob Cole's exhausted and depleted unit. The colonel ordered a roll call in an orchard where his battalion had assembled. Some 640 men had entered the death struggle for the Carentan causeway two days before; only 132 answered roll call—and many of them were wounded.

Now the remnants of Colonel Cole's battalion marched wearily back over the causeway purchased with the blood of their dead and injured comrades. The troopers moved along in silence, each immersed in his own thoughts.

It was near midnight when the exhausted airborne men reached their destination, Saint-Côme-du-Mont, a few miles to the rear. One of Cole's men remarked in a tired voice, "Say, colonel, did you know that today is Sunday?"

"Jesus Christ!" was the soft reply. "Why didn't somebody tell me?"

11

"Hold Montebourg at All Costs!"

It was pitch black during the early morning hours of Monday, June 12, as a trooper of Colonel Bob Sink's 506th Parachute Infantry Regiment was driving a horse-drawn cart loaded with mortar ammunition southward over the Carentan causeway. The cargo was on its way to the front lines in anticipation of a German attack at dawn.

The causeway, scene of a devastation in recent days and nights, was now hushed and eerie. The paratrooper driver was nervous. He had not been along the causeway before, and the absence of any sign of fellow Screaming Eagles was disconcerting. His instructions had been to drive the entire length of the causeway to a point only a few hundred yards from Carentan, then take a right turn to his unit's front-line positions.

The young trooper missed the turnoff in the blackness and continued onward—right into Carentan. Ghostly silhouettes of bomb- and shell-wracked buildings loomed starkly around him. The only sound was the horse's hooves and the cart's steel-rimmed wheels on the cobblestones. Here and there a fire glowed unattended.

Reaching the dark deserted square in the center of Carentan, the paratrooper began to have an uneasy feeling. "I don't think I'm in the right place!" he told himself. At that moment, the intense, ominous silence was shattered. An alarm clock stashed in the trooper's duffel bag and long forgotten began to ring with the utmost urgency. Its grating noise seemed to the lone American to echo throughout the town.

The Screaming Eagle hurriedly turned his cart around, slapped the horse's rump and beat a hasty retreat back out of Carentan.

A few hours later, as dawn of June 12 arrived, elements of the 101st

Airborne Division had nearly encircled the key traffic center and were poised to move to seize it. The 3rd Battalion of the 327th Glider Infantry, which had crossed the Douve River a few miles northeast of Carentan the night of June 9, had been fighting its way toward the town from the east.

Launching the final assault at 5 A.M., the 3rd Battalion glidermen, held up momentarily only by a small delaying force, entered Carentan from the east. The 2nd Battalion of Colonel Sink's 506th Parachute Infantry jumped off from the southwest at 5 A.M. and marched into town. At 7:20 A.M. the paratroopers linked up with the glidermen coming from the opposite direction.

Carentan was now in Allied hands. The Omaha and Utah beachheads had been linked. Now General Collins could launch operations to capture Cherbourg, the port Adolf Hitler had decreed must be held by the Wehrmacht if the Allied invaders were to be driven back into the English Channel.

On the morning of June 12, as General Maxwell Taylor's paratroopers and glidermen edged into battered Carentan, the Allies had 16 divisions ashore, nine American and seven British. The enormous logistical problem of supplying this large and growing force over the open beaches was becoming more difficult each day as a steady stream of reinforcements entered the Allied bridgehead. The Allied commanders were haunted by the possibility of a sudden violent storm over the capricious English Channel resulting in the destruction of the ingenious shipping facilities which were being utilized on the American and British beaches.

These portable harbors were British in concept and design and for two years had been developed under top-secret conditions. There were two types of protected anchorages. One, code-named Gooseberry, was a line of old sunken ships placed stem to stern in large numbers to provide a sheltered coastline in which landing craft and small vessels could unload in any but the most severe weather.

Code-named Mulberry, the other protected anchorage was virtually a complete harbor, constructed in England and towed across the Channel right after D-Day. The principal unit in Mulberry was a huge, concrete ship, called a *phoenix,* shaped like a box. When many of these were sunk end to end along the coast of Normandy, they provided protection against most turbulence.

A Mulberry was in operation off Omaha in the American sector and off Arromanches in the British zone. Five Gooseberries had been installed along various beaches.

Meanwhile, at his Berchtesgaden chalet perched high in the Bavarian Alps, Adolf Hitler reacted violently to the loss of the key traffic center of Carentan, which linked Omaha and Utah into one uniform beachhead stretching from the Orne River on the British eastern flank all the way westward to the vicinity of Montebourg, some 16 miles southeast of the port of Cherbourg.

On June 9, Hitler had ordered Lieutenant Colonel von der Heydte and his young paratroopers to "fight to the last man and last bullet" to hold Carentan. Now the Führer felt that he had been betrayed. In fact the German 6th Parachute Regiment had been cut to pieces in the savage struggle for Carentan, and von der Heydte had withdrawn the remnants of his unit to the flatlands a mile south of the town to prevent being surrounded by two pincers of the 101st Airborne Division.

So upset was Hitler over the capture of Carentan by the American Screaming Eagles that only a few hours after receiving the bad news, on June 12, he issued a directive to all Wehrmacht commanders in Normandy:

> Explicit orders demand that everyone at strongpoints, points of resistance and other defensive positions surrounded by enemy units must defend the position to the last man and to the last bullet, in order to allow time for preparation for the counterattack and the reconquest of the [Normandy] coast. No orders to retreat will be issued [by any commander].

At La Roche-Guyon that evening of the twelfth, Field Marshal Erwin Rommel arrived back at his headquarters after an exhausting day of touring the front in a desperate effort to halt the Anglo-American tide engulfing Normandy. He was solemn, serious, and deeply moved by the carnage being inflicted on his *Feldgrau* by smothering Allied air attacks, naval and field artillery barrages.

Now he was handed an urgent message from the Oberkommando der Wehrmacht—Adolf Hitler as transmitted by Field Marshal Keitel— which left Rommel sputtering and red-faced with anger. The OKW had heard a BBC report from London that a few German soldiers had been captured in their underwear. Now Hitler demanded an explanation. The inference was plain: the Führer believed the German army under Rommel was not fighting tenaciously.

Contributing to Rommel's rage was the fact that that day he had had to leap out of his Horch for roadside ditches no fewer than thirty times when suddenly attacked by Allied fighter-bombers. At the front Rommel had learned that infantry companies had dwindled to only thirty to fifty-five men each and that most divisions had committed their last reserves in desperate bids to halt or slow down the Allied offensive.

"I have visited the front each day and our men are performing gallantly," Rommel wrote that night to son Manfred, an army private. "It tears my heart out to see the equivalent of a regiment disappear each day in casualties."

While American paratroopers had been engaged in bloody encounters at the La Fière causeway and at Carentan, Lightning Joe Collins, VII Corps commander, had been attacking northward from Utah with other elements to secure a strong defensive position to protect the flank of other formations which would attack westward to cut the Cotentin Peninsula and isolate German forces in and around Cherbourg. All hope had vanished that the U.S. 4th Infantry Division could race northward after its D-Day assault for an early seizure of the crucial port.

The terrain over which Tubby Barton's 4th Division would have to attack toward Cherbourg was relatively flat just north of Utah but was crisscrossed by small streams and hedgerows. These provided the Germans with excellent delaying positions. It was soon apparent: the struggle for the Cotentin Peninsula and the prize of Cherbourg would be won basically by foot soldiers slogging from hedgerow to hedgerow, with gains measured in yards.

The hedgerows (*bocages*) provided a natural form of defense for the Germans infinitely more formidable than anything the wily Desert Fox, Rommel, could have contrived. For centuries the flatlands of the lower Cotentin Peninsula had been divided and subdivided into small pastures by means of thick earthen walls. Many of these were eight to ten feet high, and long, snake-like roots packed the dirt together much as reinforcing steel would for concrete structures.

A thick, thorny growth of trees, bushes, and brambles crowned each wall. The earthen mounds furnished ideal protection for defenders and the crown of vegetation gave the enemy concealment for his riflemen, machine gunners, and antitank rocket launchers.

"It's every bit as formidable as the jungles on Guadalcanal," General Collins exclaimed to his staff. Collins had been nicknamed Lightning Joe the previous year for the rapidity with which his 25th Infantry Division cleaned up the embattled Pacific island of Guadalcanal after relieving the Marines.

The *bocage* country's defense was strengthened for the Germans north of Utah by the heavily fortified areas of Crisbecq, Azeville, and Ozeville, as well as by strongpoints along the beach. In that region the Germans had constructed thick-walled, concrete blockhouses, each structure bristling with 88-millimeter guns and connected by trenches manned by riflemen and machine gunners.

Behind these strongpoints the ground rose gradually to the Quineville-Montebourg-le Ham ridge, which was to have been part of the 4th Infantry Division's D-Day objective. General Barton's men had been halted far short of that goal.

In order to secure the northern flank of American divisions set to attack westward from the Merderet River bridgehead carved out in bloody fighting by Brigadier General Jim Gavin's airborne men, Lightning Joe Collins felt he had to seize the Quineville-Montebourg-le Ham ridge. He had no way of knowing that General Karl von Schlieben, commander of the German 709th Division, had selected that precise ridgeline on which to make a stand in the coming battle for Cherbourg. Von Schlieben had organized strong defensive positions on the ridge.

On June 8 the attack northward to capture the key ridge had been launched by elements of Tubby Barton's 4th Division and the 505th Parachute Infantry Regiment of the 82nd Airborne Division, led by Colonel William E. Ekman. There were four regiments abreast: Colonel Harvey A. Tribolet's 22nd Infantry along the coast, Colonel Russell P. "Red" Reeder's 12th Infantry alongside, and Colonel Van Fleet's 8th Infantry and Ekman's paratroopers to the west of Route Nationale 13, the main north-south road running from Cherbourg to Paris and cutting through Montebourg and Sainte-Mère-Église.

Ekman's parachutists and Van Fleet's dogfaces (a term the infantrymen considered a badge of honor) made good initial progress through the hedgerow tangles and what amounted to rear guard action by small but determined groups. But as they edged closer to von Schlieben's main line of resistance, the Quineville-Montebourg-le Ham ridge, German opposition stiffened, and the Americans were pounded by the heaviest artillery barrages yet encountered in the invasion.

Perched on a rickety stool in a camouflaged tent, his battle headquarters just outside Montebourg, was a beleaguered yet confident young German major, Friedrich Küppers. His eyes were bloodshot from more than five days of almost constant fighting, and grime covered his handsome face. There had been no time to wash or shave.

Since the Allied hurricane of steel and explosives had whipped across the English Channel and lashed against the coast of Normandy at dawn on June 6, Küppers and his men had been subjected to an endless pounding by fighter-bombers from the air, naval guns from the sea, and land-based artillery and mortars. Major Küppers had seen entire companies of grenadiers (infantrymen) wiped out in only a few hours under this smothering blanket of bombs and shells. But the *Feldgrau* fought tenaciously against the Americans attacking northward from Utah, exacting a heavy toll in blood from the invaders at each earthen hedgerow.

Despite Major Küppers' modest rank and relative youth, General von Schlieben had entrusted him with command of Artillery Group Montebourg, the last strong position barring the way to Cherbourg. If the Americans broke through the hard-pressed and nearly exhausted *Feldgrau,* the way to the critical port of Cherbourg, up Route Nationale 13, would be open.

"We must stop them here," Major Küppers repeatedly told his field commanders. "Montebourg must be held—at all costs!"

Küppers had considerable firepower at his disposal. His artillery group had been formed from five different batteries for the defense of Montebourg, a previously insignificant little farming community which had languished peacefully along the road for several centuries. The artillery group consisted of 19 guns, including ones of 150-, 122- and 105-millimeter, and several of the deadly-accurate 88-millimeter, the German weapon the Allied soldier had learned to fear most.

Combined with the guns of flak group Konig and with Major Rassner's companies of the 100th Mortar Regiment, Major Küppers' artillery units were supporting the 919th Grenadier Regiment, which had been conducting a fighting withdrawal from the Utah Beach area, combat groups of the 243rd Division, commanded by Lieutenant General Heinz Hellmich, and small elements of von Schlieben's 709th Division, which had become scattered in the confusion of the Allied D-Day bombardments and landings.

Pounded by Major Küppers' artillery, the attacking Americans had engaged in bitter, hedgerow-to-hedgerow fighting for three days, inching forward. Finally, on June 12, Colonel Jim Van Fleet's 8th Infantry Regiment reached the east-west Montebourg-le Ham road. There General Collins ordered the unit to dig in. The corps commander was satisfied that his northern flank was secure and that he could proceed with the crucial task of driving westward and sealing off the Cotentin Peninsula. This operation was launched immediately.

Jumping off from the Merderet River bridgehead near La Fière on June 12, the green 90th Infantry Division under Brigadier General Jay W. McKelvie passed through 82nd Airborne Division positions. Its objective was the north-south stretch of the Douve River north of the road junction town of Saint-Sauveur-le-Vicomte. The attack floundered from the beginning.

The 90th Division had come ashore at Utah on the heels of the assaulting 4th Infantry Division, but there was no "quiet" sector in which it could be "blooded," as was the custom for green outfits. Of necessity, the 90th had been tossed right into the crucible. Suffering from acute mental shock, an affliction of all untested combat units during the first few days, and unaccustomed to the agony of mutilated soldiers and the stark reality of sudden death, the men of the 90th herded together in fear and confusion when the Germans started pounding them with mortar and artillery fire.

After General McKelvie's untested division had been in action for two days, its progress through the tangled hedgerows was virtually nonexistent, and it had taken heavy casualties from mortar and artillery fire. Alarmed and angry by the lackluster fighting of the 90th Division, on June 13 General Collins and his aide, Captain John Walsh, went forward on foot to assess the situation personally. It was not long before Collins' suspicions were confirmed: the trouble with the 90th Infantry Division was uninspired leadership at the top and in the regiments.

Collins and Walsh walked almost to the front lines and could not locate a single regimental or battalion command post. No shelling was going on, but there was no sign of efforts to move forward. The corps commander and his aide reached the front near Orglandes without seeing a single 90th Division officer. It was as though the leaders of a division of fourteen thousand men had somehow vanished.

Finally Collins and Walsh ran into Lieutenant Colonel William L. Nave, a battalion commander. Nave appeared to be the only commander operating in the field.

If Collins and his assistant had gone any farther, they would have reached German outposts. They turned around and headed back to the 90th Division command post. Nearly a half-mile from the front, Collins came upon a sergeant and several infantrymen in a roadside ditch.

"Sergeant, what are you and your men doing?" the corps commander asked.

The reply was evasive. Obviously, Collins was aware, the men were shirking. He cited the great record of the 90th Division in the Meuse-Argonne battle of the First World War and of the 82nd Airborne Division, through which the 90th had just passed, in this war. The sergeant and his men shrugged their shoulders, stared at the ground. They were not interested and said so.

Collins ordered the men to return to the front, but had to move on before he could determine if they had done so. Lightning Joe knew that there was nothing wrong with these confused soldiers that firm and inspired leadership could not remedy. The aggressive, peppery corps commander was determined that the 90th Division would get that needed leadership.

Immediately upon returning to VII Corps headquarters, Collins telephoned General Bradley, First Army commander, and gave him a rundown on the conditions he had found. He recommended the relief of General McKelvie, but stressed that he did not hold McKelvie responsible for the situation. McKelvie had been the division artillery commander and had inherited the top post only a few months before sailing from the States. Collins blamed the previous commander for not toughening the troops to face the grim realities of war.

"Whom do you recommend to replace him?" Bradley inquired evenly.

"Gene Landrum," was the reply.

"Okay, make the change."

Although Collins had not known him long, Major General Eugene M. Landrum was an experienced infantrymen who reportedly had performed well in the American occupation of Alaska's Attu peninsula the previous year. He had been assigned to VII Corps as a spare in the event a division commander were needed.

Worried about the two days lost by the floundering of the 90th Infantry Division in the attack westward to cut the peninsula, Collins made another urgent recommendation: employ Major General Manton S. Eddy's just-arrived 9th Infantry Division and Major General Matt Ridgway's 82nd Airborne Division, both battle-tested outfits, to spearhead the drive.

General Bradley promptly approved the proposal. He knew as well as Collins did that time was vital. The original plan for Neptune had called for seizure of Cherbourg on D plus 8. Now it was D plus 7 and the Americans still had not severed the peninsula to isolate the key port to the north.

Told by Collins that he was to take over 90th Division, General Landrum could hardly restrain his delight. "I'll hurry and give you a salt-water cocktail from the other side of the Cotentin!" Landrum rashly promised.

146

General Collins advised Landrum to "clean house" throughout the division, with a specific recommendation to replace two colonels whose regiments had done poorly during the past three days. Landrum promptly cleaned his house—but not thoroughly enough, as events would prove.

12

"We're Going All the Way Tonight!"

Lieutenant Mike Chester, a young platoon leader in the 82nd Airborne Division, made his way along a line of foxholes nestled against the earthen bank of a hedgerow behind the lines of the floundering 90th Infantry Division. In these holes Chester's paratroopers of the 1st Battalion of the 505th Parachute Infantry Regiment were steeling their spirits for the attack they were about to spearhead.

Many of Chester's men were veterans of last year's hard fighting in Sicily and mainland Italy, but each new attack brought butterflies to the stomach, perspiration to the palms and forehead, and deep concern to the heart.

It was June 15—D-Day plus 9—and Colonel William Ekman, leader of the 505th, had received word that morning that the 82nd Airborne would join with the experienced 9th Infantry Division in spearheading the attack to the west coast to cut the peninsula in two.

Lieutenant Chester, regarded as a tough and competent combat leader, had been given the assignment of leading a platoon in the forefront of the 82nd Airborne attack. Chester was going from man to man, giving words of encouragement, explaining the purpose of the attack, seeing that his troopers' basic combat needs were met. It would be a tough go . . . no doubt about that. Lieutenant Chester and his men would be up against an enemy dug into the tangle of hedgerows where one determined machine-gun crew could hold up an entire uninspired battalion indefinitely.

"It won't be easy," Chester told his men. "But we're going to go through them like a dose of salts through a turkey!"

The terrain over which the attack would be made was swampy in many places and most of it was covered with thick vegetation. Its streams, fields, and the *bocages* made it ideal for the defense.

149

General Collins' plan for cutting off the Cotentin and isolating large numbers of German troops to the north would be a two-pronged attack down a relatively narrow corridor, only some three miles wide. Through this corridor ran two main roads which passed over the Douve River and reached the west coast.

The southern road stretched through the key rail and road center of Saint-Sauveur-le-Vicomte, some nine miles from the west coast. The 82nd Airborne Division would use this road as its axis of advance.

Only a few miles to the north, a roughly parallel road rolled through Sainte-Colombe and on to Barneville, the picturesque little seaport perched on a hill overlooking the Atlantic Ocean. General Matt Eddy's 9th Division fighting men would push forward along both sides of the Sainte-Colombe road.

Barneville—little Barneville—was the key to seizing the port of Cherbourg. If it could be reached—and soon—Cherbourg, the major harbor Hitler had ordered held at all costs, would be doomed.

At 3 P.M. on the fifteenth, Lieutenant Mike Chester's platoon of paratroopers climbed out of their foxholes and began edging toward the enemy. It passed through units of the 90th Infantry Division as an occasional mortar shell exploded around them. As the parachutists reached the front lines of the green 90th Division, they saw that the infantrymen were huddled together alongside the earthen hedgerows, much like a flock of sheep anticipating the imminent arrival of a storm.

"Why in hell don't those silly bastards spread out?" a veteran trooper mused. "One shell could get twenty of them."

Hardly had Chester and his men, with the rest of Lieutenant Colonel Mark J. Alexander's 1st Battalion advancing on their heels, passed the 90th Division outposts than they came under intense automatic-weapons fire from small groups of Germans concealed among the hedgerows which encircled each tiny field. Several paratroopers were cut down, including Lieutenant Gerald Johnson, a bullet through the arm, and a replacement lieutenant who had joined the 82nd Airborne only a short time previously, hit in the right knee.

Mark Alexander's 1st Battalion proceeded to wipe out the opposing force, remnants of the battered and war-weary 91st Air Landing Division which had been fighting almost continually since the American paratroopers landed almost directly on its positions after midnight on July 6.

Attacking alongside Alexander's battalion was the 2nd Battalion of the 505th Parachute Infantry, commanded by Lieutenant Colonel Benjamin J.

Vandervoort. On parachuting into Normandy ten nights previously, Colonel Vandervoort had broken an ankle. But he refused to be evacuated and insisted on leading his battalion through almost constant fighting.

Mark Alexander's battalion continued to hack its way through the hedgerow tangles until it got out in front of Vandervoort's battalion. Alexander, who was the third commander of the 1st Battalion in 10 days (the previous two leaders, Major James McGinity and Major Frederick Kellam were killed within a few hours of each other two days after D-Day), got on the radio to his good friend Vandervoort.

"Ben," said the 1st Battalion commander, "we've gotten out in front of you, and I thought you might like to use the two tanks I have. We're moving through mainly trees and the goddamned hedgerows, so you can probably use the tanks to better advantage than we can."

Vandervoort, a man of action and few words, simply replied, "Send them on over."

Plodding through thickets and tangled hedgerows, still restricted to Indian-type warfare, the American paratroopers pushed on ahead steadily, halting periodically to spray a thick tangle of vegetation with Tommy guns or to toss grenades and then charge an enemy machine-gun position concealed in the heavy growth.

In their steady push westward, the 82nd Airborne men took several hundred prisoners, mainly ersatz troops impressed into the German army: Czechs, Russians, Poles. These were sacrificial pawns in the German effort to halt the American steamroller. Behind them was a wall of fanatical young German fighting men of the decimated 91st Division who, despite the pounding they had taken for more than 10 days, were determined to fight and, if necessary, die. Many of them fought savagely. And they died.

Alexander's and Vandervoort's battalions advanced until they reached the north-south flowing Douve River across from Saint-Sauveur-le-Vicomte. There they dug in to await orders.

So confused had the Germans become in this area that periodically they drove vehicles eastward across the bridge out of Saint-Sauveur-le-Vicomte and directly into the gunsights of Alexander's dug-in parachutists. Waiting until each unsuspecting motorcycle, truck, or armored car had almost reached their lines, the airborne men let loose with withering blasts of fire at point-blank range, in some instances blasting the vehicle and its unlucky occupants off the road entirely.

"Like shooting fish in a barrel!" a trooper would call out each time while gazing out at the wrecked and often smoking Wehrmacht conveyance.

Meanwhile, a couple of miles north along the corridor, Colonel Frederick J. de Rohan's veteran 60th Infantry Regiment of the 9th Division had jumped off with high hopes that day—and promptly run into a buzzsaw. Elements of the 91st Division, decimated but still fighting vigorously, supported by tanks, lashed out against de Rohan's men in a counterattack and brought the 9th Division advance to a standstill.

Late in the day Matt Eddy, the 9th Division commander, inserted the 47th Regiment, led by Colonel George Smythe, on the right of de Rohan's stalled men. That was the spark that was needed, and both regiments, side by side, plunged ahead rapidly. By nightfall the 9th Infantry Division reached the high ground west of Orglandes.

As the exhausted paratroopers of the 82nd Airborne and dogfaces of the 9th Infantry Division fell into a deep slumber in hastily dug foxholes that night of June 15, ominous events were unfolding in the darkness far to the east, along the Pas-de-Calais. At one minute after midnight 55 snorting, fire-breathing monsters roared off ramps, soared high in the air, and minutes later crashed down on the teeming center of London.

The capital of Great Britain was under attack by robots.

By daybreak, 73 of these frightening new weapons had exploded in the southeastern portion of England. Adolf Hitler, at long last, had lashed out with his "vengeance weapons"—pilotless aircraft packed with explosives and timed to cut off over the target and glide to the ground, hitting with terrific impact.

The first V-1, as they were called, was to have been launched in December 1943. But Allied intelligence spotted the ramps and they were pulverized by bombing. The date was again set for mid-February, but again the Royal Air Force and U.S. Army Air Corps smashed the ramps.

New ramps were built and Lieutenant General Ernst Heinemann, in charge of the V-1 launchings, reset the inaugural flights for the night of June 12. At 4 A.M. the first salvo of 10 V-1s roared off the ramps; five of the pilotless bombs exploded just after takeoff and the others barely got across the Channel.

General Heinemann postponed the V-1 offensive for the third time, to the night of June 15. German technicians feverishly adjusted faulty steering mechanisms. This time the launching proceeded without a hitch. London's huge civilian population was thrown into near-panic over the sudden and unexpected rain of death from the sky.

As tens of thousands of shocked and terrified Londoners pulled themselves from the wreckage created by the unexpected robot attack on the morning of June 16, across the Channel the battle for Saint-Sauveur-le-Vicomte erupted. It began at dawn with one of the heaviest artillery and mortar barrages of the Normandy campaign.

Hardly had this heavy pounding been lifted than swarms of American P-47 Thunderbolts and P-51 Mustangs, sleek fighter-bombers with wings glinting from the early morning rays of the sun, began circling over Saint-Sauveur-le-Vicomte. Suddenly, each group of four aircraft peeled off, one by one, and like hawks spotting prey on the ground swooped down to loose bombs from under their wings on targets in the battered and smoking town.

Each bomb shook the earth across the Douve where the paratroopers of Colonels Mark Alexander and Ben Vandervoort were watching the aerial show with great delight. With each ker-plunk of a bomb, the airborne men knew the resistance they would face would be diminished.

"Give the bastards hell!" a gleeful trooper shouted above the roar of exploding missiles from the sky. His comrades joined in the exhortation.

As each fighter-bomber released its lethal cargo, it would pull up sharply, then bank and return at tree-top level to strafe the hapless defenders of Colonel Eugen Konig's 91st Air Landing Division.

With his 505th Regiment dug in across the Douve from Saint-Sauveur-le-Vicomte, General Matt Ridgway, commander of the 82nd Airborne, arrived on the scene. He was told by Colonel Alexander and Colonel Vandervoort that their paratroopers had spotted the Germans pulling out of town.

Ridgway got on the radio to General Collins. "The Krauts are pulling out of Saint-Sauveur-le-Vicomte," Ridgway stated. "Can I cross the Douve and take out after them?"

The VII Corps leader promptly granted permission and instructed Ridgway to establish a firm bridgehead on the far side of Saint-Sauveur-le-Vicomte.

After the bombing from the air and the heavy barrage by artillery and mortars, at noon Captain Clyde Russell, commander of Ben Vandervoort's E Company, led a patrol over a blasted bridge spanning the lovely Douve River and entered what had once been picturesque Saint-Sauveur-le-Vicomte. But now, like many French villages, the town was chiefly pulverized masonry saturated with the ugly smell of death.

Shells and bombs had ripped homes apart, exposing in pathetic fashion their tumbled bedrooms. Gaunt and blackened by fire stood the shells of walls. A handful of civilians, terrified men, women, and children trapped in

153

the town when the gargantuan American bombing and shelling was unleashed, cringed in the rubble of their cellars.

As the Germans bolted out of town, they had left behind the litter of retreat: abandoned bedding, clothing, scattered letters and photographs, and other personal impedimenta soldiers carried into combat. Beside the door of a battered stone house hung a mirror, and crumpled in a heap beside it was a dead German with white lather on his face, his arms spread wide and glassy sightless eyes peering intently into the blue sky. Death had struck him down in the act of shaving.

As General Ridgway stood at the western end of the blasted bridge urging his troopers on, the balance of Colonel Vandervoort's 2nd Battalion pushed on into Saint-Sauveur-le-Vicomte. Vandervoort, hobbling along with the cast on his broken leg, was having a difficult time keeping up, but he did maintain pace with his able-limbed troopers and joined Ridgway in cheering his men forward.

On the heels of the 2nd Battalion, Colonel Mark Alexander and his men pushed on over the bridge and into the battered town, followed by the 3rd Battalion. Now all of the 505th Infantry Regiment was across the river.

As Alexander reached General Ridgway, the 82nd Airborne commander said: "Push on through and hold the high ground to the right. We've got fifteen batteries of artillery to support you if you need them."

"Well, that's good news, general," Colonel Alexander replied with a wry grin. He knew, as did Ridgway, that leading elements of the 82nd Airborne had moved so rapidly that they were "out on a limb" and uncertain of what enemy formations were out front of them, or on their flanks.

As the paratroopers began pushing cautiously past each dwelling and building, firing bursts from Tommy guns or rifles into those nooks of concealment which might hold enemy snipers, the familiar singsong rustle of incoming shells greeted their ears, followed seconds later by explosions. The Germans had been forced out of Saint-Sauveur-le-Vicomte, but now they were firing 88-millimeter salvos into the town, turning rubble into powder.

Just outside town on high ground in the pasture of a large, ancient chateau, terrified horses galloped about, their frenzied neighs drifting over the din of exploding German shells. The pitiful cries of French civilians, equally terrified by the German bombardment, could be heard from the shambles of the town.

Meanwhile that day the second "horse" in the double-harnessed fighting

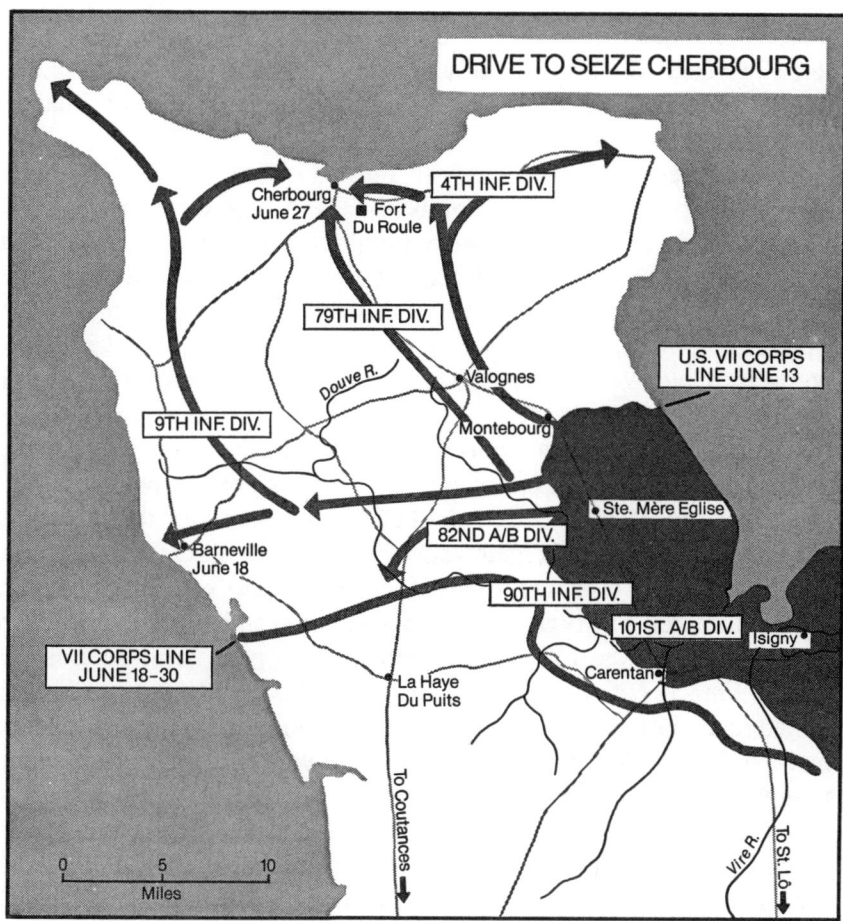

DRIVE TO SEIZE CHERBOURG

4TH INF. DIV.

Cherbourg
June 27

Fort
Du Roule

79TH INF. DIV.

U.S. VII CORPS
LINE JUNE 13

Douve R.

Valognes

9TH INF. DIV.

Montebourg

Ste. Mère Eglise

Barneville
June 18

82ND A/B DIV.

90TH INF. DIV.

101ST A/B DIV.

Isigny

VII CORPS LINE
JUNE 18–30

Carentan

La Haye
Du Puits

To Coutances

Vire R.

To St. Lô

0   5   10
Miles

tandem being driven across the Cotentin by General Joe Collins, the 9th Infantry Division, had run into heavy opposition and was hit by several local counterattacks supported by tanks, artillery, and mortars. But the 60th Regiment under Colonel de Rohan and the 47th Infantry led by Colonel Smythe smothered the enemy forces and pushed on to the Douve River near Sainte-Colombe, some three miles north of Bill Ekman's paratroopers in the vicinity of Saint-Sauveur-le-Vicomte.

As a hot June sun began its downward plunge behind the western horizon on the night of June 16, Lightning Joe Collins was conferring with his aides. "I'm convinced we've broken the German's back," he declared. "We're going to make a dash for the coast."

Collins rapidly sent out orders to General Matt Eddy: the veteran 9th

155

Infantry Division would make that run for Barneville. "Pull out all the stops," General Collins told Eddy. It was simply a reminder. Matt Eddy was accustomed to pulling out all the stops when the battlefield situation dictated such an action.

Collins directed General Eddy to move Colonel Smythe's regiment southwest from the Sainte-Colombe area and pass through the 82nd Airborne bridgehead at Saint-Sauveur-le-Vicomte. Elements of the 82nd had carved out an enclave west of the Douve for a distance of about two miles. At dawn on the seventeenth, Smythe's regiment would bolt for the west coast out of Saint-Sauveur-le-Vicomte while, three miles to the northeast, Colonel de Rohan's 60th Infantry would join in the dash for Barneville.

As darkness pulled its protective cloak over the battlegrounds, the curtain was about to rise on the final act of cutting off the peninsula.

While General Matt Eddy was shuffling his troops for the morrow's crucial attack, at far-off Berchtesgaden the German Führer fired off urgent messages to his two field marshals in the West, Gerd von Rundstedt and Erwin Rommel. The two top Wehrmacht commanders were ordered to meet the Führer the following morning at Margival, near Soissons in eastern France. Hitler, aware that the fate of Fortress Europe was being settled in the lush green and bloody fields of Normandy, wanted to learn first-hand from his commanders in the field why his legions were being trampled by the invaders.

Since D-Day, Rommel and von Rundstedt had been urging the two top officers in the Oberkommando der Wehrmacht, haughty, aloof Field Marshal Wilhelm Keitel and obedient, methodical Colonel General Alfred Jodl, to visit France personally for an on-the-spot assessment of the massive pounding being inflicted on Rommel's troops in Normandy from the ground, air, and sea.

"Our men are fighting bravely but are simply being smothered under bombs and shells," Rommel had repeated many times to the OKW.

In long evening walks in the gardens of his chateau at La Roche-Guyon, the Boy Marshal, choking on his frustration, had asked his two confidants, Admiral Freidrich Ruge and General Dr. Hans Speidel, "Why must our battles be directed by idiots far from the scene who have no conception of what's going on in Normandy?"

Now, instead of sending Keitel and Jodl to France to learn first-hand of battlefield conditions, Adolf Hitler decided to visit the West in their place. For their part, field marshals von Rundstedt and Rommel were anxious to tell the Führer bluntly that the situation in Normandy was hopeless—even though each would probably pay for his candor by relief from his post or worse.

On the morning of the seventeenth, Hitler climbed aboard a plane at Berchtesgaden and flew to Metz where he went by car to the site of the conference. The rendezvous would take place in the luxurious underground command post built at Margival in the heady days of 1940. From there Hitler was to have directed Operation Sea Lion, the planned cross-Channel invasion of England which was thwarted by the Luftwaffe's failure to seize control of the skies over Great Britain from the Royal Air Force.

Rommel, as was his practice, arrived punctually at 9 A.M. on the seventeenth for the crucial meeting with the Führer. Rommel was in an ugly frame of mind, ideal for the blunt recitation of military facts he intended to present to Hitler. The commander of Army Group B had been at the front all the previous day, had arrived back at his La Roche-Guyon headquarters at 3 A.M., then after snatching two hours' sleep was forced to drive 150 miles to Margival.

Rommel, von Rundstedt, and their aides were shown into the conference room where Hitler, looking worn and sleepless, was twirling his spectacles and nervously fingering a collection of colored pencils. Stiff, formal greetings were exchanged between the German Führer and his two famed marshals. Rommel and von Rundstedt felt anger surge in their beings—Hitler remained hunched over on a stool while the marshals had to remain standing, much like naughty schoolboys appearing before the headmaster.

The conference room reeked with defeat and disaster.

As the two field marshals stood erect before him, stern-faced and flushed with resentment over the indignity being inflicted upon them, Hitler lashed out angrily at his commanders in the West for "allowing" the Allies to get ashore in force in Normandy. He implied that his field leaders, including von Rundstedt and Rommel, were guilty of incompetence. "Cherbourg must be held at all costs!" he cried.

Hitler's figurehead commander-in-chief, West, von Rundstedt, carefully masking from his aristocratic facial features the contempt he had always felt for the Bohemian Corporal, responded first. He declared that it was impossible to mount a powerful, coordinated counterattack in Normandy due to overwhelming Allied air and sea power.

Von Rundstedt, after his brief formal introduction, turned over the floor to Rommel, who had become increasingly incensed over Hitler's slashing denunciation of German commanders in the West. Rommel testily disputed a report over the BBC from London—which Hitler had promptly labeled authentic—that Wehrmacht defenders of the Atlantic Wall had been "surprised in their sleep and their underwear" by the Anglo-American landings on June 6.

"Officers and men of the German army in Normandy have done all that duty could require of them," Field Marshal Rommel exclaimed hotly. "They have simply been overwhelmed by Allied air and naval bombardment supremacy, as well as by conventional field artillery."

Hitler's face flushed in barely suppressed anger as Rommel added, "Cherbourg will fall in a week."

Rommel, now warmed to the candid projection he had determined to present to the Führer, minced no words. "In view of the loss of Cherbourg, I propose pulling back our forces in Normandy out of the range of Allied naval guns."

Again the Führer's face clouded. This proposal was in direct contradiction of his order: "Hold every foot of ground at all costs!"

Hitler, never close to the flaming Normandy battle front, was skeptical of Rommel's assessments and spoke at length of the "mammoth destruction" heaped on London by his "secret weapons," the V-1 flying bombs which had been launched from the Pas-de-Calais only two nights previously.

"These weapons will bring England to its knees!" Hitler declared. He said that 1,000 flying bombs each week would fall on the British capital.

Rommel, knowing he had figuratively crossed the Rubicon, responded that the V-1s would contribute more to the war effort if they were directed against the ports of southern England from which supplies were brought into the Normandy beachhead. Can't be done, the Führer declared. The flying bombs were not that accurate.

However, Hitler observed, "huge masses of new jet fighters" would soon sweep the mighty propeller-driven Allied air fleet from the skies. Rommel promptly asked if "a few squadrons" of these revolutionary aircraft could be dispatched to the Normandy battleground. Not quite ready, Hitler replied. Still some "bugs" to be worked out.

The heated conference reached a boiling point when Rommel declared candidly that "the German front in the West will collapse and there will be nothing to keep the Anglo-Americans from driving on into Germany." He visualized imminent similar collapses on the fronts in Italy and Russia.

Hitler blanched as the young marshal added bluntly: "It is urgently necessary to end the war!"

"Don't you worry about the future direction of the war!" the Führer replied hotly. "You take care of your own front!"

Erwin Rommel, once the favorite general of the leader of the Third Reich, who had received a marshal's baton at an early age from the Führer himself, with that exchange sealed his own doom.

After the two disillusioned and despondent German field marshals departed Margival, and before Hitler left for Berchtesgaden, guards at the underground headquarters looked upward on hearing the throbbing putt-putt-putt of one of the Führer's V-1 pilotless bombs heading through the clear blue sky for London. Not all of the bombs reached their target. This one suddenly shifted course, its motor cut off, and the V-1 crashed with enormous impact nearby, shaking the Führer's concrete bunker.

The errant flying bomb seemed to be an omen of the disaster facing the Wehrmacht in Normandy.

As Hitler was being confronted by his two top commanders in the West at Margival, General Matt Eddy's spirited 9th Infantry Division bolted out of the starting blocks along the Douve River for the dash to the coast. Very soon the dash turned into a crawl. Just after passing through 82nd Airborne Division lines west of Saint-Sauveur-le-Vicomte, leading elements of Colonel George Smythe's 47th Infantry Regiment ran into flat-trajectory antitank, machine gun, and rifle fire. While one of Smythe's battalions dueled with his pocket of resistance on the main road leading out of Saint-Sauveur-le-Vicomte, Smythe sent his other two battalions around the flank. From that point on the southern spearhead of the two-pronged 9th Division thrust for the west coast progressed rapidly.

Just to the north, Colonel de Rohan's 60th Infantry Regiment also had tough initial going, but by early evening leading elements had fought their way into Saint-Jacques-de-Nehou. There the nearly exhausted assault troops halted for the night.

Operations in Normandy were geared to British double-summer time, so it was not totally dark until 11 P.M. A short time before dusk, a mud-splattered American armored car, trailing a towering plume of thick dust, clanked into the Saint-Jacques-de-Nehou square from the east. Out hopped Lightning Joe Collins, clad in his usual faded-salmon trenchcoat.

Collins had already put in an 18-hour day dashing about the zone of advance of the 9th Infantry Division, but his stride was brisk as he moved to the lieutenant colonel commanding the force which had been attacking all day. The battalion commander, his face a mask of grime from a combination of choking dust and perspiration, was dead tired and nearly out on his feet from lack of sleep and constant movement.

"The Krauts pulled out of town and we've lost contact with them," the lieutenant colonel told General Collins.

The corps commander had his aide, Captain Jack Walsh, clip the telephone Walsh always carried to the battalion line and put in a call for General Eddy at the 9th Division CP.

"Matt, I want you to meet me in Saint-Jacques as soon as possible," Collins stated.

Waiting for Eddy to make the jaunt to Saint-Jacques, General Collins turned his attention to the tower of the old stone church in the central square which was burning and spewing out thick clouds of black smoke. As the Germans pulled out of Saint-Jacques, they had fired an 88-millimeter round through the face of the clock on the tower, and the wooden clock supports had caught fire.

Collins and Captain Walsh, with time on their hands, could not stand idly by and watch the belfry be consumed by fire. Residents by now had begun to creep out of their cellars as fighting had halted, and stood about in dismay watching the old church go up in flames. So the American corps commander organized a water-bucket fire brigade of townspeople, and they began to douse the burning debris in the belfry.

Shortly before General Eddy sped into the town square in a jeep, the brass bell in the tower crashed down in a shower of sparks, but no one was injured. With the 9th Division commander's arrival, Lightning Joe Collins had to abdicate the role of Saint-Jacques fire chief. He may well have been the only corps commander in the war to serve as a volunteer fireman in a bucket brigade.

"The way appears open to the west coast, Matt," General Collins pointed out. "I want you to put fresh troops in the lead and continue the attack. Drive all night if you must—but get to the coast!"

General Eddy, with typical alacrity, set the wheels in motion to keep the advance rolling and the Germans to his front off balance. Spotting Colonel Frederick de Rohan and his command group along the road, Eddy halted his jeep and called out exuberantly: "We're going all the way tonight!"

Heading back to his command post near Sainte-Mère-Église, with the shadows of a summer night beginning to creep, Lightning Joe Collins was in his element. His battle philosophy had always been to keep unrelenting pressure on the enemy, particularly when the enemy was on the run and reeling in confusion.

The wisdom of Collins' decision to race on for the coast that night was confirmed by the time he reached his headquarters. There he received a jubilant call from Matt Eddy: Colonel George Smythe's 47th Infantry, which had jumped off early that morning through 82nd Airborne lines west of Saint-Sauveur-le-Vicomte, had cut the Barneville-la Haye du Puits road, less than two miles from the coast.

Meanwhile Colonel de Rohan's 60th Infantry, attacking out of Saint-Jacques where the church fire had been brought under control by townspeople, led by elements of the 3rd Battalion riding on tanks and armored cars, drove on Barneville through the night against only scattered resistance. At 5:05 A.M. on June 18, the battalion reached the hill overlooking the little port of Barneville and gazed out at the shimmering blue waters of the Atlantic Ocean.

Patrols were immediately sent down into the deserted town where they surprised and captured several German military policemen who had been ordered to direct Wehrmacht units trying to flee southward before the trap was snapped shut.

On the twelfth day of the invasion, the crucial port of Cherbourg was sealed off.

13

Phantom March Through American Lines

A thick cloud cover and fine, chilling, drizzle cloaked the German columns of marching grenadiers, horse-drawn vehicles, a few Volkswagens, and assorted radio vans as they edged stealthily through the night of June 18 heading southward. These were elements of the first-rate 77th Division which had recently been rushed into the Cotentin Peninsula from Brittany and had been cut off north of the sudden American thrust to Barneville on the west coast.

With an American breakthrough to isolate Cherbourg in sight, on June 15 Field Marshal Erwin Rommel tried to save the best divisions in his LXXXIV Corps from being bottled up in the peninsula. The Corps was ordered to reorganize into two battle groups. Rommel placed the 709th and 243rd Divisions in one group under General von Schlieben and ordered it to withdraw to the south if the peninsula were cut off.

From far-off Berchtesgaden, Adolf Hitler promptly overruled his commander in the field, Rommel, and directed these two divisions to hold fast south of Cherbourg. But with the U.S. 9th Infantry Division nearing the west coast, Colonel General Friedrich Dollmann, commander of Seventh Army, ordered Lieutenant General Rudolf Stegmann's 77th Division to withdraw to the south to the key traffic center of la Haye du Puits and there set up an east-west defensive position.

General Dollmann had no way of knowing it at the time, but his tactically sound order to salvage a first-class division from the Cherbourg trap would so infuriate Hitler that Dollmann would later be the Führer's scapegoat for the impending debacle in Normandy.

The southward withdrawal of the remnants of the 77th Division would

163

be difficult. The Germans would be under incessant air attack by fighters and would have to cut directly across the east-west corridor held by the American 9th Infantry Division.

On receiving the order to withdraw to the south on the afternoon of June 17, General Stegmann had no regrets. He felt that Cherbourg could not be held by isolated and exhausted troops, and that the port was already doomed. Stegmann was determined to lead his embattled division to the south as rapidly as possible, in battle-worthy groups, even though to do so would require slipping through the lines of an experienced, first-rate American division, the 9th.

General Stegmann ordered elements of his division to move out toward the south on the morning of June 18. Within the hour, American fighter-bombers spotted the column of marching grenadiers and horse-drawn conveyances and promptly pounced on the German formation, raking it with spitting machine guns and pounding it with bombs. Other American planes were called for and a steady stream of fighter-bombers zoomed up and down the German column. Soon utter confusion gripped the ranks of the trapped German force.

Trying to restore order out of chaos, General Stegmann was driving along the road in the midst of the carnage when his camouflaged command car was spotted by an eagle-eyed American pilot who swooped down and opened fire almost at ground level. Several 20-millimeter shells zipped through the car, one of the slugs striking General Stegmann in the head. He tumbled over onto the seat, killed instantly.

Only the day before, Lieutenant General Heinz Hellmich, commander of the 243rd Division, had been killed in precisely the same circumstances by fighter-bomber attack.

With Stegmann's death, the 77th Division was taken over by the senior regimental commander, Colonel Bernard Bacherer. The new division commander promptly summoned unit leaders. In a hurried conference under a huge, spreading tree, with background music furnished by the ominous roar of American fighter-bombers crisscrossing the sky above, Colonel Bacherer calmly put the question to his subordinate commanders: "We're cut off behind American lines. Seventh Army has ordered us to move south. What do we do now?"

A few 77th Division commanders, appalled by the steady slaughter of their men, their morale and physical strength sapped by the constant pounding by American aircraft and field guns, had reached the limits of their wills to resist. "Give up," was their explicit advice. "It's hopeless."

"Fall back into Cherbourg," others suggested.

Bacherer pondered these proposals thoughtfully. He concluded that accepting either course of action would mean captivity—or death—for his two thousand men. "They need us down south to help establish a new line," the colonel declared. "Get ready to continue the movement southward." As night fell, the beleaguered column pushed on.

Now, during the phantom march to la Haye du Puits, Bacherer's grenadiers were passing through villages occupied by American troops, and numerous surprised and startled sentries were disarmed before they realized a strong German column had slipped into their midst under the blackness of night. The Americans joined the German column as prisoners.

Bacherer's force was overtaken by daylight, but its presence still had not been detected; a blanket of low, thick clouds had grounded the omnipresent American fighters. By 11 A.M. that day, June 19, the German column was exhausted from nearly 30 hours of constant foot slogging, always under threat of sudden death from dreaded, marauding planes. Colonel Bacherer told his men to move into a long, sunken lane to sleep. He knew they could not take another step.

Patrols were sent out to reconnoiter the area and returned with an alarming report: a large American unit was bivouacked less than 600 yards away. Bacherer looked at his exhausted soldiers. Each was deep in sleep. He would allow them to slumber on despite the danger of the nearby American force. It was simply a risk he would have to take.

Convinced that all cut-off German units were pulling back northward to Cherbourg, the Americans in the bivouac routinely whiled away the day. Late in the afternoon, Colonel Bacherer roused his sleeping grenadiers—in some cases with great difficulty. They picked up their weapons and the column pushed on to the south. A few hours later Bacherer reached the narrow Ollande River and found the stream defended by a battalion of the U.S. 90th Infantry Division.

Success was almost at hand and the German colonel was determined to achieve it. He deployed elements of his column to assault the American positions. Bayonets fixed, covered by machine-gun fire, Bacherer's men closed with the American force. After a short, hand-to-hand struggle, they sent the Americans reeling and captured a large number of prisoners.

An elated Colonel Bacherer waved his column forward. It crossed over the Ollande River bridge and in a short time moved into its objective—

high ground north of la Haye du Puits. With the German column were all of their wounded, some two-hundred and seventy-five American prisoners, and twelve jeeps seized during the fight at the river bank.

The audacious Colonel Bacherer and some seventeen hundred of his men had made a clean getaway.

It was around noon on June 18 that General Omar Bradley, leader of First Army, was conferring with Major General Troy H. Middleton, a college educator from Louisiana who commanded VIII Corps. In wheeling north to capture Cherbourg, Lightning Joe Collins would have to turn his back on the enemy. So to protect Collins' rear, Bradley had strung out Middleton's corps across the neck of the Cotentin Peninsula with orders to conduct an "aggressive defense."

It was a thin corps at Middleton's disposal. The 82nd and 101st Airborne Divisions had been badly chewed up in savage fighting since D-Day, and the bewildered 90th Infantry Division, now under Major General Landrum, was still groping for its fighting spark.

Getting ready to leave Middleton's CP after discussing the VIII Corps plan for defending the 18-mile-wide Cotentin neck, Bradley clasped the professorial Middleton on the shoulder and exclaimed, "Gosh, I'll be glad when Collins takes Cherbourg and we can turn around in the direction we should be going."

Meanwhile, Lightning Joe Collins, living up to his monicker, had swiftly turned around his divisions after cutting off the Cotentin and faced them toward the north. At 3 A.M. on June 19, less than twenty-two hours after Manton Eddy's men had seized Barneville, the 4th Infantry Division jumped off without artillery preparation. Tubby Barton's D-Day veterans were on the corps' right flank, and in its zone of advance would be two towns on Route Nationale 13, Montebourg and Valognes, whose thick stone houses were made to order for enemy strongpoints.

Collins had decided to strike north for Cherbourg with three divisions abreast, so the green and newly arrived 79th Infantry Division, commanded by an old crony of Lightning Joe's, Major General Ira T. "Billy" Wyche, was positioned in the center and Matt Eddy's battle-tested 9th Infantry Division was on the left. The VII Corps plan of attack would be in the form of a double-pronged movement against Cherbourg by the 4th and 9th Divisions, with Billy Wyche's inexperienced but highly trained 79th Division and the 4th Cavalry Squadron (Mechanized) serving as a sort of linchpin to connect the two converging prongs.

Knowing that the 79th Division was new to combat, General Collins spent most of the first day at its CP to assure that it vigorously pressed the attack. It had jumped off at 4 A.M., an hour after the 4th Division on its right. Wyche's men made good initial progress against sporadic opposition; the Germans had already started a withdrawal to the north.

On VII Corps' left flank, General Eddy of the 9th Division discovered soon after the 5 A.M. jumpoff that there was no opposition in front of him, so he ordered two regiments into road-march formation. Eddy's 39th Infantry Regiment, under the grizzled old campaigner, Colonel Harry A. "Paddy" Flint, reached the outskirts of the old fortress town of Bricquebec at 7 A.M. Here American commanders had expected the Germans to make a stand, but Colonel Flint, schoolmate, drinking and card-playing crony of General George Patton, deployed his force for an attack and his men entered the town without a shot being fired.

On the morning Collins launched his corps northward, ominous weather struck the Cotentin and the English Channel. The sky was a sickly gray, leaden and foreboding. Gale-force winds ripped across the hedgerows and orchards, and a bone-chilling rain came down in thick sheets.

At his tent-complex headquarters in an orchard behind Omaha Beach, General Bradley squinted up at the gloomy sky as he moved toward the mess tent that morning. A staff aide, Brigadier General William B. Kean, fell in alongside his commanding officer. "Well," Kean said with a scowl, "this sure as hell kills Collins' chances for fighter support today."

The gods of war were about to inflict upon the invaders the worst June storm along the Channel in forty years—one that would come within an eyelash of causing the decimation of the now considerable Anglo-American force ashore in France.

By midnight on June 18, just as the intense storm started to kick up huge, frothy waves which battered against Point du Hoc, Omaha, Utah and the British beaches, the Allied high command had landed 314,514 troops, 41,000 vehicles, and 116,000 tons of supplies over the shores in the American sector, and 314,547 men, 54,000 vehicles, and 102,000 tons of supplies over the English and Canadian beaches. The flow of men and supplies had been moving smoothly over the open beaches and within the portable harbors created by Gooseberries and Mulberries. But the planned for amounts had not as yet arrived.

During the day of June 19 the northeast winds battering the assault beaches rose to 22 knots with gusts up to 32, and the Channel waters were whipped into angry nine-foot waves.

By midafternoon a crisis was reached which sent shock waves of alarm through Allied commanders in France and across the Channel in England—unloading operations, so crucial to the invaders, came to a total halt.

As heavy waves pounded the assault beaches, many landing craft, including large LCTs (landing craft tanks), were driven ashore and smashed. Small craft hovered against the concrete caissons to keep from being destroyed, and ships anchored offshore waiting to unload dragged anchor chains as they were buffeted about, fouling their anchors with adjacent vessels.

Beach engineers and quartermaster soldiers were forced to burrow into places of refuge along the sandy beaches to escape being blown over by the gale-force winds or seriously injured or killed by the debris the gigantic storm was pitching and tossing about.

The specter that had haunted the Allied planners and commanders from the conception of Overlord had suddenly struck: an Anglo-American force of nearly six hundred and fifty thousand men was ashore on continental Europe and the invaders could not unload over the open beaches and a major port was not yet in their hands. This frightening situation injected a surge of even greater urgency into Lightning Joe Collins' campaign to seize Cherbourg.

On the heels of General Manton Eddy's dash for the west coast of the Cotentin, General Karl von Schlieben received a message from Adolf Hitler at his chalet on Obersalzberg near Berchtesgaden: "You are hereby appointed commander of Fortress Cherbourg. You will defend the city to the last man and the last bullet."

It was a dubious honor at best for von Schlieben. Even the tone of the Führer's order implied doom for the critical port at the head of the Cotentin Peninsula.

Other levels down the Wehrmacht command structure got into the act, plying the already overburdened Karl von Schlieben with suggestions, warnings, and instructions on how to defend the port of Cherbourg. "Watch out for surprise American landings on the east and west coasts of the Cotentin," the Oberkommando der Wehrmacht cautioned. "Every day [you hold out] counts for the outcome of the war as a whole," Field Marshal Erwin Rommel reminded.

There was more to Rommel's ringing exhortation than mere rhetoric—under ideal conditions, it would take a week to utterly destroy the harbor facilities at Cherbourg.

At his command tent in a camouflaged hog pen just north of the key town of Montebourg, Major Friedrich Wilhelm Küppers, the young,

168

dedicated leader of artillery group Montebourg, looked up from his map as the tent flap was thrown open and a blood-smeared, begrimed figure slipped under the canvas. "For God's sake, Staake. What in the hell happened to you?" Küppers exclaimed.

Lieutenant Erik Staake of a coast artillery battery had been wounded that morning at an observation post on a hill outside Montebourg, but had refused evacuation. Staake ignored the major's question and got right to the point of his visit. "The Ami [German slang for American] tanks charged our lines and were turned back by our gunfire," the bleeding lieutenant said. "But their tanks are flanking Montebourg on both sides, and the Ami infantry is inside the town fighting with our grenadiers."

Staake paused briefly, then added: "If we're lucky, we can hold them. Otherwise, we're in a trap. We'd better get out of here, or we'll be bagged by the Americans." There was no trace of hysteria in Staake's voice, only a calm, reasoned recitation of the tactical situation. He wiped a trickle of blood off his forehead with the back of a dirt-smudged hand, then eyed his commanding officer.

Major Küppers was deep in thought. Lieutenant Staake's courage was widely known, and he was an experienced soldier from the Russian front. His analysis of the danger facing artillery group Montebourg had to be accepted as genuine and authentic. The tired Küppers hurriedly turned over the situation in his mind.

His mission was to delay the advancing Americans as long as possible. But how long was that? On the one hand, his defensive position at Montebourg was a strong one, with grenadiers of combat groups Müller, Kiel and Hoffman deeply dug in on high ground along the Quineville-Montebourg-le Ham ridge. His infantrymen had powerful fire support—Küppers's own 19 guns, some twenty weapons of the 100th Mortar Regiment, and guns of the 30th Flank Regiment.

On the other hand, the major knew that his force at Montebourg was isolated and in a precarious position, ripe for destruction. Both flanks were wide open and already American tanks were clanking around on each side to threaten his rear.

He knew that Lieutenant Staake, whose courage had been proven repeatedly, was militarily correct in asserting calmly, "We'd better get out of here before we're bagged by the Americans." Yet his orders kept surging through his being: "You are to hold Montebourg at all costs!"

Küppers looked up at the lieutenant: "Staake, our orders are to hold. We're staying."

A FORTRESS
IS DOOMED

14

The "Secret Limeys" of Station X

Camouflaged under spreading apple trees at General Omar Bradley's First Army headquarters in an orchard behind Omaha Beach was a curious-looking little truck of British make. A rigid antenna reached 26 feet into the sky from the center of the vehicle's roof. Uniformed personnel regularly rushed to and from the mystery truck, most of them wearing the blue of Britain's Royal Air Force, a handful from the Royal Corps of Signals.

The English servicemen were pleasant and polite to the Americans at the headquarters—but tight-lipped and casually aloof. Seldom would they pause to chat with their cousins from across the Atlantic. Never would the Britons drink with their hosts.

The British truck and its activities were so shrouded in a thick cloak of intrigue that its presence in the midst of an American army headquarters was a source of unrelenting interest and speculation.

"I say, old fellow," an American soldier would inquire of a comrade in his best imitation British accent, "pray tell, what is that absolutely weird looking lorry [truck] and all those Limey chaps doing here?"

"Haven't you heard the latest form?" the other would mock. "That bloody lorry was shipped in from Mars. It's Eisenhower's 'secret weapon,' don't you know."

The mystery truck and its equally enigmatic British staff had been with First Army headquarters for two weeks now—and the Americans there had been unable to unravel its puzzle. Frustrated after failing to penetrate the unit's identity, the First Army men settled for calling the personnel the "Secret Limeys."

The bewildered Americans would have been even more mystified had they known the name of the British unit's base in England—Station X—with which the Secret Limeys were in wireless contact on a round-the-clock basis.

Only a handful of top leaders and staff officers in First Army were aware that the truck and its Royal Air Force and Royal Corps of Signals staff were known as an SLU (Special Liaison Unit), and that its function was to furnish General Bradley with a continual flow of details on the German command structure and the strength, location, and morale of enemy units, often down to battalion or even company levels.

A similar SLU was in operation at General Bernard Montgomery's headquarters in the British sector.

On a regular basis, an RAF officer would hand Bradley a pirated German secret signal about a forthcoming enemy attack which had been deciphered in time for First Army to take counteraction.

The operation of which the SLUs were a component had its origin in 1939, just before the outbreak of war. British intelligence had stolen a precise copy of the highly secret and complex German coding machine named Enigma. So ingenious was the Enigma machine that Adolf Hitler and the Wehrmacht considered its code unbreakable.

A team of Great Britain's leading cryptanalysts and mathematicians, working for months under the most intensely secret conditions, solved the "unbreakable" Enigma code with the aid of another highly sophisticated British machine. From then, key German secret signals were intercepted by the British, decoded, and made available to Allied commanders—often before the signal arrived on the desk of its intended German recipient. This special intelligence was code-named Ultra. Its existence would be the most profoundly guarded Allied secret of the war.

Nerve center of Ultra was a large, stone, Victorian mansion located 40 miles north of London just outside the town of Bletchley Park, hard by the tracks of the London Midland and Scottish Railway. At this top-secret center—referred to in hushed tones as Station X—coded radio messages flowing between Adolf Hitler and his generals were intercepted, deciphered, and sometimes evaluated.

At Station X the intercepted German signals were then encoded again and transmitted to the Special Liaison Units in the field where SLU officers, sworn to secrecy under pain of a long prison sentence for violation of security, would personally take the German message to the commanding officer or his designated staff officer.

Now, at the SLU truck in General Bradley's apple orchard on the evening of June 19, the Royal Air Force officer in charge noted that a message was coming in from Station X marked with the symbol for the utmost urgency—ZZZZZ. When issued at Bletchley Park, each decrypt was marked from Z to the ZZZZZ designation, a system which would leave no doubt in the mind of the SLU officer in the field as to the degree of urgency of the message.

The officer clasped the ZZZZZ signal in one hand and slipped out of the truck. He lifted one of his flying boots and glanced at the sole, then repeated the process with the other boot. He could not risk the off chance that bits and pieces of ultrasecret material in the wireless truck had stuck to the bottom of his boots. These scraps might shake loose and be found by nonauthorized personnel at First Army headquarters.

Reaching General Bradley's tent, the RAF officer entered and handed the decoded message from Station X to the First Army commander. Bradley studied the intercepted German message as the British officer stood by silently. Without a word, the general handed the signal back to the SLU man. The message was the text of a signal from Field Marshal Erwin Rommel to General Karl von Schlieben, defender of Cherbourg: "Launch Operation Heinrich tonight."

Operation Heinrich was the code name for the withdrawal of German forces into the prepared fortifications outside Cherbourg.

Neither General Bradley nor any other top officer was permitted to retain copies of the SLU signals. In accordance with standard procedure, the RAF man in charge returned to his truck with the secret message and destroyed it. Bradley's intelligence officer passed the word on to Lightning Joe Collins at VII Corps that the Germans had been ordered to pull back all along the front that night.

General Collins promptly contacted his three divisional commanders, Barton of the 4th Division, Wyche of the 79th, and Eddy of the 9th. "The German is beginning to pull back," Collins told the three. "Get right on his heels, starting at dawn!"

Von Schlieben's depleted, exhausted, scattered units would make their first stand in the defense of the crucial port of Cherbourg in a rough semicircle, from four to six miles out from the city. Along this main line of resistance the Germans had constructed a belt of fortifications, all on high ground, which covered all landward approaches to Cherbourg.

Defensive positions were often tied in with streams which served as obstacles to tanks and self-propelled guns. Where natural barriers were lacking, ditches had been dug. Roads were blocked with huge steel gates or bars. With steep hills and rugged cliffs in many places, broken by the deep valleys of the Divette and Trotebec Rivers and their tributaries, the terrain was ideal for the defense of Cherbourg.

In some areas along the belt of fortifications were thick-walled bunkers of concrete, bristling with machine guns and backed by mortars. There were underground shelters for troops and ammunition storage chambers.

Along other stretches the fortifications consisted of more hastily built positions, with earthwork diggings often enclosing Crossbow (V-1 bomb) sites, with heavy strands of barbed wire starkly evident on three sides.

Within this formidable ring of defensive sites outside Cherbourg were swarms of 88-millimeter guns for antiaircraft purposes. But as the Americans approached the defensive line these all-purpose weapons would be lowered to fire streams of flat-trajectory shells into the attackers.

American commanders were intimately acquainted with this outer belt of fortifications. Each had been furnished with a large-scale overprint showing precise German positions—an invaluable map made possible through the efforts of the underground spy network Centurie.

One crucial factor the American commanders preparing to assault the fortified belt did not know: the strength of the enemy in these positions.

During the night of June 19, patrols from all three assaulting American divisions probed enemy defenses in front of them and reported only sporadic fire. The Germans indeed were pulling back as the Ultra message of a few hours ago had ordered. At dawn, the American infantry and tanks moved forward.

Adolf Hitler's orders to General von Schlieben had been to make a "fighting withdrawal." But so exhausted were the remnants of von Schlieben's four divisions that no rear guard action was evident during the pull-back to the fortified belt outside Cherbourg.

There was nothing in front of the 4th Infantry Division on the American right flank, yet that unit edged forward cautiously. General Collins was greatly disturbed by this battlefield lethargy and lashed out at the commander of the division, Tubby Barton, over the telephone. "Get going, Tubby," Collins exhorted.

Incensed over having his ears boxed by his superior and long-time friend, General Barton promptly called his regimental commanders and proceeded to angrily admonish them. "Your battalions aren't moving fast enough," Barton told Colonel Robert T. Foster, leader of the 22nd Infantry Regiment. "Get going!"

Colonel Foster took the tongue lashing in stride, aware that the criticism was being passed on down the pecking order of command.

"Rumor has it that the Ninth Division is in artillery range of Cherbourg," Foster told his battalion commanders. "Guess General Barton is worried someone else will beat the Fourth into Cherbourg."

On the left flank of Joe Collins' assaulting VII Corps, General Manton Eddy's veterans of the 9th Infantry Division jumped off at 8 o'clock that morning with the objective of sweeping up the west coast of the Cotentin to capture the high ground between Flottemanville-Hague and Octeville, and to block the principal road into the Cap de la Hague peninsula, which jutted out into the Atlantic Ocean like a long, sinister finger.

Matt Eddy's men made good initial progress northward against sporadic pockets of resistance until they reached the outer belt of fortifications around Cherbourg in the vicinity of Flottemanville-Hague, four miles due west of the port and only three miles below the northern coastline of the Cotentin. There the 9th Division veterans ran into a buzzsaw.

Eddy's men were pounded by mortars and artillery. Dug-in machine guns raked the advancing Americans as they edged ahead over open fields. Arms and legs were blown off as the 9th Division infantrymen set off mines. A flank outfit lowered its rapid firing 20-millimeter and all-purpose 88-millimeter guns to pour flat-trajectory fire into the attackers. The Americans were forced to pay a bloody price for each yard of ground purchased.

Casualties were not limited to dogfaces head-to-head with the Germans in the front line. Lieutenant Colonel James D. Johnston, commander of the 2nd Battalion and one of the most popular men in the 47th Infantry Regiment, was moving forward with his command group when he approached a crossroads that had been under repeated heavy enemy fire. A salvo of 88-millimeter shells hissed into the intersection and Colonel Johnston was killed. Other members of his staff were mortally wounded by the same shell bursts.

In the attack on German defenses at Flottemanville-Hague, Lieutenant John E. Butts was leading his platoon in an assault against a well-fortified and strongly defended hill. Enemy gunners entrenched in thick-walled pillboxes poured withering bursts of fire into his men; artillery and mortar shells exploded around Lieutenant Butts and his platoon as they tried to edge up to the death-dealing concrete bunkers.

Butts was weak from two painful wounds received in recent days. As a platoon leader in the 60th Infantry Regiment, the young officer had been

177

struck by shrapnel during the 9th Division's westward attack to cut off the Cotentin Peninsula. The lieutenant refused an order to be evacuated and, his uniform saturated with blood, continued to lead his platoon against the enemy.

Two days later, on June 16, Butts was wounded again. This time he refused medical aid and remained to fight.

Now, one week later outside Flottemanville-Hague, Lieutenant Butts was still on his feet at the head of his platoon. Under the intense German fire from the hill he and his men were assaulting, some faltered and began to fall back. Butts scrambled to his feet to rally his men and a burst of machine-gun fire stitched bullets across his stomach, knocking him to the ground.

Writhing in excruciating pain, the young officer ordered a squad to move off to one side and flank the enemy strongpoint. To draw German attention away from this flanking movement, Lieutenant Butts pulled himself up to his knees, then onto his feet and, holding in his bloody intestines with one hand, charged the enemy bunker alone.

Another burst of fire struck Butts, and he went down again. But he pulled himself forward to within 10 yards of the spitting machine gun, where a point-blank fusillade ripped through his body. He lay still— forever.

Lieutenant Butts' actions served the purpose he had intended. Enemy attention had been diverted to this lone bloody figure edging toward the bunker, and his men succeeded in flanking the strongpoint and wiping out its defenders.

Meanwhile at his underground headquarters in Cherbourg, the beleaguered General Karl von Schlieben was being bombarded—not by American guns but by orders from the Oberkommando der Wehrmacht in Berchtesgaden: "Hold the outer perimeter belt of fortifications at all costs!" "Hold the Joburg peninsula in the northwestern corner at all costs!" "Hold the hills around Brix!"

On paper, von Schlieben had been given a free hand to defend Cherbourg. In reality, Adolf Hitler, totally removed from the stark battlefield reality on the Cotentin, was directing the operation, through orders issued by the OKW.

Where, von Schlieben wondered, was he to get the men to carry out this flood of fanciful orders from the Führer? Many of his battalions in the outer belt of fortifications had been chopped down to fewer than 175 men. The German defender of Cherbourg knew the fortress was doomed. Now his main mission was to gain time—time to demolish the harbor and time to bring up German reinforcements to defend the neck of the Cotentin once Cherbourg had fallen.

Reluctantly, General von Schlieben sent out orders to his commanders: "Dig in and hold!"

In the corridors of von Schlieben's underground command post, it was nearly impossible to take a step without treading on the mass of humanity gathered there. Over 1,000 men had squeezed into the subterranean chambers, sitting idly, staring into space, cursing and ranting. These were not all fighting men, but Luftwaffe ground staff, naval gunners with no guns to fire, construction workers, crews of *Schnellboot* (PT boats) with no craft to man. An overpowering stench of sweat, urine, feces, and exhaust fumes from motors saturated the choking tunnels. Shells exploded just outside the entrances, causing naked light bulbs inside to flicker and masonry powder from the ceilings to shower the miserable occupants of the tunnel. Above all this hovered an impending sense of doom, for Fortress Cherbourg and for the Germans trapped inside its confines.

Unrealized by the defenders of the crucial port, the Wehrmacht had a new partner—Mother Nature. The violent storm, the worst June up-heaval in 40 years, continued to batter the English Channel for the second straight day. Omaha and Utah beaches, over which the large American force on the continent had to be supplied, were shambles. The beaches were strewn with wrecked craft which formed junk piles on the shore. The giant concrete caissons towed from England to form break-waters off Omaha were now scattered across the sand.

Unloading operations on the Allied beaches were still at a standstill, as gigantic waves pounded the shore. Crucially needed ammunition to replace the huge amounts of shells and bullets being expended in Lightning Joe Collins' drive against Cherbourg could not be unloaded.

It was a frightening situation for the invaders, who had only a three-day stock of ammunition in Normandy dumps. There was only one thing to do—ration General Collins' VII Corps. The mission to quickly seize Cherbourg was jeopardized. And the port's purchase price in American blood would soar.

15

A Steel Noose
Is Tightened

As the storm-devils continued to shriek and howl over the Channel, General Joe Collins' three infantry divisions and supporting troops edged steadily ahead, probing the outer defenses of mighty Cherbourg. The enemy reacted savagely to the advance. The battered defenders were now entrenched in the highly formidable outer belt of fortifications. But there was another reason for the stiffening of German resistance.

That morning, June 21, with the Americans closing in on all sides of the 31-mile-long perimeter of Cherbourg, General von Schlieben issued an order to all commanders which reflected his desperation:

> Withdrawal from the present positions is punishable by death. I empower all leaders of every grade to shoot on sight anyone who leaves his post because of cowardice. The hour is serious. Only willpower, readiness for fighting and heroism to the death can help.

Shortly after dawn that day, some 10 miles south of where the harassed General von Schlieben was seeking to steel his men's spirits, Captain Brian Dumond and 14 of his 79th Infantry Division men were drowsily stirring in a field where they had spent the night. A member of headquarters company of his battalion, Captain Dumond the evening before had been ordered to establish a command post behind the unit's assembly area. The advance had been so rapid on the heels of the withdrawing Germans that Dumond lost contact and set up the CP in the darkness at a position he thought was to the rear of his battalion.

Now, as he awoke and looked around in the light of day, Captain Dumond was startled to see that he and his men were sleeping near enemy pillboxes. Believing that the battalion had gone forward and already cleaned out the pillboxes, Dumond forged ahead with Sergeant Robert Corley and a wire sergeant as the "point." The other twelve men followed in approach march formation.

The small group drew a few bursts of fire from a distance but pressed on, keeping close to what cover was available. It was a highly fluid situation, Dumond knew, as the attack on Cherbourg was so urgent the infantry often bypassed German pockets and left them to be cleared out later.

Captain Dumond and his men started up the slope of what appeared to be a grass-covered mound, green and lush. It looked like any other grassy elevation in Normandy. Suddenly German automatic weapons opened up on the little band of Americans from the front and the flanks. Dumond and the others flopped to the ground as bullets hissed past them.

Clinging tightly to the ground, the captain peered out from under the rim of his steel helmet and could detect that he and his men were under fire from three machine guns. The strident shouts of German officers could be heard over the intense chatter of the automatic weapons. Minutes later explosions rocked the ground around the prostrate and helpless Americans —mortars had opened up.

Deceitfully unwarlike, the green mound, under its layers of sod, held one of the toughest German forts yet faced by the invaders in Normandy. On each side of the mound loomed supporting concrete pillboxes, ominous machine-gun barrels protruding from apertures.

Captain Dumond and his men, armed only with light hand weapons and a few grenades, opened fire in the direction of the concrete fortifications, but it was an uneven match. The Germans had automatic weapons, were protected behind thick concrete, and outnumbered Dumond and his men. Five minutes after the firefight began, the Americans were on the verge of having to surrender or be killed where they lay; they were nearly out of ammunition.

Glancing over his shoulder behind him to seek a possible covered route of withdrawal, Captain Dumond saw a sight that sent renewed hope surging through him: coming up the slope was the battalion spearhead, a patrol commanded by Captain Ben Rhodes. Only then did Dumond realize that he had not been *trailing* his battalion, he had been out in front of it, leading the attack.

Captain Rhodes and his patrol joined Dumond and his men in the firefight, and mortar and artillery fire was called in. The German defenders had had enough. White flags began waving from the underground fort and seconds later 22 enemy soldiers emerged with hands in the air.

While the Wehrmacht prisoners stood sullenly to be searched for concealed weapons, the entire group, German and American alike, were raked by fire from the rear. Again the Americans flopped to the ground—a split-second after their twenty-two prisoners had flung themselves to the earth. The firing was coming from an underground chamber, which was promptly the target of withering smallarms blasts from the 79th Division men.

Covered with fire by his comrades, Captain Dumond crawled up to the enemy position and saw that entry to the subterranean compartment was through a large hole. Dumond shouted down into the opening, in a mixture of English and pidgin German: "Raus up mit youse or we'll kill every one of you goddamned sons of bitches!"

Seven Germans squeezed through the hole and out onto the ground, including one wounded man. "They're cocky bastards, aren't they?" observed a GI in disgust.

One of the latest batch of prisoners spoke English. He was defiant. "You'd never have gotten us if there weren't so many of you!" he spit out.

An American responded in an internationally recognized form of communication—he raised his combat boot and kicked the English-speaking grenadier in the seat of the pants.

Captain Dumond and his men began moving forward once more, taking their new prisoners along. Reaching a wooded area, six Germans suddenly bolted. Dumond shot four of them and his men cut down the other two. The remaining twenty-three prisoners had terror in their eyes, fearing that their captors, angry over the escape attempt, would gun them down also. A look of relief flooded the Germans' faces as Captain Dumond nodded for the column to move out.

After Dumond left Captain John McCabe went to the top of the grassy mound to examine the just-captured fort. An artillery officer arrived and said he wanted the elevation for an observation post. McCabe wanted to blow it up, but the artillery officer hoped to preserve the 40 tons of ammunition found inside, so it remained intact. On inspecting the layout of the camouflaged fort, the 79th Infantry Division officers murmured silent thanks that the position had not been more fully manned. Its concrete walls were four feet thick. Outside this was 35 or 40 feet of hard packed earth. Inside were two-inch thick steel doors operated by an electrical mechanism. The fort mounted one 88-millimeter gun and two 40-millimeters in the top turret. Protecting its flanks were several other artillery pieces and machine guns, and four smaller pillboxes.

When McCabe and his men emerged from the underground fort they came under intense fire from another pillbox apparently bypassed by advancing infantry battalions, and mortar explosions began to pop all around them. McCabe and his men withdrew to the rear.

Almost as soon as the Americans left, a German force moved back into the underground fort and when trailing 79th Division units approached they came under heavy fire from the grassy mound. Air support was called in, and an hour later dive bombers worked over the fort and its nearby pillboxes. Then the infantry moved in again. They captured forty-two more Germans and found three dead. Taking no chances that the underground fortification would have to be seized for the third time that day, division engineers blew up the structure.

At an adjoining pillbox, a call to come out went unheeded and the succeeding blast tossed a German soldier who had been inside high into the air. Four more dead Germans were found in the bottom of a connecting tunnel.

The Battles of the Grassy Mound had sent a signal to the Americans, loud and clear. The final few miles to Cherbourg would be difficult and bloody.

Not all the Wehrmacht were willing to go along with General von Schlieben's order to fight to the death. In the 9th Infantry Division's zone of advance in the western portion of the Cotentin Lieutenant James B. Fahy was guarding a group of bedraggled men in civilian clothing. These had recently defied being shot by their officers or noncoms and had doffed their German uniforms and put on civies to escape from the steel noose tightening on Cherbourg. Only a few were German nationals; the rest had been conscripted into the Wehrmacht against their will.

In order to minimize the possibility that his prisoners would decide to suddenly jump him and his two men, Lieutenant Fahy ordered the enemy soldiers to turn their backs. As they complied, most began weeping. They were convinced Fahy intended to execute them.

Even though the prisoners had recently been fighting against his division, the American felt a twinge of pity for these shaking, crying figures. "Goddamn it," he called out. "Quit your damned bawling. I'm not going to shoot you!"

A short distance away, Private Matthew Budieselich, a communications man, and Private Hubert Leslie, whose job it was to guard prisoners, were seated in a foxhole waiting for an attack to be organized. They were joined there by John H. "Beaver" Thompson, a bearded correspondent for the *Chicago Tribune,* who had gained wide fame, and his nickname, when he parachuted into Sicily with the 82nd Airborne Division a year previously.

Indiscriminate shellfire was falling in the area, but the foxhole occupants ignored it.

"Damn. I like seeing all these German prisoners coming in," Budieselich remarked enthusiastically while chewing reflectively on a blade of grass.

Whereupon Leslie turned to the war reporter and said, "Speaking of large numbers of prisoners, Mr. Thompson, how about putting my name in the paper so my mother can see my name in print?"

Thompson, at thirty-four, squirmed slightly at the *mister,* an implication that he was in the senior citizen category. To the teenagers with him, he was —especially with the "maturity" given his face by a bushy beard.

"You can tell her," Leslie added "that I helped capture one hundred and fifty Germans yesterday."

Beaver Thompson's nose, tuned to newsworthy events, sensed a good story.

"How did you capture them?" he inquired.

"Well, the Krauts came up the road and gave up to me and another guy."

Meanwhile that day, several swift American fighter planes knifed in low over smoking, besieged Cherbourg. Out of the aircraft were tossed thousands of leaflets intended for the Wehrmacht in the dying city. Knowing that the Germans were aware that they were trapped with no hope for escape, the leaflets took aim at their dilemma. The enemy soldiers were presented with "an honorable alternative to sure death"—surrender. Exploiting the fact that German rations in Cherbourg had been cut in half, the punch line read: "And don't forget to bring along your messkit!"

As VII Corps continued to fight its way forward, General Collins, wearing what had become his trademark—a faded salmon-colored trench coat—was relentlessly dashing up and down the battle lines, urging his men on to greater things. "Faster! Faster!" was his battlecry. "Keep them reeling back!" Collins lived and fought by the creed that constant pressure on the enemy was the key to battlefield success at the minimal cost in lives.

By that evening of June 21, Collins had tightened the noose around the port city. On the off chance that General von Schlieben would capitulate without further heavy bloodshed on both sides, Collins broadcast a surrender ultimatum in four languages in order to reach all in the garrison's multilingual force:

> You and your troops have resisted stubbornly and gallantly, but you are in a hopeless situation. The moment has come for you to capitulate. Send your reply by radio, on a frequency of 1520 kilocycles, and show a white flag or fire white signal flares from the naval hospital or the Pasteur clinic. After that, send a staff officer to the farmhouse on the road to Fort du Roule to accept the terms of surrender.

General Collins threatened that the garrison would be wiped out unless von Schlieben surrendered by 9 A.M. the following day.

As Collins had expected, the Cherbourg commander did not reply. In the meantime, Lightning Joe continued to put the final touches on the plan for the all-out assault against the doomed "gateway to Europe."

General Collins called in his three division commanders—Generals Eddy, Wyche, and Barton—that night to outline the coordinated attack, which was set for the period of noon to 4 P.M. the following day, June 22. The precise time would depend upon the capricious weather; the storm that had halted unloading operations on the beaches continued to hover over the Channel.

Collins would mass gigantic firepower for the attack, requesting "air pulverization" of some 20 square miles before the jumpoff, more to demoralize the Germans and force surrender than to pave the way for ground advance. The massive air strike would employ the entire IX Bomber Command (medium bombers) as well as hundreds of American and British fighter-bombers.

The actual penetration by ground forces into Cherbourg itself was to be made by Billy Wyche's 79th Infantry Division from the south and Matt Eddy's veteran fighting men of the 9th Infantry Division from the west. Tubby Barton's 4th Division was to seal off the doomed port from the east.

For the pre-H-Hour air attack, troops were to be pulled back at least 1,000 yards from the bomb line—a safety factor that, by implication, stressed the precariousness of mass bombing in front of a battle line.

That night General Omar Bradley, commander of First Army, was listening to the latest war news over the BBC from London. He was shocked by one item: General Collins of VII Corps had issued an ultimatum to the commander of the German garrison in Cherbourg. That was the first Bradley had heard of the ultimatum. The First Army leader was furious and called in his chief of psychological warfare for an explanation.

"How did BBC get the story of that damned ultimatum?" Bradley demanded to know.

"Seventh Corps released it, general."

Bradley winced, but he knew there was nothing he could do about it. "Let's see if we can't get Collins' staff to keep these things under their hats," he declared. "When the German turns that ultimatum down, he's going to look like a hero instead of the fool that he is."

Late that afternoon, staff officers at First Army headquarters received a copy of the day's London *Times,* which had been flown over from England. The Americans were enraged by a one-inch headline across page one:

MONTGOMERY'S TROOPS DRIVE ON CHERBOURG

"Goddam it," one staff member roared, "outside of the Secret Limeys in that damned battered old wireless truck, there's not another Englishman in sixty miles of Cherbourg!"

Another added: "Yeah, and who the hell said we were *Montgomery's* troops? The last I heard we belonged to the American army."

It was not the first time in the war that the British press had irritated American commanders with misleading headlines. It would not be the last.

That same afternoon, General Bradley was handed a ZZZZZ Ultra by a young British RAF officer. It had initiated at the headquarters of the German Seventh Army at Le Mans. Scanning the secret signal, Bradley saw that the *Abwehr* (German army counterintelligence) had discovered American passwords for the period June 21 through 26, and had filtered this vital information on down the chain of command.

General Bradley promptly changed the passwords for this period. As a result, the hapless *Abwehr's* credibility plummeted as soon as German soldiers tried to use this knowledge of American passwords to their tactical advantage—and were promptly greeted with heavy bursts of fire by Americans who had received revised watchwords.

At General von Schlieben's headquarters in an underground fortress, the Cherbourg commander was firing off an indignant protest to the OKW at Berchtesgaden. Von Schlieben two days ago had radioed an urgent need for *panzerfausts* (anti-tank bazookas) for his beleaguered troops. The Luftwaffe promptly readied a mission. Containers were loaded with *panzer-*

fausts and that night several JU-88s parachuted the crucial weapons—not over Cherbourg, but into the Channel Islands of Guernsey and Jersey.

Von Schlieben immediately protested the Luftwaffe error and that night a supply mission was again mounted. The results were the same—the parachuted containers landed on the Channel Islands.

"*Mein Gott!*" spluttered a staff officer in the underground port headquarters, "the Luftwaffe can't even hit Cherbourg!"

16

"Fight to the Last Pillbox!"

As a timid sun peeked cautiously over the eastern coast of the Cotentin Peninsula on the morning of June 22, Cherbourg, battered, bruised, and smoking, lay fearful and silent in its topographic saucer, surrounded on three sides by stark hills and cliffs. Perched 302 feet in the sky on a rugged, rocky escarpment, impregnable Fort du Roule frowned down on the city by the Channel.

Cherbourg was built on the site of an ancient Roman camp named Coriallum. In the 11th century the town became known as Carusbar. It was sacked by the British in 1295 and in the next two centuries withstood several British sieges. Projects to build fortifications around the port began in the 17th Century, and later were improved upon and expanded by French Emperor Napoleon Bonaparte. When Nazi Germany's Todt Organization, its national builders, began construction of the Atlantic Wall in 1942, these old fortifications were incorporated into the modern defensive belt.

Inside the doomed city, six thousand civilians now cringed in cellars, fearfully anticipating the deluge of steel and explosives which was about to engulf them. Out of a population of 40,000, only they had been unable or unwilling to depart their homes and flee to the relative safety of the countryside.

French leaders for two days had pleaded with German military authorities to evacuate the innocent civilians, but the pleas were turned down. The Germans were fearful that American intelligence would obtain valuable information from those who had been in the besieged city.

In Cherbourg hospitals, clearly marked with large red crosses on fields of white, more than one thousand injured members of the Wehrmacht,

189

wounded in the fighting withdrawal up the Peninsula, overflowed wards and lay on stretchers in the corridors. German nurses, working around the clock, were near exhaustion from their labors and lack of sleep. German army surgeons, swamped by the deluge of patients, hovered constantly over tables in the operating theaters.

During the dark night, American long-range artillery had pummeled Cherbourg. An occasional exceptionally loud blast rocked the city and echoed off the surrounding cliffs: German demolition troops had set off another huge charge of dynamite in the relentless, feverish effort to destroy forty-two hundred acres of harbor facilities in France's second busiest port.

That was the whole purpose of thousands of young Germans (and impressed aliens) fighting, suffering, bleeding and dying in the outreaches of the port—to buy time to deny an operating major port to the Allies.

Now, on the summer morning of June 22, a thin haze gently caressed Cherbourg. Far below ground in suburban Octeville, General Karl von Schlieben, his ever present Iron Cross earned for gallantry in Russia adorning his throat, had set up his headquarters for the final violent showdown along the northern coast of the Cotentin. There Vice Admiral Walther Hennecke, the high-living naval commander for Normandy without a navy to command, had also installed his nerve center.

Throughout doomed Fortress Cherbourg, an eerie calm had enveloped the wrecked city. Not a single American gun could be heard. Stern-faced Wehrmacht troops, knowing there would be no escape from the trap, resignedly waited for the cards Fate would deal them. It was the calm before the storm.

During the night, a black Luftwaffe aircraft knifed in low over the city and in the vicinity of General von Schlieben's headquarters released a parachute with a large container. *Feldgrau* who rushed to recover the package took it to their commanders who quickly ripped it open. It contained Iron Cross decorations—hundreds of them. The medals had been parachuted in at the personal direction of Adolf Hitler to steel the will of Cherbourg's defenders.

Meanwhile at Hitler's Berchtesgaden headquarters, there had been feverish discussions of the advisability of reinforcing the Cherbourg defenders. It was proposed that a parachute regiment be brought in by air, and that another regiment be sent by sea from Brittany. These recommendations were soon abandoned: the Luftwaffe did not have the planes available and it was agreed that the powerful Allied naval force lying off the northern Cotentin would intercept and demolish any troop convoy approaching Cherbourg.

190

Early that morning, while tranquility still reigned in the besieged port, General von Schlieben was handed a signal from Adolf Hitler himself:

> I expect of you that you will conduct this action as Gneisenau once conducted the defense of Kolberg. As long as you still have ammunitions and rations, every enemy attack must be shattered by your inflexible will, the strength of your wisdom, your skill and the bravery of your troops.
>
> Even if the worst should happen, it is your duty still to defend the last pillbox and to leave the enemy not a harbor but a field of devastation.

Karl von Schlieben tossed the message onto his desk resignedly. He knew that no amount of the steel will, wisdom, skill, and bravery about which the Führer spoke could match the hundreds of airplanes, scores of artillery batteries, and powerful offshore naval guns which would soon be heaping death and ruin on Fortress Cherbourg and its exhausted, decimated defenders.

In bunkers and pillboxes along the deep belt of fortifications outside the port on this crisp yet pleasant June morning, solemn, tight-lipped *Feldgrau* nervously fingered triggers on Schmeissers and machine guns and braced for the unleashing of the American hurricane which they knew was about to engulf them. West of Cherbourg, Lieutenant Colonel Franz Müller sped from strongpoint to strongpoint along the sector his combat group was to defend, inspecting positions, giving orders, offering words of encouragement to his hard-pressed fighting men.

The young lieutenant colonel, a veteran of the Russian campaign, in common with other German officers on the Cotentin was bitter at the high command—and even at the Führer. It was well known down through the ranks that top Allied officers had visited the Americans in Normandy in recent days—American Chief of Staff George Marshall, the British Chief of the Imperial General Staff, Field Marshal Alan Brooke, and Winston Churchill himself.

But not a member of the Oberkommando der Wehrmacht had come to Normandy to give a boost to sagging Wehrmacht morale—not Hitler, not Keitel, not Jodl. None of these high functionaries had any conception of the smothering effect of Allied air, sea, and land artillery power, Lieutenant Colonel Müller confided privately to a few confidants in moments of extreme depression.

However, Müller, as well as the commanders of the other three combat groups defending the outer reaches of Fortress Cherbourg, would fight to the end for the Fatherland, expending his life in the process if necessary. He was ready, willing, and able to personally shoot the first *Feldgrau* who bolted in the face of the enemy.

In his underground bunker, General von Schlieben was particularly concerned with the hodgepodge troops he had sprinkled among his four combat groups—naval and Luftwaffe security units, headquarters staff, quartermaster soldiers, all green and untrained in front-line fighting.

Early that morning he fired off a signal to Colonel General Friedrich Dollmann, commander of Seventh Army, at Le Mans: "Am especially concerned about performance of miscellaneous troops. Good treatment of prisoners on the part of the enemy is very dangerous."

The implication was clear: he expected large numbers of these inexperienced troops to surrender at the first opportunity.

On the other hand, the defender of Fortress Cherbourg was not concerned about supply: there were ample stocks of ammunition stored in the myriad of underground chambers. General von Schlieben's spirits would have soared had he been privy to a closely guarded secret of his foe: Lightning Joe Collins' three divisions, poised for the assault, had been rationed to three shells per gun due to the mighty storm that had been howling in the Channel for four days.

At 11 A.M. that morning of June 22, some five miles south of Cherbourg, an American platoon of 4.2-inch mortars, deadly, accurate weapons whose rate of fire was so rapid the Germans had previously mistaken them for a revolutionary type of automatic artillery, was dug in alongside a narrow, dusty road leading northward into the port. All morning crewmen had been lugging up ammunition and placing it alongside each of the four mortars.

Although corps orders had limited the rate of fire to only three rounds per mortar per day, the unit's officers had winked at that restriction, having "secretly" hoarded a larger supply of shells for the final assault on Fortress Cherbourg. Most of the rounds being placed by the mortars were WP (white phosphorous). The initial mission for the platoon was to fire smoke-producing WP on specified German strongpoints to mark targets for P-47 and P-51 dive-bombers, soon to appear over the battleground.

Idly waiting for action to commence, Sergeant Robert "Red" Jones, a freckled 22-year-old leader of one of the mortar squads, pointed up the road toward Cherbourg and called out to his comrades with a straight face: "Look, we're being attacked by our own guys!"

Coming down the road toward the mortar position was a company of infantry of the 79th Division, spaced out and marching in two files, one along each side of the road. As Sergeant Jones and his comrades knew, these riflemen and machine gunners were being pulled back 1,000 yards as a safety factor prior to the imminent "pulverization" of German front-line positions by swarms of Allied aircraft. American infantry was following this procedure all along the 30-mile front.

As the infantrymen of Billy Wyche's 79th Division moved on past the 4.2 mortar position, hollow-eyed, stepping methodically, huffing and wheezing under the heavy loads that were the lot of the combat riflemen, Red Jones remarked, "Well, now we're the outpost line." The files of infantrymen marched back along the road for a few hundred yards past the mortars and there fell out to await the arrival of Allied bombers and dive bombers. There would be nearly 1,000 of them.

At this point Providence intervened in the battle for Fortress Cherbourg—on the side of the Americans. For the first time in days the skies cleared, just in time for the aerial blitz to begin. The storm-devils who had been venting their wrath on the Channel coast disappeared into thin air.

It was 12:40 P.M. when the relative silence over the battleground along the 79th Infantry Division's central sector was shattered as the first Allied fighter planes and fighter-bombers swept in at treetop level. The mighty roar of their motors echoed and re-echoed across the lush green landscape, pockmarked here and there with the ugly black circles left by exploding shells.

A half-hour before the air bombardment opened, General Joe Collins had gone forward to a position along the Valognes-Cherbourg highway to witness the spectacular event. With him were 39-year-old Major General Elwood R. "Pete" Quesada, scion of a wealthy and influential family and commander of the U.S. 9th Air Force, and Quesada's aide, Brigadier General Richard E. Nugent. The Air Corps generals had flown from England to view the massive attack by the warplanes under their command.

Quesada was obviously delighted with the efficiency of his winged warriors. Above the ear-splitting din of swarms of powerful airplane motors, he looked at General Collins, pointed to his wristwatch, and shouted: "Right on time!"

The white-banded bodies of the P-47s, P-51s and British Typhoons twinkled in the noonday sun as they flew over the battlegrounds, then pounced on targets down below on the faceless green terrain. There was a thud of delayed-action bombs striking the ground; then quick bursts from machine guns before the fighter-bombers sped off toward England. Some ten or fifteen seconds later, the bombs would explode, rocking the terrain around the impact site.

As sweep after sweep of Allied fighters appeared overhead, the staccato of German machine-gun and machine-pistol fire against the winged tormentors rattled across the landscape. Here and there the intense German fire caught a fighter-bomber in a vulnerable spot. The plane would veer crazily for a few seconds, then plunge grotesquely to earth. Often the doomed plane exploded on impact, sending large balls of flame and black smoke spiraling into the air, blowing the luckless pilot into tiny fragments.

At their forward observation post, General Joe Collins and the two visiting Air Corps generals were engrossed by the aerial extravaganza, peering through binoculars and excitedly exchanging views on the sky action. Above the intense racket of exploding bombs and roaring airplane motors, Collins and the Air Corps officers became aware of an especially loud and close noise. They looked to one side and saw a flight of British Typhoons bearing down on them at treetop level. Then the alarming coarse chatter of belching machine guns as the Typhoons raked the hedgerows around the three generals.

They quickly flopped to the ground as the squadron of sleek-bodied Typhoons, all guns blazing, swept past the prostrate American commanders.

The three generals got to their feet, brushed the dust and leaves from their clothing, and peered over the hedgerow toward the front. Nearby soldiers were frantically tossing out yellow smoke grenades, the designated signal to mark American lines.

Much as a flame would attract a moth, the yellow smoke apparently caught the eye of American fighter-bombers, and several P-47s peeled off and strafed the hedgerows around General Collins and his two visitors who again dived to the ground.

When the final strafing plane soared off into the distance. Lightning Joe Collins got to his feet and cast an icy stare at General Quesada, whose fighter planes had just strafed their commander and the leader of the U.S. VII Corps. Quesada, expressionless, said nothing.

A short distance away, Sergeant Jones, the big redhead from Texas, and other members of his 4.2 mortar platoon were methodically dropping white phosphorus shells into the yawning mouths of the deadly weapons. The barrels had been lowered to maximum range because the WP shells were marking targets off in the distance for the fighter-bombers.

"Good God, here comes one of them!" Corporal Walter Makara called out. He pointed skyward to a dive bomber plummeting downward, and the mortarmen ceased firing as a bomb released from the P-47 and headed in their direction. They leaped into foxholes and in seconds heard a loud explosion. The 500-pound bomb had crashed into a ravine only a hedgerow away.

Climbing out of their holes, the mortarmen shook their fists at the errant P-47 pilot and turned the sky blue with creative oaths.

For over an hour, wave after wave of P-51s, P-47s, and rocket-firing Typhoons bombed and strafed German positions on the outer belt of fortifications. Twenty-four of the fighters were shot down by enemy antiaircraft fire.

As the last Allied fighter-bomber turned and headed for England, an eerie lull settled over the battle lines. It did not last for long. Just before 2 P.M. a faint hum was heard in the west and high in the blue sky could be seen an approaching flight of two-engine medium bombers, their sleek white hulks glistening in the afternoon sun. The engine roar became increasingly louder, and those on the ground could see bomb-bay doors open and scores of lethal missiles begin tumbling toward German positions far below. It was what General Quesada of the 9th Air Force called "pinpoint bombing."

Told previously that there would be little danger to ground troops because of the pinpoint technique, a skeptical 79th Division infantrymen had spoken for his comrades when he observed wryly: "I only hope we don't look like pins to those goddamned flyboys."

High in the sky, heavy German antiaircraft fire burst around the first wave of American medium bombers, blotching the air with thick puffs of black smoke. Inside the aircraft, crewmen heard what sounded like a handful of rocks thrown against a tin wall—shrapnel was splattering against the bombers.

Down below, the tense infantrymen, who soon would have to go forward to root out the Germans from their concrete bunkers and pillboxes, looked up in fascination at the aerial fireworks. A brief surge of euphoria raced through the long-suffering dogfaces on the ground as the hail of bombs fell on German positions. Clouds of smoke and dust rolled up over the woods where the German pillboxes were hidden by trees.

At the 4.2 mortar position where Red Jones and his comrades were peering into the sky, one man called out, "Hitler, count your goddamned soldiers!"

"Give those Kraut bastards hell!" shouted another.

As the long stream of bombers bored methodically through the sky, bright and twinkling lords of war, the early elation felt by the men on the ground turned to concern. Far off in the distance, at first merely black specks in the bright blue sky, a flight of sleek, black-painted fighter planes was racing toward the American bomber formation. The long-absent Luftwaffe had finally made an appearance over the Cotentin killing grounds.

From out of the bright sun, the swarm of German fighters pounced on the slow-moving American bombers and promptly knocked two of the twin-engine Marauders out of the sky with machine-gun bursts. One bomber, burning brightly, plunged to earth in a grotesque swirl. GIs on the ground looked on in dismay. No parachutes were sighted.

No sooner had the Luftwaffe flight made its first pass at the bomber formation than large numbers of American P-47 Thunderbolts and P-51 Mustangs sped to the scene and proceeded to pounce on the German fighters. Soldiers on both sides of the line gazed upward as a fierce series of dogfights broke out.

In the cauldron in the sky, rapid-firing German machine guns dueled with the slower-paced automatic weapons in the wings of the American fighter planes. The dogfights lasted for a quarter of an hour. Then the Luftwaffe pilots, far outnumbered, their ammunition low or expended, turned and fled for home bases.

Wave after wave of the American mediums—627 in all—swept in over the outer defenses of Cherbourg. Most of the explosives landed in enemy territory, but the targets were close enough to U.S. lines to make sweating, swearing dogfaces hug the ground.

In the 9th Infantry Division sector to the west of Cherbourg, a battalion commander who would take his outfit forward in a few minutes fought with a bulky field telephone, trying to find out whether the air operation was running on schedule. He got a connection to regimental headquarters, bellowed into the mouthpiece: "Hello, hold it! Is this goddamned air show over or not? I don't like this pinpoint bombing crap. There're too goddamned many 'pins' near our front line!"

The line went dead. The lieutenant colonel cursed loudly. It rang on again—the bombing was over in the battalion commander's area. "But there'll be more just ahead," the voice on the other end of the line said. The infantry officer cursed again. "What in the hell do you mean by 'just ahead?'" he roared into the telephone.

The battalion moved its command post 50 yards forward up a road.

There it halted abruptly as the ripping-silk burst of a German machine pistol sent bullets hissing past the lieutenant colonel's head. The Germans were still on the job and ready for business.

By midafternoon one company had worked its way ahead through a wide field and come in sight of a long concrete fort ringed with mines and dominating a ridge barring the way to Cherbourg. There the battalion used time and explosives to save men. Instead of assaulting the fort and its bristling machine guns, the commander called for drenching artillery and mortar fire, then sifted in his infantry cautiously to wipe out what resistance was left.

On all three sides of the city the advance on Cherbourg was like that—methodical and cautious. Ground soldiers were now in the heart of the Germans' outer belt of fortifications.

All three of the attacking divisions made slow advances during the afternoon despite the heavy bombings which were to have "pulverized" enemy defensive positions. West of Cherbourg, Lieutenant Colonel Franz Müller's combat group, largely fighting from the protection of thick-walled concrete bunkers, fought General Matt Eddy's 9th Infantry Division almost to a standstill. The resistance was steeled by determined young German officers and noncoms who, with pistols in hand, threatened to shoot anyone who bolted to the rear or tried to surrender to the Americans.

General Billy Wyche's 79th Infantry Division, attacking with three regiments abreast in the central sector, ran up against the stubborn 919th Regiment and the 17th Machine Gun Battalion, formed into a combat group under Lieutenant Colonel Günther Kiel, and elements of Colonel Walter Koehn's 739th Regiment. Wyche's regiment making the main effort up the Valognes-Cherbourg highway was stopped by fierce resistance shortly after its jumpoff at the les Chevres strongpoint which straddled the road.

In its methodical but short advance that day, elements of the 79th Division moved past a bunker which was well concealed and not detected. The concrete structure was a communications bunker which contained a switchboard for the entire Cherbourg *Landfront.* The bunker was not discovered by following troops and would function for two days behind American lines, placing regular calls to General von Schlieben in the besieged port with details of American troop movements in that area.

East of Cherbourg, General Barton's 4th Infantry Division was bitterly contested by the combat group commanded by Colonel Helmuth Rohrbach, although it had been nearly decimated in many days of action. Its ranks were heavy with naval and Luftwaffe security units and headquarters staff, kept fighting by the junior officers and noncoms vigilant for any sign of defection by individual *Feldgrau.*

Assault elements of the 4th Division had to pay dearly to gain a few hundred yards of ground during the day. One battalion, trying to outflank an enemy strongpoint, was caught in the open by murderous machine-gun fire from concrete bunkers and by artillery tree bursts. In that single action, the battalion lost 31 killed and 92 wounded.

As the June sun began its daily journey behind the western horizon on that first day of the "final" assault on Fortress Cherbourg, American commanders were shocked by the fierce resistance put up by the beleaguered German defenders. The enemy had taken a bloody toll, and American gains were measured in yards. But, as field leaders concluded, the day's bloody fighting and the heavy air and artillery pounding of German positions in the belt of fortifications had also exacted a heavy price among the defenders of Cherbourg. The fact remained however: the breakthrough hoped for by American commanders had not occurred.

At 11 P.M., in his underground command post in suburban Octeville, General von Schlieben, weary, depressed, harassed by armed Americans and armchair tacticians in the upper reaches of the German high command, sent a coded signal to his superior, Field Marshal Erwin Rommel at La Roche-Guyon:

> The troops of 709 division who have taken part in the fighting are numerically and spiritually exhausted. Fortress garrison itself not fit to withstand a severe strain. Men are over age, untrained and pillbox-minded . . . Reinforcement regarded as absolutely necessary for a task which the Führer has declared to be decisive.

No reply was received from headquarters, German Army Group B.

That night, as soldiers from both sides licked their wounds like two prehistoric beasts bloody and mutilated after a savage encounter, the German Transocean News Agency broadcast over Radio Berlin: "German troops have recaptured several positions within the fortified area of Cherbourg."

This was news to General von Schlieben. He knew that his exhausted and decimated combat groups were barely holding on by their toenails as they braced for another American avalanche which would strike them with renewed fury on the morrow.

17

Attackers Fought to a Standstill

Shortly after dawn on June 23, General Joe Collins was standing before a large map of the Cherbourg region, gazing intently at the tangle of blue lines and red arrows. Collins was a worried commander. Only twenty-four hours before, he had launched a full-scale attack on Fortress Cherbourg by all three of his divisions, supported by a massive air operation and a pounding of enemy positions by a thousand guns and hundreds of mortars. Hopes had been high for a breakthrough into the port.

The cold military fact was evident in the light of a new day and reports from front-line commanders: the Americans had been stopped cold.

The "breakthrough" attack of the previous day had been conducted in the classic form an army could mount when it had overwhelming air power, plenty of good artillery, and adequate numbers of well-trained infantrymen. But despite Army Air Corps leaders' use of such phrases as *pinpoint bombing, carpet bombing,* and *rolling aerial barrages,* the Allied air crews had not achieved the desired results. American bombs had been clustered around key enemy strongpoints, but Germans inside their thick-walled concrete bunkers had been largely unscathed.

Nor did the thousand-gun artillery barrage that followed the air attack succeed in weakening German positions prior to the jumpoff by weary, grimy American infantrymen. Most gun batteries had to ration shells due to the howling hurricane-force storm which had halted unloadings on the landing beaches for four days and left the portable harbors in shambles. Shells that did crash into German positions bounced off concrete bunkers, much like a flea bouncing off the thick hide of a rhinoceros.

Once the aerial bombing and artillery barrages were lifted, the Germans had fought back savagely with concrete-protected machine guns, heavy coastal guns, field artillery, and multiple-barreled heavy mortars, whose projectiles sailed through the air with an unearthly noise which sounded to the Americans like gigantic horses whinnying.

Despite the pall of gloom that hovered over VII Corps headquarters on this morning, staff officers tuned to the BBC in London for the war news heard an upbeat report on the fighting: "American forces which have a large German garrison trapped in the port city of Cherbourg pushed ahead steadily yesterday in the face of determined resistance . . ."

At Field Marshal Rommel's headquarters at La Roche-Guyon, in the Paris region, the commander of German Army Group B was wrestling with red tape at a time his armies were being cut to pieces in Normandy. During the past two days, with Cherbourg's death knell apparently about to ring, Adolf Hitler and his confidants at the Oberkommando der Wehrmacht had been bombarding Rommel with sharp and pointed inquiries. Each signal contained a new demand for information and explanation:

What were the troop dispositions around Cherbourg? How many combat effectives did von Schlieben have to defend the port? What provisions did the port have? Who was responsible for seeing that it had been supplied prior to the D-Day landings? Had sufficient ammunition been stored at Cherbourg?

Erwin Rommel was furious. The sudden deluge of demanding signals not only taxed communications channels needed for the conduct of the Normandy battle and angered field commanders, who had more crucial matters to attend to, but the implication was transparent: Hitler and the OKW were searching for a scapegoat for the coming military disaster.

Meanwhile early that morning, in a 79th Infantry Division regimental bivouac area a short distance behind the front lines, an American captain was kneeling before a small mirror hooked on a hedgerow branch. Before him was his helmet filled with water, and a thick lather adorned his face. The officer was in his OD undershirt with a towel around his neck, so there was no insignia of rank.

The young company commander was in a foul mood. The day before he and his men had been engaged in savage pillbox fighting, trying to root out the stubborn, concealed, and protected enemy with grenades and bayonets. Many of his fighting men had been killed or mutilated. Now his men were in reserve, a brief respite from the omnipresent perils and hardships of face-to-face combat.

Out of the corner of his eye the captain detected a tiny group of figures moving across the field toward him. He looked up in annoyance as they halted beside him—into the beaming face of the Supreme Commander of the Allied Expeditionary Force, Dwight Eisenhower. The startled captain, with the towel still around his neck and lather on his face, stumbled to his feet, saluted and gave his name and rank.

The supreme commander, continuing to beam, returned the military greeting. His freshly pressed and immaculately clean summer worsteds were in sharp contrast to the sweaty, grimy attire of the front-line soldiers in the bivouac area.

Eisenhower began circulating among the infantrymen dotting the field, followed by his two companions, General Omar Bradley and General Ira Wyche, commander of the 79th Division. The captain, chagrined at being caught in a state of disarray by the unexpected sudden appearance of the supreme commander, sheepishly fell in behind.

The erstwhile Kansas farm boy, now one of the world's most powerful men with massive Allied land, sea, and air forces under his control and endowed with almost unprecedented authority to employ them, was in his element—chatting casually with the men carrying the heaviest burden of all, the front-line combat soldiers.

For most of the 18 days the Allies had been ashore in Normandy, General Eisenhower had been itching to get out of the suffocating atmosphere of his SHAEF headquarters and visit the men who were in the front lines doing the fighting. Now, early in the morning of June 23, despite the protests of his staff, the supreme commander had fled the confines of SHAEF and dashed across the Channel to mix with his combat soldiers.

In his jeep on the way back to an airfield for the return trip to England, Eisenhower's face was constantly lit with his world-renowned smile as soldiers waved vigorously at him. Some of the more daring ones shouted, "Hi, Ike!" Eisenhower would grin even more broadly and return the wave.

Determined to keep pressure on the German defenders, Lightning Joe Collins that morning again sent his three attacking divisions forward. Fighting was savage and confused. Now the dogfaces of the 9th, 79th, and 4th Infantry Divisions were battling the stubborn enemy inside the belt of fortifications outside Cherbourg.

In the 9th Division zone to the west of the port, two regiments cleared out several bunkers and other strongpoints, aided by Pete Quesada's dive bombers and heavy artillery and mortar fire. By evening General Matt Eddy's men were firmly dug in astride the ridge leading to Cherbourg.

Billy Wyche's 79th Division in the center sustained heavy losses during the day and failed to reach its objective, the enemy strongpoint at la Mare aux Canards, astride the Valognes-Cherbourg highway. Another regiment of the 79th spent the day rooting out German forces which had infiltrated behind forward lines. As darkness approached, most of the regiment assaulting la Mare aux Canards was pulled back to await air support.

Closing in on Cherbourg from the east, Tubby Barton's 4th Division assault elements, with two Sherman tanks attached to each of the forward companies and backed by heavy artillery support, were unable to reach the objective, the town of Tourlaville. The 12th Infantry Regiment spent the day in hand to hand combat with Germans who had either infiltrated behind division lines or who had been bypassed by assault companies.

General Joe Collins was becoming increasingly concerned. The attacking corps, for the second straight day, had been fought almost to a standstill. Hundreds of Wehrmacht prisoners had been taken during the two days of savage fighting, but the front-line American soldier could detect no slackening of enemy resistance nor will to fight to the end. Most of these prisoners were bitter over the failure of the Luftwaffe to join in the fight. "If we are supposed to die to defend Cherbourg," a seriously wounded German told his captors, "then why can't the Luftwaffe come out and die with us?"

Unknown to that bitter and agonizing German soldier and to thousands of his comrades, there was good reason for the absence of the once-vaunted Luftwaffe—it had been virtually destroyed by the Allied air forces. On June 23 Ultra intercepted a lengthy signal from Flight Corps 9 summarizing conclusions reached at a conference of senior German air commanders in the West: Undertrained pilots were jettisoning their bombs. Reinforcement pilots from within the Third Reich were "useless" as their training was inferior. The minimum for a "safe" strike into the Cotentin (because of Allied air superiority) was 12 to 15 fighters. Any smaller number would be "dangerous." And finally aircraft should avoid flying over German troops as they were in danger of being shot down by jittery Wehrmacht gunners conditioned to conclude that anything flying would be American or British.

Other details of the Luftwaffe woes in Normandy poured forth in the Flight Corps 9 signal—into the eager electronic ears in the confines of Station X at Bletchley Park, north of London: Shortage of fighters and bombers. Lack of fuel. Low morale. Pilots consider sortie over Normandy "suicide mission." Airfields in arc around Normandy unserviceable due to Allied bombings.

202

With starkly clear indications that the Germans were about to turn Cherbourg into a miniature Stalingrad, Lighting Joe Collins looked to an untapped source for assistance—the United States Navy. The VII Corps commander requested Admiral Morton Deyo, skipper of Task Force 129, to shell the coastal batteries in and to either side of Cherbourg. Lean, bushy-browed Mort Deyo, aggressive commander of three battleships, four cruisers, and seven destroyers, leaped at the opportunity.

Deyo would be taking on a considerable task—neutralizing 20 case-mated German batteries, 15 of them of 150-millimeter or greater caliber, including three of 280-millimeter. In addition there were many clusters of 75- and 88-millimeters which could fire out to sea or inland. Together, they would represent enormous firepower. These waterside batteries bore such names as *Hamburg, Bromm, Yorck,* and *Landemer.*

Collins, eager to break into Cherbourg, requested Admiral Deyo to go into action the following day, June 24. "Cannot comply with suggested date," the admiral signaled. "Earliest date for mission is Sunday, twenty-fifth."

Admiral Deyo could not bombard German batteries the following day for a simple reason: when the hurricane-like storm struck the Channel on June 19, he had ordered Task Force 129 to sail for the relative security of English ports. Now he would have to reassemble his warships from various harbors between Plymouth and Portsmouth.

Elated at going into action in such a crucial role, Mort Deyo, from his flagship *Tuscaloosa,* signaled Task Force 129: "This port is going to be ours, so we don't want to mess it up any more than we have to."

Admiral Deyo need not have been unduly concerned with damage caused by his warships' gunnery—German demolition experts from the army and navy had been feverishly involved in "messing up" the port for more than a week.

A great pall of smoke hung over blackened and seemingly deserted Cherbourg in the waning light of June 23 as the Germans ignited buildings and other installations that might be of value to the Americans. Flames dotted the port city. The sharp sound of explosives regularly rent the summer air.

During the night German demolition men backed an entire freight train loaded with dynamite to the Gare Maritime. A mighty roar erupted which could be heard for miles as the dynamite was ignited, blowing the train and the Gare Maritime into splinters. Great fireballs billowed into the dark sky, illuminating the area for vast distances. In foxholes several miles away, American soldiers could feel the ground tremble around them.

Hitler's stern orders to General von Schlieben had been: "If worst comes to worst, leave the enemy not a harbor but a vast field of devastation." The commander of Fortress Cherbourg intended to do just that.

During the night of June 23, von Schlieben sent a signal to Rommel's headquarters at La Roche-Guyon which painted a dismal picture of the German situation in the bitter struggle for the port the Führer ordered must be kept out of Allied hands "at all costs." Even though his patchwork units had stalled the full American assault for two days, von Schlieben knew that his losses in men, guns and equipment had been massive.

Von Schlieben declared gloomily in his signal to Rommel:

> I have no more reserves to throw into the battle. Have given orders to troops to defend to the last cartridge. The fall of Cherbourg is inevitable. The only question is whether it is possible to postpone it for a few days.

Early on the morning of June 24, General Joe Collins again launched his three attacking divisions toward the besieged port. The 9th Division on the west overran three defended Luftwaffe installations and slogged its way to the outskirts of Octeville, the suburb in which, unknown to the Americans, General von Schlieben was directing the last-ditch defense of Cherbourg.

In the 79th Division zone in the center, the bitterly defended strongpoint of la Mare aux Canards, astride the Valognes-Cherbourg highway, was finally cleared by infantry with tank, artillery, and fighter-bomber support. Billy Wyche's forward elements then pushed on to within sight of Fort du Roule, which hung on a steep cliff overlooking Cherbourg.

Three attempts were made to break through to Fort du Roule, but all were driven back by heavy fire. The Americans would soon learn that the diabolically constructed fort would be one of the toughest nuts of the war to crack.

On the east, the attacking 8th Infantry Regiment of the 4th Division, Colonel Jim Van Fleet's force, which had made the initial D-Day seaborne assault at Utah, ran into bitter last stands by isolated German forces and became bogged down in heavy fighting. From the protection of concrete bunkers and deeply dug fieldworks, the Germans plastered Van Fleet's men with light artillery, antiaircraft guns, mortars, and machine guns, and threw back the American assault.

Colonel Van Fleet sent a battalion to outflank the German strongpoint, and the defending force withdrew. But the day's cost had been heavy for the 8th Infantry. Thirty-seven men were killed and some 106 wounded. One of those killed was Lieutenant Colonel Conrad Simmons, the 1st Battalion commander, who had huddled with Brigadier General Teddy Roosevelt shortly after H-Hour on D-Day to hurriedly form a plan to attack inland after it had been determined that the 8th Infantry had landed a mile from its designated beach.

Another 4th Division unit, the 12th Infantry Regiment, attacked Tourlaville and became engaged in a savage fight with a German force defending an artillery position. With the aid of Sherman tanks and a dive-bombing attack by a dozen P-47 Thunderbolts, the infantry overran the position. The fleeing Germans left behind six field pieces and large quantities of shells.

In the day's advance, 4th Infantry Division elements captured 800 prisoners and by night occupied the high ground outside Tourlaville from which the city of Cherbourg was visible. The German defenders had exacted a high price in American blood for modest gains that day. Among those killed leading his men in the attack was Lieutenant Colonel John W. Merrill, who had taken command of the 1st Battalion of the 12th Infantry only the day before.

As darkness pulled its ominous cloak over the battleground on June 24, General Joe Collins' three divisions had closed in on the doomed port. The German outer ring of fortifications had been pierced in numerous places. True to his Lightning Joe monicker, the VII Corps commander would hardly pause before unleashing further sledgehammer blows on the battered defenders of Fortress Cherbourg. And on the morrow, the dazed Germans in the port would be struck from yet another direction: Admiral Mort Deyo's Task Force 129 would bombard Wehrmacht defenses from the sea.

A weary General von Schlieben, from his underground command post in suburban Octeville, that night signaled Field Marshal Rommel at La Roche-Guyon:

> Concentrated enemy fire and bombing attacks have split the front. Numerous batteries have been put out of action or have worn out. Combat efficiency has fallen off considerably. The troops squeezed into small area will hardly be able to withstand an attack on the 25th.

While von Schlieben's latest report to his superiors was being radioed to

Rommel—and being decoded by British agents at Station X north of London—General Matt Eddy, the energetic and aggressive leader of the U.S. 9th Division, was issuing Field Order 9: "This Division ... will attack on 25 June and capture Cherbourg." The Grand Prize of the Great Invasion was ready to be plucked. The plucking would prove to be a bloody one.

Meanwhile, some hundred miles from Cherbourg as the crow flies, Field Marshal Erwin Rommel, grimy and exhausted, drove up in front of his La Roche-Guyon chateau in his mud-splattered Horch. It was less than an hour until midnight. As was his custom, the commander of Army Group B had been touring the front lines since daybreak, some 18 hours before.

He was particularly bitter at Hitler over the debacle now entering its final phase at the tip of the Cotentin Peninsula. Before the U.S. 9th Division had sealed off the peninsula on June 18, Rommel had constantly pleaded for withdrawing the Cherbourg garrison to the south, but the plea had fallen on Hitler's deaf ears.

Rommel's normally buoyant spirits, already flagging, were hardly elevated when General Hans Speidel, his astute chief of staff, handed him the second signal of the night from von Schlieben in besieged and blackened Cherbourg:

> [My headquarters] communications to several battalions no longer available. Phosphorous shells have put eight batteries out of action. Tomorrow [June 25] heavier enemy attack expected ... Completely crushed by artillery fires. Losses of unit leaders heavy. Morale low.

Shortly after 7 A.M. on the pleasant Sunday morning of June 25, two 9th Infantry Division GIs were on outpost duty on a hill overlooking Cherbourg from the west. "Look!" one man called out, pointing his finger down the road toward German lines. Approaching were two figures, one waving a large white flag. The pair of Americans motioned the advancing men into their lines.

Holding the white flag was a young German medical lieutenant, adjutant of the naval hospital in Cherbourg, and his companion was an American air corps pilot who had been shot down over the city and taken prisoner. The German and pilot were escorted back to regimental headquarters.

Speaking to the colonel, the German medical officer said that American artillery shells had been falling constantly around the hospital where hundreds of German and 150 American wounded were being treated, even though the facility was marked with large red crosses. He asked that shelling near the hospital be halted. When it was pointed out to him that the Germans had established an ammunition dump next to the hospital, the emissary agreed to see that it was moved.

The German also asked for plasma, which was supplied to him to take back to the hospital for treating the American wounded.

On his return trip into Cherbourg, the enemy medical officer was accompanied by Captain John B. Jackson, assistant intelligence officer of the 9th Division who was fluent in German and had been acting as interpreter. Jackson carried with him another surrender ultimatum which was handed to a German colonel:

> The fortress Cherbourg is now surrounded and its defenses have been breached. The city is now isolated . . . You are tremendously outnumbered and it is merely a question of time when Cherbourg must be captured. The immediate unconditional surrender of Cherbourg is demanded . . .

Captain Jackson was told there would be no reply. Time, that's what the Germans in Cherbourg were buying. Time. Time to continue demolishing port facilities. Time for Field Marshal Rommel to bring up reinforcements to hold a line across the neck of the Cotentin Peninsula. Jackson shrugged his shoulders and returned to 9th Division lines.

At 9 A.M., after having issued orders for the attack to smash into Cherbourg to jump off shortly after noon, General Collins was attending Mass in a stable formerly occupied by a German field artillery battery, which had departed suddenly a few days before. Collins was tired. He had not gotten to bed until 1:30 A.M. after spending 19 hours dashing about the front in his rolling CP, an armored car.

When he returned to his nearby headquarters in a fashionable chateau, Collins found a visitor waiting for him—Omar Bradley. Omar the Tentmaker, as he was called by war correspondents, had come forward to discuss with Collins final plans for the reduction of German defenses inside Cherbourg.

Preparing to leave, the soft-spoken Bradley, not one of British General Bernard Montgomery's ardent fans, turned to Collins and remarked with a chuckle, "Joe, you'll love this. Monty has just announced that Caen is the key to Cherbourg!" Caen, 12 miles in from the British beaches and Montgomery's D-Day objective, had not yet been captured. The city was nearly 75 miles east of Cherbourg.

"Well, Brad," Collins replied, "let's wire Monty to send us the key."

In the interest of Allied harmony the wire was not sent.

At his First Army headquarters behind Omaha Beach, Bradley was handed a message from the Supreme Commander, Dwight Eisenhower:

> I most earnestly hope that you get Cherbourg tomorrow [June 26]. As quickly as you have done so we must rush preparations for the attack to the southward with all possible speed. The enemy is building up [there] and we must not allow him to seal us up in the northern half of the [Cotentin] peninsula.

Pressure for the quick seizure of Cherbourg, especially after the disastrous storm that had wiped out the portable harbors on the American landing beaches, was patently being exerted down the chain of command. Eisenhower "hoped" Bradley could take Cherbourg by June 26. Bradley had gone forward to "discuss" plans for eliminating German pockets in the port. Collins was back in his rolling CP "urging" his division commanders onward. Eddy, Wyche, and Barton, the division chiefs, were lashing regimental colonels to "keep moving."

After Bradley departed, Collins raced to the CP of Barton's 4th Infantry Division to the east of Cherbourg. General Teddy Roosevelt took Collins in tow and guided him to a position just captured from the Germans. It was on a high hill overlooking the surrounded port. Collins viewed a magnificent panorama. A short distance to the right, the corps commander could see hundreds of German prisoners being rounded up in another enemy position just seized by Barton's foot sloggers supported by tanks.

Off to the left were the steep cliffs of the highlands that ran right up to the back door of Cherbourg. Collins could see fires started there by American artillery and knew that Billy Wyche's 79th Division was closing in from that direction. Far off to the right were the inner and outer breakwaters with their old French forts guarding the entrance to Cherbourg from the sea.

Within this frame, the city itself lay as in a bowl from which billows of thick black smoke rose. The Germans were demolishing stores of oil and ammunition. Joe Collins felt a thrill surge through his being at this awesome view and the historic action being unfolded before his eyes.

As General Collins and his escorts watched, a heavy American battery far off in the distance out of sight fired a perfect concentration onto a German position just west of Fort des Flamands, along the docks. The target area appeared to lift off the ground and dissipate in an ugly cloud of thick smoke and dust.

Awed by the sight, Lightning Joe turned to Teddy Roosevelt and said, "Cherbourg is ours!"

Then to the 4th Division commander, General Barton, Collins said, "Tubby, push one of your regiments on into Cherbourg by night fall!"

It was a sudden switch in the plan to capture the port. Initially Barton's 4th Division was to hold fast on the east while the 79th Division from the south and the 9th Division from the west drove on into the city. But now the corps commander had a change of heart; the 4th Division had fought so long and hard since making the D-Day assault that Collins did not want it to be excluded from the honor of being in on the final kill.

18

An Impregnable
Bastion in the Sky

It was 8:03 A.M. on June 25 and a thin haze hovered over smoking, blackened Cherbourg. High in the sky, their white bodies reflecting the early morning sun, a squadron of P-47 fighter-bombers was circling above the German bastion of Fort du Roule, the cornerstone of the Wehrmacht's defensive line around the threatened port.

High and secure in the steep rock promontory which stood immediately south of the city, the fort dominated the entire harbor area and was an awe-inspiring, ominous edifice whose very appearance chilled the blood of those whose job it was to capture it. Fort du Roule was primarily a coastal fortress, with its guns housed in the lower levels of the fort pointing seaward.

But the fortress was also defended against land attack from its top level, which mounted automatic weapons and mortars in concrete pillboxes, and enjoyed a favorable defensive position due to the fact that it could be assaulted only along a narrow ridge from the south. On the west, north, and east, sheer cliffs dropped off around the fort.

Only the top level of Fort du Roule was visible from the land side. Along the solitary approach route the Germans had sewn thick mine fields and built heavy barbed-wire entanglements. A few hundred yards southeast the defenders had dug an antitank ditch, and a short distance south there was a stream bed.

Now in the skies over Cherbourg, the flight of P-47 Thunderbolts had sized up the target down below, and one after the other peeled off to drop two bombs each on Fort du Roule. Troops of Colonel Warren A. Robinson's 314th Infantry of the 79th Division looked on intently from positions about a thousand yards south of the fort. Grim-faced, tight-lipped, clothing soiled and torn, these were the foot sloggers who, in minutes, would have to pit their flesh and whatever luck they could muster against the thick concrete walls and spitting machine guns of impregnable Fort du Roule.

There was no question of cunning military masterminding, of feints, outflanking maneuvers, or infiltration. These solemn fighting men would have to cross open ground in a "frontal attack from the rear." They knew it. The Germans knew it. The Germans would be primed and waiting.

Warren Robinson's fighters felt a dull sense of hope for survival as plane after plane let loose with its lethal cargo. In all, two dozen five hundred-pound bombs were dropped in the air attack by 12 Thunderbolts. To the infantrymen, the ones who would carry the ultimate load, the bombs seemed to be hitting Fort du Roule directly. Unknown to them, all the bombs had missed the comparatively small target entirely and plunged harmlessly into the flatlands down below.

As the last P-47 pulled up into the blue summer sky and headed for its home base, a mighty roar erupted along and behind the infantry lines as the guns of the 311th Field Artillery Battalion and a platoon of 4.2-inch mortars began to send salvo after salvo onto Fort du Roule. With forward observers calling the shots, the artillery and mortar barrage was pinpoint accurate. Cluster after cluster of shells exploded violently upon the ramparts of the bastion in the sky.

Other than to informally announce to the German defenders that an attack was about to be launched, the thunderous barrage achieved nothing. The heavy concentration of shells exploded harmlessly atop the five-foot thick roof of the fort. Here and there some concrete was chipped off.

As the artillery and mortar pounding of the fort continued, there were shouts along the lines of the 314th Infantry Regiment. "Okay, let's go! Let's hit 'em!" Wearily the dogfaces struggled to their feet, and elements of two battalions began moving toward the fort the German commanders had termed "impregnable."

The leading 3rd Battalion was moving down into a draw only minutes after jumping off when they were suddenly raked with automatic-weapons and smallarms fire. There were cries among the attacking Americans as bullets plowed into vulnerable flesh. Pellets—thousands of them—hissed and sang past Robinson's foot sloggers. Here and there was a sickening thud as a slug found its mark. Shouts of "Medic! Medic!" rang out above the din of battle.

Robinson's men had run into a buzzsaw while still 700 yards from Fort du Roule. A force of Germans was dug in along an east-west trail on the forward slope of the draw the Americans were just moving into. As the Wehrmacht soldiers continued to rake the trapped attackers, who could only hug the ground and pray, all machine guns in the 2nd and 3rd battalions were rushed forward to concentrate their fire on the enemy force along the trail. This heavy volume of American automatic-weapons fire soon resulted in a diminishing of resistance from the German outpost position, and then the enemy firing ceased entirely.

A number of Germans were seen edging out of their foxholes and dashing for the relative safety of the fort to their rear. Most were cut down. Their comrades lay dead or seriously wounded in their field fortifications where, in accordance with the Führer's orders, they had fought savagely to the last man.

With the assaulting 3rd Battalion badly chewed up by the deeply dug-in German force, the 2nd Battalion took over the attack. It overran several other outlying positions, and then went forward along the broad ridge toward Fort du Roule. In the advance, the two assaulting companies were under continuous fire, not only from the Germans in the fort but also from artillery on the heights of Octeville across the Divette River to the northwest.

As the Americans edged their way forward, suffering heavy casualties along the way, the attack became a methodical use of Bangalore torpedoes to blast gaps in thick strands of barbed wire and satchel charges of TNT to root the Germans out of concrete pillboxes defending the approaches to the fort. Almost ceaselessly, the Americans were raked by automatic weapons and pounded by mortars.

In the forefront of the assault, the platoon of Corporal John D. Kelly was pinned down on the slope by enemy machine-gun fire. Kelly saw that the withering blasts were coming from a pillbox and, without orders, armed himself with a 10-foot pole charge with 15 pounds of dynamite, and began inching his way up the slope under heavy automatic-weapons fire. Had the assistant squad leader had time to reflect on his action, he would not have considered himself a hero. Only that there was a job to do—and someone had to do it.

As his comrades peppered the apertures in the pillbox with covering fire, Corporal Kelly reached the enemy position and placed the TNT charge at the base of the strongpoint. He hurriedly wriggled along the ground to a safe distance. A mighty roar erupted from the pillbox site as the dynamite exploded. When the thick cloud of black smoke dissipated, Kelly and his comrades farther back saw with dismay that the TNT charge had hardly made a dent in the thick-walled structure.

Kelly refused to admit defeat. He crawled back to his platoon, secured another TNT charge and braved the fire-swept slope again to repeat the process. This time the ends of the enemy guns were blown off, and the murderous firing from the pillbox slackened to reports from several rifles.

Again the corporal returned to his lines for another TNT charge and returned to the concrete bunker. There he exploded the dynamite at the rear entrance, then edged around to the front and tossed two grenades in through an aperture.

Now Kelly's comrades moved forward and outside the pillbox shouted, "Come out, you sons of bitches!" Seconds later the badly damaged metal door creaked and groaned as it was forced open and several *Feldgrau*—pitiful looking creatures covered with masonry dust, their ears and mouths bleeding from Corporal Kelly's dynamite blasts—emerged trembling and ashen-faced with hands held in the air. Inside the bodies of some 15 comrades lay sprawled on the concrete floor which was awash in a sea of blood.

Meanwhile the 3rd Battalion moved up to clear resistance on the left flank of the assaulting 2nd Battalion and promptly ran into murderous flat-trajectory fire from dug-in German 88-millimeter guns and automatic weapons. The advance ground to a halt.

Lieutenant Carlos C. Ogden, who just that morning had taken over Company K from the wounded company commander, armed himself with a Garand rifle, a grenade launcher, and several rifle and hand grenades. He began edging up the slope alone toward the enemy strongpoint as heavy fusillades of machine-gun fire swept past him. One of the pellets struck Ogden, but after a momentary halt he continued to pull his way along the ground.

With blood saturating his grimy uniform, Lieutenant Ogden reached a point from which he could see the 88-millimeter gun firing rounds into his company of dogfaces behind him. The wounded officer got to one knee, attached a rifle grenade, and fired it into the enemy gun position. There was an explosion and cries of pain from the German gunners. The gun fell silent.

Ogden then set out in search of the German machine guns. Again he was struck by one of the thousands of bullets whistling through the area. But he continued forward, located the spitting automatic weapons, and crawled toward them. Only some 10 yards away, Ogden began hurling grenades into the enemy position. Again the screams and the firing halted.

Now the assaulting American companies, having clawed their way over a 700-yard path strewn with the lifeless bodies of comrades and Germans alike, fought their way into the upper level of Fort du Roule. Inside they discovered that the bastion was a tangled maze of compartments where *Feldgrau* fought tenaciously from room to room. Only a few hours before some of the German occupants had argued violently among themselves over whether to fight or surrender. The debate was settled when officers and noncoms drew pistols and threatened to shoot any German soldiers who tried to surrender.

The chambers of the old French fort echoed with the sound of Tommy guns, grenades, and TNT as the Americans rooted out the defenders. Some sections held out until 10 P.M., but by then the top level of impregnable Fort du Roule was solidly in American hands. Colonel Warren Robinson's assaulting infantrymen had captured 457 Germans in the bitter fighting before the fort and one hundred and six more had been taken when the first level was secured. Exhausted American foot soldiers collapsed in deep sleep on the top level. Unknown to them, in the rabbit warren of rooms in the levels underneath, several hundred armed Germans were ready to continue the fight for Fort du Roule.

While Colonel Robinson's men had been busily engaged in rousting Germans out of the top level of the fort that evening, John Thompson, the correspondent of the Chicago *Tribune* who had made it a habit through many campaigns of reporting on the war from the front lines, and a fellow reporter, Tex O'Reilly of the New York *Herald-Tribune,* were walking briskly across a field a few hundred yards to the rear of the fighting. They were heading for embattled Fort du Roule.

Thompson and O'Reilly became aware that several 79th Division infantrymen ahead were vigorously waving their arms and looking in the direction of the pair of oncoming newsmen. Reaching the waving men moments later, Thompson inquired, "What in the hell are you fellows motioning at so hard?"

"At you," one replied. "You guys have just walked through a German mine field."

South of Fort du Roule, along the vegetation-covered route just crossed by the assaulting 314th Infantry Regiment, Sergeant Rudolph Halasy, a communications man, together with several comrades was laying wire.

Suddenly Halasy looked up and saw ten Germans coming out of some brush toward him—with their arms raised in surrender. The group had been bypassed in the assault on the fort.

Aware that the enemy had been fighting tenaciously for Cherbourg, Sergeant Halasy asked one of the English-speaking Germans, "What in the hell are you guys fighting for, anyhow?" The German shrugged his shoulders and replied, "Damned if I know. We were told to fight."

Meanwhile on the 79th Division's right flank, a thirty-man patrol, unshaven, weary, grimy, of the 313th Infantry Regiment, led by Lieutenant Shirley Landon, pushed down through the hamlet of Haut Gringor. This was to be a preliminary probe of German defenses there before the big show was launched.

Nearing the village, Landon's men spread out among the hedgerows and cautiously edged into town. Haut Gringor was to have been an enemy strongpoint, but the patrol drew no fire so started back for its own lines. Passing an old house, Platoon Sergeant Arthur J. Uber spotted an elderly French couple tapping on a window. They appeared to be terrified and motioned toward the back yard, holding up 10 fingers.

Figuring there were 10 Germans there, the patrol, weapons at the ready, edged cautiously around the house. As they came into view, up from the tall grass and the sparse woods came a flutter of white flags. Eighty-one Germans, all members of a labor battalion pressed into front-line duty as riflemen by General von Schlieben, had emerged with their hands held high in surrender.

As the patrol started to form up the prisoners for the march to the rear, Private First Class William K. Petty saw three of the Germans reach over to pick up their rifles. "*Nein, Schweinehund!*" (no, you sons of bitches) an American shouted, and the three Germans quickly straightened up.

"Hell, they weren't planning on starting anything," a 79th Division man mused to a comrade. "Some goddamned Kraut officer told them to hang on to their rifles, and they were only following orders."

"And how about that old Frog holding up ten fingers?" another observed. "Apparently the French count different than we do. In France, ten means eighty-one."

The patrol reached American lines with its large batch of prisoners at 12:35 P.M. Minutes later—far too late—the enemy reacted to the patrol's probe into the edge of Haut Gringor. With a chilling scream that split the warm summer air, German rockets and mortar shells raced through the air and crashed down onto the precise spot in Haut Gringor which Lieutenant Landon's patrol had left 20 minutes earlier.

216

Now Colonel Sterling A. Wood, commander of the 313th Infantry, received orders to push into the outskirts of Cherbourg in force. He assembled his battalion commanders and other key officers.

"When you get into the goddamned place," Colonel Wood said, "Don't send your tanks in between buildings if you're fired on. Let the tanks stand back and blow the goddamned buildings to bits. Take no unnecessary chances. Take your prisoners with you if you have no time to send them on back. There will, of course, be no looting. Okay, start the attack!"

While Wyche's 79th Division infantrymen had been engaged in the savage fight for Fort du Roule, on the west, the 47th Infantry Regiment of Eddy's 9th Division jumped off for Cherbourg—and promptly ran into a hornets' nest at the ancient fortress of Équeurdreville. Surrounded by a dry moat with a single bridge, heavily fronted by barbed wire and located atop a high hill, the old fortification had overhanging observation rooms and tunnels connecting with coastal batteries to the north. The road fronting the hill had been mined.

Before the 2nd Battalion under Major Woodrow W. Bailey assaulted the formidable strongpoint, tank destroyers shot up the mined road and sent flat-trajectory fire into the fort. A squadron of Thunderbolts bombed and strafed the enemy position, and at 9:30 A.M. Major Bailey's infantrymen moved forward behind a heavy mortar and artillery barrage.

Fortunately for the assaulting foot soldiers, the German defenders at this formidable defensive position had no disposition to continue the fight. Fifteen minutes after the attack was launched, eighty-nine Germans in the medieval fortress emerged under white flags with hands thrust to the sky.

With the suburb of Equeurdreville in his hands, Major Bailey called in dive bombers before pushing his men on into Cherbourg. As the Thunderbolts finished bombing and strafing, Company E of the 2nd Battalion began advancing. A couple of hundred yards from the port's city limits, Private First Class John T. Sarao and his platoon leader spontaneously burst forth in a two-man foot race for the honor of being the first American to enter the primary objective of Operation Neptune, the invasion of continental Europe.

Huffing and wheezing under the burden of their weapons, heavy boots, and combat gear, the pair of 9th Infantry Division men were neck and neck through most of the race, but during the last few yards Sarao pulled out in front and dashed past a sign indicating Cherbourg city limits.

At his headquarters outside Octeville, Matt Eddy, commander of the veteran 9th Division, was jubilant to learn that elements of Colonel George Smythe's regiment had broken into Cherbourg against sporadic resistance, although Eddy's right regiment had run into a buzzsaw just south of the city and was engaged in bitter fighting. Eddy looked up to see General Collins enter the room. Collins was anxious to learn of the 9th Division situation as most of Cherbourg lay in Eddy's zone.

The division commander took Collins to a former German antiaircraft position which had been pulverized by a dive-bombing attack the day before. Hardly had the two generals reached the position than there was a ssswwwiiissshhh-CCRRAACCKK. A loud explosion nearby as the flat-trajectory 88-millimeter shell exploded sent Collins, Eddy, and their aides scurrying for the protection of a German communications trench. For several minutes round after round tore into the observation post as the Americans hugged the ground at the bottom of the trench.

Then silence returned. The German battery had stopped firing. With as much dignity as they could muster, Generals Collins and Eddy picked themselves off the bottom of the trench and continued with the inspection tour.

While heavy fighting was taking place all around the outskirts of Cherbourg that morning, a weary, despondent, harassed General Karl von Schlieben, commander of Fortress Cherbourg, was sending off a report to Field Marshal Erwin Rommel at La Roche-Guyon:

> Enemy superiority in material and enemy domination of the air overwhelming. Most of our own batteries out of ammunition or smashed. Troops badly exhausted, confined to narrowest space, their backs against the sea ... Loss of town unavoidable in nearest future as enemy has penetrated outskirts. Have 2,000 wounded without possibility of moving them. Is there any point, in view of the overall situation, in having our remaining forces entirely wiped out, as seems inevitable in the absence of effective counter-weapons? Request urgent instructions.

Von Schlieben, in his subterranean office, could hear the grating rattle of smallarms engaged in a firefight in the near distance. Periodically he could hear the muted crash of American shells outside. He looked on expressionlessly as intelligence officers drew in red arrows which pierced through the blue lines and circles representing German lines and strongpoints. On his desk lay a carbine for his personal use in the last-ditch fight now in progress.

At 3:52 P.M. an aide entered von Schlieben's office and handed the fortress commander a piece of paper. "Field Marshal Rommel's reply to your signal this morning, *Herr General*," the staff officer said solemnly.

Von Schlieben reached out for the reply and read: "In accordance with the Führer's orders, you are to continue fighting to the last round. Rommel. Field Marshal."

Wordlessly, he handed the message back to his aide. Now von Schlieben knew for sure: not only was Fortress Cherbourg doomed, but so was every Wehrmacht man in it. What is the purpose of this continued bloody sacrifice? von Schlieben anguished. He had carried out the Führer's orders to "leave the enemy not a port but a field of devastation." Why must the hopeless fight go on?

Meanwhile, at dawn that day, Admiral Mort Deyo's 14-ship Task Force 129 sailed from Portland on its way to bombard German strongpoints in and around Cherbourg. The Channel was now dead calm after the storm. There was a light haze which, as the warships neared the French coast, was enhanced by smoke from artillery fire, German demolitions, and demolished bomb targets.

Even though the shelling mission was only hours away, Admiral Deyo was not certain as to what First Army wanted from him. All he knew was that the naval task force had been ordered not to commence firing before noon, to fire for only 90 minutes instead of the three hours Deyo had planned, and to shoot only at targets designated by the army.

With minesweepers in the van, Task Force 129 made landfall at 9:40 A.M., about 15 miles north of Cherbourg. Deyo flashed word to his skippers that they were not to fire before noon unless fired upon. The naval flotilla began idly steaming in circles, its commanders furious over the restrictions the army had put on them. For more than an hour all was quiet. Shore fire control parties (SFCP) made no requests, the enemy remained silent.

Ten minutes later the suspense was broken. There were flashes on the beach near the village of Querqueville, three miles west of Cherbourg. Minutes later, four German 150-millimeter shells whistled into the water around three minesweepers, followed quickly by another salvo. British Captain C. P. Clarke, skipper of the group under attack, flashed an immediate order from his flagship, the cruiser HMS *Glasgow*: "Engage with direct fire the batteries firing on the minesweeper." At 12:14 P.M. several of Admiral Deyo's ships, belching flames and thick black smoke from gun muzzles, opened fire on the distant flashes near Querqueville.

The enemy coastal battery continued to pour shells at the warships offshore, concentrating on the *Glasgow* and *Enterprise,* and the dust stirred up at the German gun site by the salvos of shells falling on it had become so thick that a British Spitfire spotter plane could not see the target.

At 12:50 P.M. those on the *Glasgow* heard the chilling rustle of large-caliber shells heading directly at their ship and moments later a 150-millimeter round crashed into her hangar. Within minutes another exploded in her superstructure, killing several men and seriously wounding many others.

Now Admiral Deyo's task force was being flooded with requests for fire support from army troops fighting their way into Cherbourg who were often running up against intense artillery fire from concrete-enclosed gun sites. In answer to the first call, the ancient battleship *Nevada* opened up with her 14-inch guns on a battery two miles southwest of Querqueville. With each belching salvo, the old warship shook and shuddered from bow to stern, but its shells landed directly on the battery.

"You are hitting on target and digging in!" a naval fire observer on shore shouted jubilantly into his transmitter.

More of the enormous 14-inch shells were heaped onto the German battery, each salvo sounding to those near the impact area like a freight train racing through a tunnel. After twenty-five minutes of firing, the shore spotter called to the *Nevada,* "The bastards are showing a white flag, but we have learned not to pay any attention to that. Continue firing!"

Minutes later came the voice over the radio once more, "Okay, you can cease fire. You left only a pile of dust. Good shooting!"

On both sides of Cherbourg and at Fort de l'Est, guarding a harbor breakwater in the city, Mort Deyo's warships blasted away at shore installations and in turn were kept under constant shelling from *Kriegsmarine* coastal batteries. The spirited duel had been a Mexican standoff—there was no clear-cut winner. As the 90-minute firing period drew to an end, the aggressive Admiral Mort Deyo was deeply disappointed. He knew that the bombardment had fallen short of expectations.

The admiral was in no mood to retire from the scene of battle, so at 1:20 P.M. he signaled General Collins on shore: "Do you wish more gunfire? Several enemy batteries still active."

While Admiral Deyo paced back and forth on the bridge of the *Tuscaloosa* like a caged tiger, impatiently awaiting a reply from the army, the German Querqueville battery, which was thought to have been silenced, suddenly came to life and fired salvos which straddled the destroyer *Murphy* four times in 20 minutes. The fighting heart of Mort

Deyo would not allow him to stand by idly while the army decided what it wanted. He ordered his flagship *Tuscaloosa* and several other warships to close within range of the Querqueville battery and open fire.

A direct hit on the shore battery sent a spiral of flame and smoke soaring into the sky, but the German guns kept firing at a slower pace. A salvo by the *Nevada's* 14-inch guns fell squarely on the target, cloaking it in a thick mixture of smoke and dust. A navy spotter on shore radioed, "No need for further firing!"

It had taken the combined efforts of a battleship, four cruisers, and five destroyers to silence "target 308"—the Querqueville battery. As the task force retired, target 308, like a cat with nine lives, defiantly fired a few more shells at Deyo's warships.

After the spiritual duel had concluded, Admiral Deyo was handed General Joe Collins' reply to Deyo's inquiry: "Thanks very much. We should be grateful if you would continue firing until 3 P.M."

An urgent call was received on the *Tuscaloosa* from the 4th Infantry Division which was fighting its way into the city from the east: Fort des Flamands, at the eastern end of the inner breakwater, had been inflicting heavy casualties on an attacking regiment with its eight dual-purpose 88-millimeter guns. The regiment had been brought to a halt by the flat-trajectory fire of these lethal German weapons. The destroyer *Hambleton* and cruiser *Quincy* responded to the request for help, and began pounding the strongpoint. Fort des Flamands fell silent—for the time being.

Meanwhile the old battleship *Nevada* had been dueling with German batteries on the west side of Cherbourg, and was straddled twenty times by large-caliber shells. One missed her by only 25 feet and two passed through her superstructure before splashing into the water, deluging sailors on deck. But the pre-World War I warship led a charmed life. Not a single casualty was sustained.

While Admiral Deyo's warships were battling with German batteries west of Cherbourg and within the city, a group under Rear Admiral C. F. Bryant, consisting of the battleships *Texas, Arkansas,* and five destroyers, had been engaged in a shootout with the most powerful and strongly protected German battery in Normandy, known to the Germans as Hamburg.

Sited on a hill near Fermanville, six miles east of Cherbourg, Hamburg had a force of more than 1,000 members of the *Kriegsmarine.* Four 280-millimeter guns, powerful weapons which could fire accurately for 25 miles, were protected by more than five feet of reinforced concrete and by steel shields much like naval gun turrets. Clustered around these 11-inch guns were 12 antiaircraft guns and six 88-millimeter guns.

From a brush-covered hill overlooking Hamburg, a fire control party asked the antiquated battleship *Arkansas* to close in and open fire on the German strongpoint. As other warships edged toward shore to get within range, German gunners in Hamburg bided their time, secure in the knowledge that they were relatively safe in their concrete bunkers.

Suddenly, the powerful guns in Hamburg began firing. The second salvo straddled the destroyer *Barton.* A 240-millimeter shell struck the water next to the *Barton* and ricocheted into her hull, then smashed into the engine room after plowing through several bulkheads. It finally came to rest inside the ship—a dud.

Minutes later the destroyer *Laffey* was struck by a 240-millimeter shell on her bow near the anchor. It buried itself into a bulkhead—also a dud. An apprehensive team of damage-control men, aware that a dud could explode at any second, gingerly pried the huge missile loose and tossed it overboard.

Firing between the ships offshore and battery Hamburg now became intense. The battleship *Texas* was straddled by a cluster of shells and swerved hurriedly just in time to avoid three shells which whistled over her stern.

Now Hamburg concentrated its fire on the destroyers and mine sweepers. A shell plowed into the destroyer *O'Brien,* hacked away the ladder to her bridge and smashed into the combat information center where it exploded, killing thirteen sailors and wounding nineteen. Under a smoke screen, the *O'Brien* retired out of range.

Admiral Bryant, a bold commander but a realistic one, realized his group of warships was getting the worst of it in the duel with powerful Hamburg. Three quick hits on his destroyers and near-misses around his battleship convinced Bryant that it would be prudent to withdraw out of range of Hamburg's powerful and securely protected guns.

Meanwhile the battleship *Texas,* with heavier guns and a better fire-control system than the ancient *Arkansas,* was sent into range to take on the batteries at Hamburg once more. The *Texas,* with a pair of destroyers screening her with smoke, opened fire. But the wind quickly dissipated the smoke screen, leaving the *Texas* sitting naked on the calm blue Channel in plain view of Hamburg.

The 280-millimeter guns in the German strongpoint roared and belched smoke as they sent round after round toward the hapless *Texas.* One shell struck the conning tower and crashed into the pilot house. There was a tremendous explosion, which destroyed the bridge, killing one man and wounding eleven.

Captain C. A. Baker, skipper of the *Texas,* was hurled violently to the deck. Dazed but not seriously injured, Baker retired for a short period of recuperation and his executive officer took over command temporarily. The battleship continued to fire at its tormentor on the shore.

Perseverance was rewarded when a shell from the *Texas'* 14-inch guns crashed into Hamburg, knocking out one of the 280-millimeter guns. But the other three kept blasting away at the American battleship.

At midafternoon, a navy spotter on the hill overlooking Hamburg radioed the *Arkansas* offshore: "Hamburg a mass of rubble."

Overhead, an American pilot in a spotter plane heard the report and interjected: "Maybe so, but the mass of rubble is still shooting like hell."

As if to prove the pilot's point, the *Texas* wandered back into range of Hamburg and was greeted by a violent burst of firing from the casemated strongpoint. During a lull, an officer on the *Texas* returned to his cabin. Walking through the doorway, he was dumbfounded to see, nestled against his bunk, one of Hamburg's calling cards—a 280-millimeter dud. Personnel on board had been so busily engaged dueling the enemy batteries that no one had been aware of the huge shell striking the *Texas.*

As Task Force 129, battered but all ships afloat, entered Portland harbor that night, Captain Clarke on the HMS *Glasgow* radioed Admiral Deyo: "Hope to have the honor of holding the captains' conference on board this ship."

Deyo and other task force commanders accepted the invitation. At 9 P.M., with the shadows of night starting to creep, the American admiral and others boarded the *Glasgow,* weary, but definitely quite thirsty. There, in Captain Clark's cabin, the day's heavy dueling was ardently discussed as the commanders' parched throats were soothed by appropriate liquid from His Majesty's stores.

The captain's quarters proved to be a most suitable site for the impromptu "conference." It had been riddled by shell fragments from Hamburg.

19

"We've Nabbed the Head Kraut!"

D uring the night, with American soldiers on top of old Fort du Roule taking in the fascinating pyrotechnics unfolding in the bowl down below, the Germans worked feverishly to destroy remaining port installations. Fort des Flamands, badly damaged that day by Admiral Mort Deyo's gunboats offshore, went up in flames, followed by the Amcot aircraft works, and buildings around the already demolished Gare Maritime, which had contained the electrical control system and heating plant for the port.

Enormous blasts rocked the hills around Cherbourg as piers and jetties were wrecked by 35 tons of dynamite. The city's famous stone tower was blown into fine pieces and toppled into the harbor basin where it joined 20,000 cubic yards of masonry already dumped where, in peacetime, ocean liners docked.

General von Schlieben anguished at length before giving the order to blow up the ancient tower. His decision was based on military considerations: the huge amount of masonry it represented would add to the invaders' difficulties in clearing the harbor. With one tremendous blast, Cherbourg's centuries-old landmark disappeared in the night.

Unseen in the darkness, the harbor was strewn with a wide variety of mines. All basins in the port were blocked with sunken ships. Quay walls were severely damaged by large charges of TNT. The breakwater for the inner harbor was cratered so that the waters from the Channel poured through. The entire port looked as though some huge force had wreaked vengeance—bending, breaking, smashing, destroying.

As dusk had started to enfold embattled Cherbourg the evening of June

25, General von Schlieben could hear other types of blasts. American engineers armed with TNT charges were blowing up bunkers less than 100 yards from the entrance to the Cherbourg commander's underground headquarters. The general issued orders for all secret papers to be destroyed. An aide to the commander sent out a final message by radio: "Last phase of fighting begun. General von Schlieben fighting side by side with his men."

An hour later a short reply was received from General Friedrich Dollmann, commander of Seventh Army at Le Mans: "We are with you."

Resigned to his fate as a dead or captured fortress commander, von Schlieben tossed the signal aside and smiled wryly. "This whole ridiculous nightmare is being played out to the bitter end!" he was thinking.

Outside von Schlieben's office, crammed in the maze of tunnels and chambers of the underground complex, were hundreds of gaunt, exhausted *Feldgrau,* stragglers who had made their way to the relative security of the subterranean headquarters. Hollow-eyed, bearded, uniforms torn and often blood-caked, they sprawled about. Those who were not sleeping were staring into space with the haunted look of those who had just escaped death.

Trying to force a passage through the tangle of arms, legs and bodies, junior officers and sergeants were lugging boxes of ammunition to the entrances where, with the arrival of dawn and the certain assault by American tanks and infantry, they would take up positions to carry out Adolf Hitler's order to Fortress Cherbourg: "Fight to the last cartridge!"

Unseen by Karl von Schlieben and others in the underground complex, American units all around the outskirts of Cherbourg were reorganized during the night in order to launch the attack in the morning which would overrun the entire city. The curtain was about to go up on the final act of the melodrama at Cherbourg.

Off toward the east, the dark sky, illuminated periodically during the night by flames shooting upward from German demolition blasts, now began to show patches of gray as another summer dawn arrived over the tortured Cotentin Peninsula. High above the dying city, in the top level of old Fort du Roule, Colonel Warren Robinson was walking about, contemplating his next move.

It was quiet in the hollow, musty confines of the thick-walled fortification. In the midst of its shambles wandered grimy, rain-soaked infantrymen of the 79th Division's 314th Infantry who had taken the top level the previous day in a bloody assault. Their eyes were red-rimmed, their bodies leaden from fatigue and constant fighting. Robinson, their commander, looked just like one of them. Because of snipers the colonel had removed his insignia of rank.

"This is the goddamnedest situation you ever saw," Colonel Robinson was telling a visiting officer. "We captured this fort yesterday and took one hundred and six prisoners. On the approach we had taken about four hundred and fifty," he related in a puzzled tone. "Then this morning when we were searching through the tunnels we nabbed one hundred and fifty more Krauts. We spent several hours in the night sleeping here with all those armed Heinies practically right beside us."

Colonel Robinson paused briefly, then continued: "A Kraut captain was flushed out of one of the rooms and said that was all the Germans. When I ordered a bazooka shot into his cavern he had a change of heart and said that he would bring the others out. We thought that cleaned up the works, but damned if some more of those Nazis didn't start firing their big guns from way down the cliff below us."

As there were sheer cliffs on all three sides, and Germans on the lower levels were blasting away with 88-millimeter guns at Americans down below in Cherbourg, Colonel Robinson pondered how his men could get at the enemy remaining in the fort.

"Let's try dropping hand grenades and dynamite charges over the face of the cliff and down on the Krauts," Colonel Robinson told his men on the top level. A brigadier general from division had arrived and joined Robinson and others in leaning out over the sheer drop and letting loose the explosives. Looking down, they could see the muzzles of 88s sticking out of apertures in the lower levels and the muzzle blast as the guns fired at American targets in the streets of Cherbourg.

As the one-star general and Colonel Robinson were stretched out trying to see the effect of the explosives below them along the cliff face, a violent blast rocked the upper level. One of the TNT charges had exploded prematurely, blowing off the general's and Robinson's helmets and knocking them to the ground. At the same moment, a sniper down below had leaned out of an aperture and fired at the two officers, the bullet coming so close that it punctured the brigadier's ear drum.

Next four sergeants were sent scrambling down the face of the cliff hanging onto dangling ropes and carrying explosives. With other ropes, they lowered the charges to the openings where the 88s were being fired and scrambled back to the top. The TNT was detonated and exploded with a mighty roar. The guns fell silent.

"We got the bastards!" a soldier observed jubilantly. Minutes later the 88 muzzles could be seen from above poking out of the apertures and several rounds were fired at 4th and 79th Division infantry and tanks in streets far below.

As Colonel Robinson pondered his next move, pacing about the upper level, he spotted what appeared to be fresh concrete in one wall, indicating, he thought, that the Germans had sealed themselves in the lower levels after it became obvious the previous day that the Americans were about to seize the upper part of Fort du Roule. The colonel decided to blast open the new cement in the hope that it would lead his men into a passage where they could get at the Germans in the lower levels.

Two bazooka men, Private Robert Dalzier and Private Edward J. Campbell, drew the job. They entered a narrow room inside the reinforced concrete tunnel and set to work.

"They're going to kill themselves," Captain William Hopper whispered to one of his men. Hooper, who had led one of the two assault companies which had taken the fort's top level the previous day, was in a nearby chamber.

There was a sharp blast from the tunnel; the bazooka team had fired a rocket into the freshly installed cement. Smoke poured out of the narrow confines in which the bazooka men were operating. Captain Hooper dashed through the smoke into the tunnel and returned moments later. He merely nodded his head—Dalzier and Campbell were all right.

More sharp blasts rang out from the tunnel. Then Dalzier and Campbell emerged, their hands stained with gray powder from the bazooka discharges. As comrades crowded around, Dalzier spoke with effort. He was nearly exhausted from lack of sleep.

"We shot rockets through two brick walls, a concrete wall, and a steel wall," he related in a low monotone. "Then we hit the sardines."

Sardines? The others stared at him in puzzlement.

"Yeah, sardines," he resumed. "We shot our way into a Kraut storeroom packed with sardines."

Colonel Robinson shook his head wearily from side to side. He knew those guns down below had to be silenced. "Get some more explosives up here!" he called out "We might as well turn our TDs (tank destroyers) down below loose and see what they can do with them."

Then for 17 minutes the Americans on the top level endured yet another curious phenomenon. Crouching in the protection of German built pillboxes inside the fort, they listened as the 75-millimeter guns on the TDs down in Cherbourg pounded the German gun positions built into the face of the cliff 100 feet below. Occasionally the aim of the American tankers was faulty and TD shells exploded on the top level, sending whining pieces of shells around the 79th Division men there.

When the TD barrage lifted those on the top level went to the edge of the cliff to peer down the rock edifice. They saw gashes all around the gun apertures. Finally the 88s in the cliff face appeared to have been silenced. As the Americans above started to turn away there came the roar and belch of the 88s banging in defiance, their shells falling in the city.

An effort was made to extract information from prisoners taken on the top level of Fort du Roule which might furnish a clue to a secret passage to get at the Germans down below. The quest was fruitless. In organizing the defense of the fort, the Germans had not let the men in one section of the mammoth complex know anything about the setup in the other sections. The prisoners taken in one part of the fort knew nothing about the defenses in other parts.

Still hoping to root out the Germans holed up halfway down the cliff, Colonel Robinson sent a patrol under Captain Robert Kirkpatrick on a roundabout route back around the fort to the bottom in the belief there was an exit at ground level. Down on the ground, Kirkpatrick located a small railroad spur which led to an entrance at the base of the cliff. The patrol followed the track into a tunnel in the cliff and found an electric elevator. But hopes of getting by this means at the Germans more than 200 feet above were dashed. The elevator had been put out of commission.

The dilemma faced by the Americans on the top level appeared insoluble. They had taken Fort du Roule and its supporting pillboxes, key to Cherbourg's entire system of defense. Yet they were unable to blast their way down into the bowels where Germans, well stocked with food and ammunition, remained defiant.

While Americans high above were trying to blast the stubborn Germans out of the lower levels of Fort du Roule, several men in regulation GI uniforms and steel helmets backed up a jeep and trailer to the lower entrance to the old fortification at the base of the cliff. These men wore arm bands with the letters WC (war correspondent). One of the reporters was Red Knickerbocker, a veteran of World War I who worked for the Chicago *Sun-Times.*

The newsmen hopped out of the jeep, scarcely bothering to look up at explosions along the face of the cliff, and hurried into the entrance. It was as though they were engaged in a precise military drill—and these men indeed were skilled in carrying out missions of this type. They were searching for caches of Wehrmacht booze. "I've got a nose for these things," Knickerbocker had told his pals.

Indeed he had. Inside the entrance the correspondents began hurriedly but methodically searching the premises and soon there was a shout of triumph: "I've found it!" The others dashed to the room and the gleam of victory lighted their eyes: the chamber was stocked from floor to ceiling with spirits of many kinds.

Knickerbocker and his comrades hurriedly began tossing cases of wine, cognac, schnapps, and vodka into the trailer and jeep. "Load it up good, fellows!" the veteran Chicago reporter called out. "It might be a long war."

The task completed, the newsmen jumped into the jeep and sped triumphantly away. They considered the mission "journalistic research." "Who knows," one observed, "our editors might some day call on us to do a piece on German booze supplies."

As elements of the 9th, 79th, and 4th Infantry Divisions pushed through the streets of Cherbourg on June 26, von Schlieben's cornered defenders continued to resist tenaciously at many points. Eighteen-year-old youths of the Labor Service, hurriedly handed guns and formed into small combat groups, stood and fought to the end. They fired *Panzerfausts* (bazookas) at American tanks and Schmeisser machine pistols at advancing infantry until their ammunition ran out. Some then fought the attackers with spades. But with no further means to resist, most came out with their hands in the air, convinced that they had carried out the Führer's orders to fight to the last cartridge.

Veteran Wehrmacht combat groups, decimated, exhausted, scattered, were steadily chewed up as they fought stubbornly from pillboxes. Colonel Kohn's 739th Grenadier Regiment, Lieutenant Colonel Rohrbach's 729th Regiment, Lieutenant Colonel Kiel's 919th Grenadier Regiment, and Colonel Müller's men of the 922nd Grenadiers had to yield ground steadily. Yard by yard, General Collins' foot soldiers and tankers were crushing the defenses in Cherbourg.

In the underground hospital which was a component of General von Schlieben's headquarters in Octeville, three hundred and fifty seriously wounded members of the Wehrmacht had been jammed into a ward designed to hold fifty. Low moans and groans sifted over the chamber. Occasionally a sharp scream pierced the ward. The stench was overpowering—sweat, urine, feces, festered wounds, stale air. A few of the wounded were on cots, others on the concrete floor, and still more were seated and propped against the wall. Some were murmmuring over and over, "*Mutter! Mutter!*" (Mother. Mother.)

An aide to von Schlieben stuck his head into the ward, flinching involuntarily when the stench blasted him in the face. "How are things?" he inquired of a pretty German nurse, her once immaculate uniform splattered with blood.

She shrugged her shoulders resignedly. "They're dying off like flies."

In the northwest portion of Cherbourg, patients at the large Naval hospital heard a rattle of gunfire outside and moments later shouts in English echoed loudly somewhere in the facility. Elements of Matt Eddy's 9th Infantry Division had burst into the hospital where they took charge of twelve hundred wounded Germans and liberated one hundred and fifty American patients.

Lightning Joe Collins's men had been fighting inside Cherbourg for 26 hours, and the old Maginot-type forts of the city's perimeter, begun by Vauban in the 17th Century, improved by Napoleon in 1808, and perfected by the Todt Organization in the early 1940s, still blazed with resistance. The beleaguered Germans were fighting from machine-gun nests, rooftop strongpoints, cellars, and windows.

As clouds of smoke rolled over Cherbourg, General Eddy, commander of the 9th Division, and Colonel Flint, the up-front leader of the 39th Regiment, were standing on a hillside near Octeville, on the southwest approaches to the port. Eddy and Flint were peering over the barrel of a machine gun which was sending tracers across a large quarry. Following the line of fire they could see the mouth of a tunnel. A number of American tank-destroyers had clanked around to the rear and sent several rounds from their 75s into the rear entrances.

Minutes later a loud voice called out in German from the front entrance of the tunnel, "Cease firing! Cease firing!" After much difficulty, General Eddy and Colonel Flint managed to get the assaulting battalion to be quiet.

Eddy then turned to a German-speaking soldier: "Tell the bastards we'll give them two minutes to come out." The American shouted out the command.

Almost instantaneously, a German soldier carrying what General Eddy thought was the largest white flag he had ever seen emerged from the tunnel. He turned right and dipped the flag, turned left and dipped the flag, faced in the direction of Matt Eddy and Paddy Flint and dipped the flag.

Despite their ugly mood from the heavy losses suffered in the bitter street fighting, the American foot soldiers taking all this in could hardly restrain themselves from snickering at the formal display of precision surrendering.

One hard-bitten, bearded GI called out with a straight face to his comrades: "Somebody tell that Kraut bastard to act sloppier. Our goddamned officers might start getting ideas!"

Hard on the heels of the flag-carrying German a lieutenant, ramrod straight and walking stiffly, emerged. He asked to see "the ranking officer present" and was directed to General Eddy. As the 9th Division commander eyed the German stonily, the emissary presented the compliments of Lieutenant General Karl Wilhelm Dietrich von Schlieben, commander of Fortress Cherbourg, and of Vice Admiral Walther Hennecke, naval commander in the port, and asked that an officer be sent to the tunnel to conduct them out to surrender.

In the meantime, the tank-destroyers' shells had created so much thick dust and choking fumes in the tunnel that the Germans inside, knowing that a surrender was taking place, stampeded out of the pit and nearly trampled von Schlieben and Hennecke who were emerging at the same time.

Von Schlieben, a black helmet clamped on his head and the Iron Cross earned in Russia at his throat, was a beaten man. His flabby, worried face was a tired gray. His gray-green greatcoat was wrinkled and splotched with mud and dusted with powdered masonry. The starch had gone out of both the soldier and his clothes.

Spotting the formidable figure of General von Schlieben, an astonished GI nearby called out in jubilation: "Goddamn, we've nabbed the head Kraut!"

Brusque Admiral Hennecke looked haughtily down his hawk's nose. His morale had sky-rocketed only hours before when Hitler awarded him the Knight's Cross to the Iron Cross. Hennecke "performed a feat unique in the history of coastal defense," read the radioed citation. "He carried out an exemplary destruction of the port of Cherbourg."

Von Schlieben, who had sent out Hitler's orders to fight to the last cartridge and the last man, surrendered although his underground headquarters contained large stores of ammunition. Altogether 842 Germans poured out of the tunnel. They were not a cohesive fighting force, but rather a beaten, exhausted ragtag assortment of grenadiers, elderly navy headquarters ratings, Luftwaffe staff members, Labor Service troops, and medics.

General von Schlieben promptly informed his captors that he was surrendering only himself and those in the tunnel. He refused to order other strongpoints in Fortress Cherbourg to give up. General Eddy drove his two high-ranking prisoners to his headquarters and served them his best brandy. By radio he notified VII Corps headquarters of the capture of the two German commanders. Collins was on top of embattled Fort du Roule, where a determined enemy force was still holed up and defiant in the lower two levels, when a radio message reached him that Eddy was sending von Schlieben and Hennecke back to VII Corps. An elated Collins hurried back to his CP at the Chateau de Servigny, at Yvetot Bocage, near Valognes.

Meanwhile, General Eddy was trying to engage his two important captives in small talk. Von Schlieben was taciturn and sullen. Hennecke, buoyed by the decoration from the Führer, joined eagerly in the conversation.

Members of the press, notified that the Cherbourg commanders were at Eddy's headquarters, descended on the CP. Robert Capa, a photographer for *Life* magazine, prepared to snap the austere von Schlieben's picture. "*Nein!*" he called out, holding his hand in front of his face. He said he was tired of being photographed.

Capa, who had lived in Austria and fled the takeover of that small nation by Hitler, responded tartly: "And *I* am tired of photographing captured German generals!"

With all the pomp and deference due their rank, von Schlieben and Hennecke were escorted back in a command car to VII Corps headquarters where General Collins was awaiting their arrival. Amid formality as stiff as an inspection on the fields of West Point, a grim-faced Collins and a sullen von Schlieben saluted each other. The American general, with blue eyes and a bulldog chin, stood in dress shirt and tie to receive the helmeted German general.

Through an interpreter, Collins asked von Schlieben to surrender the entire Cherbourg garrison. The answer was a quick, emphatic "*Nein!*"

Collins asked, "From a moral point of view, General von Schlieben, how can you surrender personally while your troops still are fighting a hopeless battle?"

The German pondered the question thoughtfully, then replied slowly that it had been his experience in Russia that determined groups of soldiers could hold out and cause much damage and delay. For that reason, he said, he would not ask his troops to surrender.

Joe Collins set his long jaw, stiffly dismissed his two high-level captives. He permitted them to wash up, then sent them under armed guard back up to the next notch of command—General Omar Bradley at First Army.

Collins promptly ordered loudspeakers to be set up in Cherbourg and German soldiers learned that their commander had saved his own skin but allowed them to continue to fight and die. Many would.

As General von Schlieben and Admiral Hennecke were on the way to First Army headquarters, a spirited debate broke out among Bradley's aides. A few of them had suggested that General Bradley invite von Schlieben to be his guest at supper. Others vehemently opposed the idea. Bradley, in typical fashion, listened to the arguments, then made his decision: "If the bastard had surrendered four days ago I'd have asked him. But now that he has cost us a pile of human lives—hell no!"

En route to First Army headquarters behind Omaha Beach, General von Schlieben had to endure further indignity. A trunk carrying his uniforms and decorations fell off his truck and flew open on striking the road, scattering his personal belongings. Before an aide could retrieve them, eagle-eyed American soldiers along the road pounced on the uniforms and decorations and in seconds Von Schlieben's belongings had been whisked away.

The full impact of the disaster which had befallen General von Schlieben's force at Fortress Cherbourg was driven home to him as he rolled along the Cherbourg-to-Paris highway. The road was lined with marching columns of German prisoners. At one point he passed some five hundred of his bedraggled men, now so thoroughly whipped that they were guarded by only two grimy, mud-splattered Americans with rifles who looked every inch as exhausted as their prisoners.

In Cherbourg itself, where Lightning Joe Collins' men were methodically edging ahead from house to house and street to street, rooting out stubborn German pockets with rifles, bayonets, grenades, and flame-throwers, enormous explosions began to periodically rock the city. Some 18 miles to the west, carefully concealed among the rolling ridges of the Cap de la Hague, German long-barreled 280-millimeter railroad guns were sending huge shells screaming into the city.

That evening, with Americans and Germans still fighting and dying in the streets and among the pillboxes, the London *Times* headline reported:

MONTGOMERY'S TROOPS CAPTURE CHERBOURG

At Cherbourg's heavily fortified city hall, where tunnels radiated to other German strongpoints, the 2nd Battalion of Colonel Paddy Flint's 39th Infantry laid siege. The building was raked with automatic-weapons fire and the three-inch guns of tank destroyers. Then Lieutenant Colonel Frank Gunn, battalion commander, demanded surrender of the force defending the city hall. Preceded by a German carrying a large white flag, the colonel in command and four hundred of his men trouped out with hands in the air.

In the meantime, about two miles away as the crow flies, Colonel Warren Robinson of the 79th Division had spent the day on the upper level of battered Fort du Roule, still trying to find a way to blast the Germans out of the two lower levels. The enemy 88s continued to menace Americans in the streets of Cherbourg.

An engineer outfit was ordered to bring portable jackhammers to the fort and holes were laboriously hacked out in the floors. TNT charges widened the holes, and then 15-pound dynamite charges were dropped through the openings. The blasts in the lower confines shook the sturdy structure, and screams were heard echoing through the corridors down below. Soon cries of "*Kamerad!*" were heard, and the entire force in the bowels of Fort du Roule, some four hundred men, surrendered.

That night in far-off Berchtesgaden, Adolf Hitler was livid. He had just learned of von Schlieben's surrender to the Americans. "A disgrace to his uniform and the lowest form of German general!" the Führer shouted.

At Army Group B headquarters at La Roche-Guyon that night, Field Marshal Erwin Rommel and his staff dined in almost total silence. The debacle of Cherbourg, about which Rommel had constantly warned the Führer, was coming to an end. After the meal, the Army Group commander and his naval aide and confidant, Admiral Friedrich Ruge, strolled on the grassy, forested heights overlooking the peacefully flowing Seine.

Erwin Rommel on this beautiful summer evening was nearly choking from emotion—sorrow for his *Feldgrau* who were being slaughtered in Normandy, bitter anger that those at the top around Hitler were endeavoring mightily to place the blame squarely on Rommel's soldiers for the Normandy disaster, and anguish that he could not do more to rid his beloved Germany of the man he was convinced was determined to bring the Third Reich crashing down in utter ruins—Adolf Hitler.

Dejected and seeing no clear-cut means for ridding Germany of the Führer and gaining a separate peace with the United States and Great Britain, Rommel wondered if the best way out for a commander who had just suffered a disaster at Cherbourg would be "to shoot yourself."

Rommel promptly rejected the thought—it was too negative.

20

Death Throes
of a Citadel

As the commander of Fortress Cherbourg, General Karl von Schlieben, brooded in a comfortable farmhouse near Omaha Beach where he was being held under guard, the port's assistant commander, Major General Robert Sattler, was agonizing over his course of action. Sattler and 400 assorted German military men were barricaded behind the thick walls of the *Port Militaire* (naval arsenal) on the western edge of Cherbourg's inner harbor as dawn broke over the Cotentin on June 27.

Sattler was aware that von Schlieben had surrendered the previous afternoon, a fact he could hardly have avoided knowing. The night before and earlier that morning American loudspeakers had been calling on the defenders of Port Militaire to follow the example of their leader. "Why die for a hopeless cause?" the amplifiers blared out repeatedly.

To reinforce the surrender pleas over loudspeakers, hundreds of photographs of von Schlieben giving up to the 9th Division's General Eddy were dropped by airplane over the arsenal.

General Sattler's conflict was between his conscience and his military obligations. Adolf Hitler, the commander in chief, had ordered each strongpoint in Cherbourg held until the last cartridge and the last man. Yet, Sattler reflected, was there any military advantage to be gained by permitting his four hundred men to be systematically slaughtered by overwhelming power?

There was no doubt in Sattler's mind that he could extract a bloody price before the Port Militaire and its garrison was destroyed, as inevitably it must be. The arsenal was a fortress within a fortress, some 1,300 yards square, with thick, reinforced concrete walls surrounded by a deep moat. On its parapets was a bristling display of firepower—antitank, antiaircraft, and machine guns. Artillery was mounted to cover land as well as sea approaches. Food and ammunition were plentiful, enough to withstand a long siege.

At 7:30 A.M. Colonel George Smythe, commander of the 47th Infantry Regiment of the 9th Division, had all three of his battalions ready to jump off to assault the formidable bastion. Smythe and everyone else in the impending attack knew that taking Port Militaire would be a bloody affair.

Intent on probing the enemy's determination to fight, Colonel Smythe at 8 A.M. sent a platoon against the arsenal. Halfway to the bastion, the patrol was raked by machine-gun fire and returned to its lines. Smythe radioed his battalion commanders: "Prepare to attack."

Minutes after the order was given, Germans were observed walking on the arsenal wall, unarmed and carrying white flags. General Sattler, with an aide holding a white piece of material aloft, emerged from the arsenal, and Colonel Smythe went out to meet him. The German commander was taken to General Matt Eddy who had come forward to view the assault on Port Militaire.

"I refuse to accept your surrender until you inform me precisely of the location of mines and booby traps outside and inside the arsenal," the 9th Division commander sternly warned General Sattler.

Sattler balked. "Very well," Eddy replied, "I'll turn our artillery, tank destroyer guns, and mortars onto the arsenal."

The German pondered this threat, then relented. "I give you my word as a German officer that there are no mines or booby traps in or around the arsenal."

"If that bastard knows what's good for him, there goddamned well better not be any!" a bearded infantry officer who would have to enter the arsenal muttered.

On the basis of General Sattler's word, Eddy accepted the surrender, and nearly 400 Wehrmacht members streamed out of Port Militaire and into captivity. They were nearly trampled by a surging mass of tattered, disheveled men and women, slave laborers from Eastern Europe, who had been held in a building inside the walls.

Meanwhile, along the battered Cherbourg docks near the arsenal, Captain Hans Witt was determined to continue the fight. He supervised the demolition of a few remaining facilities, then ordered eight officers and thirty men to climb aboard a small boat and two dinghies. With Americans on all sides, the tiny flotilla headed across a basin to Fort West on the outer mole.

Fort West was a crucial site, Captain Witt knew. There was located the firing panel for the extensive minefields blocking entrance to the western harbor. Witt could, with one finger, blow up any Allied ship which tried to enter Cherbourg harbor.

Belatedly detecting the German captain and his little force holed up in the concrete strongpoint on the mole in the harbor, American commanders began pounding it with artillery, direct fire from tank destroyers, and mortars. Dive bombers were called in and one by one they swooped down to drop lethal cargoes onto the casemated fort. But Captain Witt, with one finger literally on the firing panel, refused to surrender.

Only a short distance from where the tenacious German captain and his *Feldgrau* were angrily defying the enormous power bent on destroying them, pretty young French women, freshly scrubbed and with their Sunday finest on, were strolling arm in arm with their liberators, grimy, mud-splotched, bearded American fighting men. Other citizens casually strolled the streets. From the windows hung the red, white and blue of American, French, or British flags.

Cherbourg's outer perimeter of houses and shops bore scars from American shells directed at German strongpoints, but the center of the city was relatively untouched, due mainly to the speed with which American foot sloggers and tankers rooted out the enemy in street fighting.

At 4 P.M. the sun-dappled Place de la Republique began filling with French men and women, Cherbourgeois who had weathered the man-made storm of steel and explosives or who had returned to the city. The windows in the buildings around the square were filled with the olive drab or green fatigue uniforms of the conquering soldiers and with the gayer colors of French women's dresses. Together with the masses crammed into the square, they had come to witness one of the most significant ceremonies of their lives.

At one end of the square, surrounded by rolls of barbed wire put there by the Germans, was a statue of Napoleon on a horse. Symbolically, it appeared to many, one of the emperor's bronze hands was pointing toward England—the direction from which the invading Allies had recently come.

Massed on the steps of the *Hôtel de Ville* (city hall) were the commanding generals of the five American divisions which had taken part in the campaign to seize Cherbourg: General Ridgway of the 82nd Airborne,

General Taylor of the 101st Airborne, General Eddy of the 9th, General Wyche of the 79th, and General Barton of the 4th.

In front of the commanders stood one company of American fighting men, many freshly shaven and wearing clean uniforms for the occasion. They represented selected combat men from the divisions which had made the final four-day assault on Fortress Cherbourg. Before them, fluttering majestically in the light breeze, were the American flag and the blue and white flag of VII Corps.

Suddenly there was a murmur from the crowd and all eyes turned toward the side of the square where Napoleon serenely surveyed the scene. An armored scout car drove into the square and General J. Lawton Collins, the most recent captor of Cherbourg, hopped briskly out of the vehicle. The band struck up "The General's March" as Collins took his place before his commanders on the city hall steps.

It was time for the ceremony to begin. Lightning Joe Collins was about to formally turn the city over to its elected city officials. A black-coated Frenchman with a drooping white mustache, Eugene Simon, introduced Mayor Paul Reynaud, the venerable, long-time mayor of Cherbourg. Choking with emotion, tears glistening in his eyes, Reynaud expressed the deep gratitude of his townspeople at being freed from four years of Nazi control.

As Reynaud was speaking, a loud explosion was heard in the direction of the western suburbs. The Germans, as if to remind all that bloody fighting lay ahead, had fired in a salvo of shells from a mammoth railroad gun more than 15 miles to the west.

A murmur ran through the crowd, but Reynaud continued his short talk as though nothing had occurred. Off in the distance to the east could be heard the periodic muted chatter of machine guns—Barton's 4th Division fighting men were still digging out entrenched and fiercely resisting Germans.

Head bare, General Collins spoke in passable West Point French: "I thank you warmly for the joyous manner in which you have received us American soldiers." Later he said, "We Americans are proud to return to our sister republic the first major city to be liberated by the Allies."

Collins handed the mayor a French tricolor flag made from the silk of parachutes used by the 82nd and 101st Airborne Divisions in the drop onto the Cotentin a few minutes after midnight on June 6.

"This flag is particularly fitting in that the first Americans to land in the invasion were paratroopers," Collins stated.

Hundreds of Cherbourgeois wept unashamedly.

240

At the conclusion of the ceremony, Mayor Reynaud invited the American generals inside the *Hôtel de Ville* for a glass of champagne. Turning to General Collins, Reynaud said feelingly, "I assure you, my friend, I never offered the Nazis champagne."

On the way in, General Billy Wyche edged up to his old friend and present corps commander. "Joe," he said, "I didn't know you spoke French. I could understand every word you said!"

"That's bad news, Billy," Collins replied with a straight face, "because if the Americans could understand me, the Frenchmen could not."

High on the cliff overlooking Cherbourg, 79th Division soldiers and engineers were still trying to solve the mysteries of the intricate system of underground tunnels in old Fort du Roule. Vast quantities of stores of all kinds, worth millions of dollars, were found in the subterranean chambers: food, ammunition, whisky, cognac, and wine. If necessary, the German defenders of Fort du Roule had planned to fight it out there all winter.

Although more than one hundred prisoners had been taken in the top level and some 400 finally flushed out of the bowels of the cavernous structure, Americans thought more of the enemy might be concealed inside.

Meanwhile that day, some American soldiers in Cherbourg, with the enthusiastic help of citizens, were searching for Gestapo agents who had been trapped in the town. The Gestapo chief in Cherbourg had fled soon after the D-Day landings, but his underlings hung on and their headquarters not far from the *Hôtel de Ville* was one of the last strongpoints taken by the invaders.

When the Americans had stormed their pillbox the Gestapo agents fled through a tunnel to the city hall which had another bunker outside. There the Gestapo men hid but were discovered and captured. Much to the relief of the German agents, who thought they would be turned over to a vengeful French citizenry, they were held in custody by American military police.

That evening Omar Bradley put in a call to the supreme commander. "Ike, we've captured a few trainloads of Wehrmacht booze in Cherbourg," the First Army commander said. "I've ordered it put under lock and key until we can distribute it to the troops."

"I think that's a good idea, Brad," General Eisenhower responded.

In the farmhouse near Omaha Beach where he was being held, the recently deposed commander of Fortress Cherbourg was complaining bitterly to those guarding him. He declared he was not being accorded the perquisites of his rank. Von Schlieben was particularly unhappy about being served K-rations for breakfast, the same meal thousands of officers and men of the American First Army were eating. He also protested the fact that there was no shower for his use in the farmhouse.

Meanwhile, elements of the 4th Infantry Division were engaged in a bitter fight for Maupertus airfield east of Cherbourg. The attack had started the previous day with three battalions abreast and a troop of cavalry on each flank. The fighting went on through the day and into the night before the last German was killed or surrendered and the airfield occupied.

Colonel Robert Foster's 22nd Infantry Regiment then pivoted north and speedily overran *Batterie Hamburg,* the naval coastal fortification which two days previously had engaged in the spirited duel with Admiral Mort Deyo's warships. Battered by continual shelling from sea and land, Hamburg's garrison was demoralized by the fall of Cherbourg and the surrender of von Schlieben—990 *Kriegsmarine* became American prisoners of war.

With the downfall of Hamburg, major organized resistance northeast of Cherbourg collapsed. Patrols were sent east to the tip of the peninsula at Barfleur, where the Germans had mysteriously left burning all night one of the world's most powerful searchlights as massive Allied convoys were streaming across the Channel three weeks before to assault Normandy. The Barfleur area was found to be unoccupied.

Although General Joe Collins and Cherbourg Mayor Paul Reynaud were exchanging toasts on the liberation of the city on the evening of June 27, several German forts on the *digue,* the outer breakwater, were holding out defiantly and periodically firing at American troops with their 88s.

As the sun sank behind the western horizon and a mixture of haze and smoke rolled over embattled Cherbourg, an American PT boat, skippered by Lieutenant Commander John D. Bulkeley, was racing across the calm blue water toward the line of concrete strongpoints along the *digue.* Alongside was another of the swift torpedo craft, while some five miles offshore four other PT boats waited in reserve.

Darting and twisting, the oncoming pair of PT boats charged to within 100 yards of the *digue,* then opened up with withering bursts of machine-gun fire against the concrete structures. Secure behind thick walls, the Germans returned the fire with 88-millimeter rounds at point-blank range. For thirty-five minutes the PT boats zigzagged at high speed back and forth in front of the forts, raking the strongpoints with their automatic weapons as shells from the 88s hissed into the water around them.

One of the deluge of enemy missiles exploded next to the PT boat accompanying Bulkeley, and for nearly 10 frightening minutes the crew made emergency repairs as the craft lay dead in the water virtually under the noses of German gunners in the *digue* forts. Bulkeley's boat began racing in a circle around the disabled craft, concealing the lame PT boat with smoke.

Sensing the kill of two valuable PT boats, gunners in all the breakwater forts aimed at the craft. Collective sighs of relief were almost audible on the two American vessels as the motor on the damaged PT boat began to sputter and cough, finally breaking out in a full-throated roar. "Let's haul ass!" an officer called out over the communications network, and the pair of PT boats, firing a few defiant rounds, sped away from under the muzzles of the 88s. Enemy shells plunged into the water around them until the speedy craft were far out in the Channel.

Seven miles east of the *digue,* German Major Friedrich Küppers was in his command post in a bunker inside powerful Fort *Osteck,* a complex of deep underground fortifications, tank traps, thick mine fields, deep trenches, heavy strands of barbed wire and mortars and flamethrowers which could be touched off electronically by the press of a button. Only the day before Major Küppers had received a startling message from his artillery commander in Cherbourg: "We're giving up. Can do no more. All the best."

That was all. No order for *Osteck* to surrender nor to keep fighting. Obviously that decision was to be left up to Küppers. He chose to fight.

Osteck's powerful guns and diabolical fortifications could cost the Americans much blood. But the fort was now isolated and its garrison was a hodgepodge collection of officers and men who had made their way to its confines after their positions or gun batteries had been smashed or overrun. Major Küppers, an energetic and determined junior commander, immediately organized his garrison into infantry units.

Now, on June 27, Major Küppers was standing in his bunker with one eye glued to a periscope through which he was methodically inspecting the surrounding terrain. He could see swarms of American infantry, backed by tanks, edging toward him on three sides. Küppers knew these had to be members of the U.S. 4th Infantry Division—he had been fighting against this outfit from the first minutes of the D-Day assault at Utah Beach.

The German commander saw through the periscope that a white flag had been hoisted over one of the southern outposts of *Osteck,* one manned by elderly supply soldiers who had suddenly found themselves front-line infantrymen. Küppers, furious, barked out orders over his communications system to one of his 88-millimeter batteries: "Shoot that damned white flag down!" The guns opened up and within a few rounds shot the sign of capitulation off its staff.

Infantry of Tubby Barton's 4th Division had now closed in on the well-camouflaged ramparts of *Osteck*, unknowingly passing through a thick German mine field. Not a single mine exploded—someone had failed to attach the detonators. Sherman tanks, after sustaining losses from the direct fire of 88s in *Osteck*, had worked their way across ingenious tank traps and joined the infantry in front and on top of Küppers' grass-camouflaged underground CP bunker.

Major Küppers ordered other batteries in the complex to fire on his own position, as the Americans were out in the open and he and his men were shielded under several feet of concrete. Soon German salvos were screaming into the ranks of the attackers and the advance was brought to a halt.

For the balance of the afternoon and on into evening, a bitter struggle for *Osteck* raged. Barton's 4th Division dogfaces, backed by engineers exploding demolition charges to blast out the stubborn enemy and by tank gunfire, and Küppers' hodgepodge collection entrenched behind thick concrete, their positions camouflaged by grass, fought it out.

At 10 P.M. Major Küppers received an alarming report: *Osteck* had run out of shells.

Silence fell over the fort. In a captured underground chamber, an American officer rang a field telephone and was startled to hear it answered at Major Küppers' command post. "We demand your immediate surrender," the American told Küppers. "Your position is hopeless. If you don't surrender, at dawn our planes and heavy artillery will blow you all to hell!"

Küppers banged the telephone down without reply. Outside he detected the blare of loudspeakers: the Americans had set up amplifiers and were reminding *Osteck* that the commander of Fortress Cherbourg had already surrendered. "Why should you die for a hopeless cause while your general is comfortable and safe?" a voice in German called out.

Major Küppers, knowing he was out of artillery shells and that his situation was indeed hopeless, solemnly consulted his key officers in the underground fort. A decision was made: wait and see what the morning would bring—perhaps a miracle of some sort.

The balance of the night passed quietly. American attackers and German defenders were at a standoff.

At about 8:15 A.M. General Barton of the 4th Division, a driver, and an aide were jeeping toward the main entrance to underground *Osteck*.

244

Waving in the breeze at the front of the vehicle was a large white flag. Barton had come to personally demand the surrender of the besieged fortification.

Major Küppers came out to meet his opponent. Curiously, a friendly conversation developed between the foes and Barton reminisced at length on his World War I experiences as a young officer in occupied Germany near Küppers' home town of Wiesbaden. Finally General Barton's aide tapped him on the shoulder and reminded him that time was running out. A powerful American attack to smash *Osteck* from the land, sea, and air was ready to be launched.

Promptly leaving his fond memories of post-World War I Germany behind, General Barton solemnly reminded Major Küppers of the hopelessness of his situation. "Your troops have fought with great skill and courage all the way from the beaches," the American commander said. "You are about to be hit from all sides and the air, so why resist further?"

Barton called for his combat map and spread it out on the ground. Drawn in were the positions of strong American units poised on three sides of *Osteck*. "I would remind you that you will also be struck heavily from the sea and air," the general observed.

A solemn Major Küppers asked to look at the map. What he saw astounded him. Shown with absolute accuracy were German strongpoints in the area and the entire elaborate *Osteck* defense network, in greater detail than carried on Küppers' own maps.

"Turn the map over," General Barton suggested, staring intently at the German's face to detect his reaction. On the back Küppers saw a listing of the guns at each strongpoint, their caliber, fields of fire, and amount of ammunition. Also enumerated were the names and ranks of top officers at each defensive position.

Küppers raised his eyes from the map, astonishment in his face. General Barton could not tell his foe that the detailed map was the result of the work of hundreds of French civilians, agents of the underground network Centurie, who had labored for months, often at the cost of their lives, to obtain the bits and pieces of information that resulted in this depiction of German defenses.

For several moments Major Küppers and General Barton stood in silence, staring solemnly at each other. How, Küppers wondered, how could the Americans have conceivably come up with this detailed information, much of which he did not have himself? How? Where did it come from?

Friedrich Küppers' steel will, which had kept him going through three

245

weeks of constant fighting against overwhelming odds, now was totally shattered—not by the deluge of American bombs, shells, and bullets which had rained on him and his men for 21 days and nights, but rather through the enigma of an American military map.

Küppers held a hurried conversation with a few key officers. Each knew further resistance would result only in the German defenders of *Osteck* being wiped out. The major returned to General Barton and the two soberly shook hands. The bitter struggle for the key fortification had ended. Several hundred *Feldgrau,* battered and weary, straggled out of *Osteck* and into prisoner of war compounds.

Meanwhile inside Cherbourg that early morning of June 28, two days after the city had been officially captured, Commander Quentin R. Walsh of the U.S. Coast Guard was going about his mission of reconnoitering a portion of the dock area to determine what steps would be needed to allow Cherbourg to receive vessels. At the head of a force of fifteen sailors who were armed to the teeth with Tommy guns and grenades, Walsh penetrated deep into the confines of the *Port Militaire.*

Suddenly a machine gun opened fire on the naval men, who promptly dived for cover. A German sailor who had volunteered as a guide told Walsh that pockets of die-hard Wehrmacht soldiers, most of them uproariously drunk, were lurking in the arsenal and along the adjoining waterfront. As the American sailors remained under cover, nearby army men wiped out the machine-gun post, after which Commander Walsh and his men continued with the reconnoissance.

During the next hour Walsh's sailors killed several snipers in the arsenal and received the surrender of a German captain and nearly one hundred and eighty of his men who came out with their hands in the air. Four sailors escorted the captives to the rear.

Walsh, Navy Ensign Daniel Laner, and the seven remining sailors were inspecting demolished facilities along the nearby inner harbor when eighty-five more Germans came out of a bunker to surrender. One of the captives told Commander Walsh that some fifty American paratroopers were being held prisoners in Fort du Hamet, a strongpoint along the inner harbor. Guarding the fifty parachutists was a fanatical German force, which, the enemy soldier declared, had vowed it would never capitulate.

Ordering their sailors to remain behind, Walsh and Laner approached within 150 yards of Fort du Hamet carrying a piece of white cloth. There they remained as a German officer emerged from the fort under a white flag and escorted the American officers into the strongpoint. Walsh and

Laner were taken to a room on the second level where the German colonel in command and six of his officers were seated.

The enemy colonel, stiff, cold, and formal, promptly announced that he would never surrender Fort du Hamet and refused to give up his paratrooper prisoners. He bitterly condemned his chief, General von Schlieben, and other officers who had given up.

Walsh, with all the conviction he could muster, told the colonel that he had 800 assault troops outside Fort du Hamet ready, on Walsh's signal, to storm the fortification and wipe out the German force holed up inside. Actually, the "assault troops" available to the Coast Guard commander consisted of seven sailors.

Out of communication with other strongpoints for two days, the colonel fell for the bluff. He surrendered the entire force in Fort du Hamet. The 50 captive paratroopers, members of the 101st Airborne Division who had been dropped near Cherbourg by mistake in the early-morning darkness of D-Day, were free men once again.

It was not until the next day, June 29, that the forts along the outer breakwater, the *digue,* finally gave up after being pounded by artillery for three days and subjected to repeated dive bombings by P-47 Thunderbolts. Captain Witt in Fort West gave in only after a shell pierced the firing panel for the mines in the harbor entrance and after he had been wounded. Fort du Centre, the largest of the strongpoints, surrendered and the others followed this example.

A bit of comedy accompanied the proceedings. American Navy Captain Norman Ives, whose country had the most powerful naval force in the world, was unable to locate a warship. Finally he made the short journey to the *digue* in a tiny sailboat, the only craft he could locate, to accept the German surrender.

At this point, American prisoner of war compounds were running over. Some thirty-nine thousand Wehrmacht personnel had been taken into captivity in and around Cherbourg. But six thousand German troops had managed to pull back into the Cap de la Hague, the finger of land thrusting out into the Channel at the northwest tip of the Cotentin Peninsula.

Leaving the security of Cherbourg in the hands of the 4th Infantry Division, General Joe Collins sent his veteran 9th Division into the Cap de la Hague. The country was open ground and the Germans had studded their commanding positions with gun emplacements and tank barriers as formidable as those in the outer ring of Cherbourg.

Paced by P-47 dive bombers, Matt Eddy's men jumped off on June 29.

The tired infantrymen were promptly greeted with intense fire from mortars and artillery, but pushed steadily ahead and took several hundred prisoners. Lieutenant Colonel Kiel, the tenacious commander whose battle group had been destroyed in the fighting around Cherbourg, had taken command of the mixed bag of German soldiers defending the Cap de la Hague. Kiel was determined to make the Americans pay a heavy price in blood.

Raked by machine-gun fire and pounded by mortars, 88s, and even two railway guns, Matt Eddy's men fought from ridge to ridge. The 9th Division suffered some of its heaviest casualties of the campaign in fighting to seize key towns and road junctions. At 4 A.M. on July 1 Paddy Flint's 39th Infantry Regiment broke into Auderville, overlooking the Channel at the very fingertip of the Cap de la Hague peninsula.

An intense firefight broke out in the early morning darkness, but by 5 A.M. the Germans had finally been crushed. The American battalion commander radioed a laconic message to regiment: "Everything here is giving up."

The final shot had been fired in the 24-day struggle to seize mighty Cherbourg, the port Adolf Hitler had decreed must be held at all costs, to the last man, to the last cartridge. "If we can deny the Anglo-Americans a major port, we can smash the invasion!" the Führer had said repeatedly to his generals.

Now from Auderville eastward past Cherbourg to Barfleur at the northeast tip of the Cotentin and south to Barneville and Utah Beach silence hung like a blanket over the lush green meadows, pulverized provincial towns, and ominous hedgerows where only recently violence, noise, and sudden death had been the norm.

For three and a half weeks, exhausted, mud-splattered, unshaven American fighting men had plodded relentlessly through the *bocage,* across streams, up wooded hillsides, into marshy wastelands, always in the face of determined enemy opposition. When they were too weary to continue, they somehow got to their feet and pushed on. They were raked by tree bursts, hugged the ground as mortar shells crashed around them, endured the anguish of the screams of wounded comrades. There were only two ways out of this nightmare for the combat soldier—a disabling wound or death.

But now, with the capture of Cherbourg and the silencing of all opposition in the northern Cotentin, thousands of Americans looked forward to a long period of rest, relaxation, maybe even clean uniforms. A holiday from the brutalities of war.

The same afternoon that Paddy Flint wiped out the last armed German at Auderville, General Omar Bradley placed a call to General Collins at VII Corps headquarters.

"Joe, the German is building up rapidly at the base of the Cotentin," Bradley observed. "How soon can you turn your corps around and head south?"

Epilogue

When Hitler learned of the fall of Cherbourg and surrounding defenses, he flew into a rage. A scapegoat for the debacle was urgently needed. Field Marshal Rommel would not do; he was a hero in the Fatherland second only to the Führer himself. Field Marshal von Rundstedt would not fit the bill; he had led German legions to too many brilliant victories in previous years. So the accusing finger of Adolf Hitler was pointed at Colonel General Friedrich Dollmann, commander of Seventh Army and responsible for the defense of Normandy and Brittany.

Dollmann was highly regarded by his Wehrmacht peers, but he was not widely known on the home front. The Führer ordered von Rundstedt, Commander in Chief, West, to court-martial General Dollmann. Von Rundstedt refused, telling the Führer bluntly that he would do no more than a factual routine inquiry into the loss of Cherbourg. The aging marshal then proceeded to hand over the probe to Rommel.

As a result, von Rundstedt and Rommel found themselves in the peculiar position of investigating themselves for the loss of the key port. Rommel, burdened with massive problems on the battleground, did nothing. General Dollmann saved Hitler and all others concerned a great deal of trouble: on June 29 he dropped dead of a heart attack.

The capture of Cherbourg sent sighs of relief through Supreme Headquarters Allied Expeditionary Force in England. For days there had been whispered remarks in secluded corners of "another massive Dunkirk" as Americans battled from hedgerow to hedgerow against a stubborn foe and British and Canadian forces were bogged down in front of Caen, on the left flank of the bridgehead.

As final German die-hards were mopped up in Cherbourg, it became starkly evident to the Americans that Hitler's orders had been carried out with great skill and thoroughness—"leave the Allies not a port but a field of devastation." Major General Cecil R. Moore, chief engineer of SHAEF, said Vice Admiral Walther Hennecke had "knocked hell out of the port."

Other American engineers were aghast by what they found. Colonel Alvin G. Viney, who had prepared the original plan for rehabilitation of Cherbourg port facilities, declared: "The demolition was masterful, beyond a doubt the most complete, intensive, and best-planned demolition job in history."

Estimates based on experience at the harbor in Naples the year before were that Cherbourg could begin operations three days after its capture. But it was almost three weeks before the port was opened at all. Little by little the port capacity was increased until in November Cherbourg handled more than half of all the cargo landed in France for the American armies.

Seizing one of Europe's finest commercial ports exacted a toll in human lives. Battle casualties sustained by General Joe Collins' VII totaled 22,119, including 2,811 killed, 13,564 wounded and 5,665 missing (most captured, some drowned). Best estimates available for German losses in the Cherbourg campaign were 47,070 killed, wounded, or captured, including six generals and 826 officers.

The two American airborne divisions (the 82nd and 101st) suffered particularly heavy losses—41 percent of VII total casualties. The 82nd Airborne sustained 4,480 men killed, wounded, missing, or captured, and the 101st had an almost identical total—4,670. In addition, in the airborne assault in the early hours on D-Day 60 percent of all supplies and heavy equipment dropped by parachute or landed by glider were destroyed, damaged, or missing.

The contribution of the airborne assault to the overall success of the VII Corps landing on Utah Beach was incalculable. Casualties in the seaborne attack by the 4th Infantry Division were astonishingly low—12 men killed and 46 wounded. Events proved General Omar Bradley totally right in his ongoing duel with SHAEF's commander for air, Marshal Trafford Leigh-Mallory, in threatening to call off the Utah seaborne assault unless the 82nd and 101st Airborne Divisions jumped behind the landing beaches.

For his part, on the morning of D-Day when initial reports indicated the two airborne divisions had not been "slaughtered," as he had predicted,

Leigh-Mallory telephoned General Eisenhower to apologize for "any added burden I may have caused you."

Following his capture in the Cap de la Hague where he was one of the final German commanders to hold out on the Cotentin, Lieutenant Colonel Günther Kiel told his captors that the speed with which the 4th Infantry Division assaulted Utah Beach and American units pushed inland had been far greater than German commanders had estimated. Each time the Germans behind Utah tried to assemble on D-Day, they were disrupted by bands of American paratroopers, Colonel Kiel declared.

On nearby Omaha Beach, where the veteran 1st Infantry Division and attached elements of the 29th Infantry Division went ashore, no airborne troops dropped inland. There the amphibious situation was much different. Seaborne assault troops were raked with withering fire even before many had gotten out of their landing craft. Only after a bloody struggle and through the courage and resourcefulness of individual officers and men did the Americans claw their way off Omaha late in the afternoon. V Corps lost 2,374 men killed, wounded, or missing on D-Day alone.

Two key actions by the American airborne divisions were crucial to the success of Neptune, the assault phase of Overlord, and were among the bloodiest involving American troops in World War II. Years later, General Matt Ridgway, commander of the 82nd Airborne, wrote: "The La Fière causeway fight was the hottest single incident I experienced in my combat service, in Europe and later in Korea."

Brigadier General Jim Gavin, who led the La Fière causeway attack, told the author in 1983: "It is impossible to put into words the holocaust that took place there. But the attack was crucial to gain a bridgehead for the drive west to cut off the peninsula."

The 101st Airborne Division later would receive immortality for its stand at Bastogne during the Battle of the Bulge. But veterans of both actions maintained that the attack over the Carentan causeway which linked Utah and Omaha beaches was the bloodiest, most difficult of the war for the Screaming Eagles.

While the man with the rifle and machine gun bore the brunt of the ordeal, as is always the case in war, many factors were involved in the seizure of crucial Cherbourg. The work of the Centurie underground in Normandy provided American commanders with a tremendous advantage—knowing in precise detail German defenses along and behind the Atlantic Wall. Ultra, whose very existence was cloaked in utmost secrecy until 30 years after the war, was an enormous plus factor for the Allies. Learning in advance about German intentions and actions was a tactical and strategic bonanza which defied measurement.

Operation Fortitude, the ingenious Allied deception plan to convince Hitler that the Normandy landings were but a prelude to the assault by the phantom Army Group Patton against the Pas-de-Calais succeeded beyond even the wildest dreams of the most optimistic Allied strategist. When the American flag was hoisted over Cherbourg more German divisions were sitting idle along the Pas-de-Clais and the coasts of Belgium and Holland than were in action against the enemy on the invasion front.

On June 29 General Collins wrote Admiral Mort Deyo: "I witnessed your naval bombardment of the coastal batteries and the converging strongpoints around Cherbourg—the results were excellent and did much to engage the enemy's fire while our troops stormed into Cherbourg from the rear."

With tongue in cheek, Collins added: "Fortunately we did not ask the Navy to shell Fort du Roule—fortunate in that it contained, among other things, a well-stocked wine cellar."

The 90th Infantry Division, which floundered so badly in Normandy that SHAEF considered breaking it up for replacements, soon found the spark it needed—spirited and resourceful leadership at the top and at the regimental level.

Major General Raymond S. McLain, a banker turned fighting man, took over the 90th Division after the Normandy campaign and breathed new life and spirit into the sagging, bewildered formation. When McLain was promoted to corp commander, Brigadier General James Van Fleet, who led the assaulting 8th Infantry Regiment of the 4th Division onto Utah Beach, took over and continued to mold the 90th into a first-class fighting machine.

Van Fleet performed so admirably that he too was promoted to corps command, being replaced by Major General Hubert Earnest. The 90th Division became one of the finest divisions in the European Theater of Operations.

Shortly after the capture of Cherbourg, Brigadier General Teddy Roosevelt, the diminutive, game fighting man who insisted on leading the Utah assault regiment ashore, died of a heart attack while resting in a captured German truck. Two hours before his death, the fifty-seven-year-old assistant commander of the 4th Infantry Division had received a visit from his son, Captain Quentin Roosevelt.

Earlier that day he had been to front-line positions, encouraging
254

officers and men who were finding the going difficult. Teddy Roosevelt never learned that he was in line for promotion to major general and command of the 90th Infantry Division. Nor did he know that he would be awarded the Congressional Medal of Honor for his D-Day heroics.

Death took another unorthodox and game fighting man on July 23. Colonel Harry "Paddy" Flint, General Patton's drinking and card-playing crony, was shot through the head while out in front leading an attack by his 39th Regiment of the 9th Infantry Division. At the time, Flint was in his normal battle garb—stripped to the waist, a black silk scarf around his neck, as he waved his men forward with a Garand rifle.

Cautioned many times of the peril of exposing himself in dangerous situations, Paddy Flint would merely point to the enemy positions just ahead and declare, "The German bastards couldn't shoot in the last war, and the sons of bitches still can't."

A "lucky" shot brought down the little fighting man. Soldiers nearby said later he "died with a smile on his face."

Corporal John D. Kelly of the 79th Infantry Division, who cleared a path for his comrades to capture "impregnable" Fort du Roule by blasting a German bunker with TNT charges after being seriously wounded, never would know that he would be awarded the Congressional Medal of Honor for that action. He died of wounds received in another battle the following November.

Lieutenant Carlos C. Ogden, also of the 79th Division, who knocked out a German bunker housing an 88-millimeter gun and adjoining machine guns in the Fort du Roule action, survived the war and personally received his Medal of Honor, in April 1945.

Lieutenant Colonel Robert H. Cole, who led a bayonet charge which turned the tide in the bitter Carentan causeway fight, was killed in Holland the following September by a sniper's bullet the second day after parachuting with the 101st Airborne Division. He would receive the Medal of Honor posthumously for his role in the causeway battle.

On July 17, Field Marshal Erwin Rommel was returning from his daily visit to the front when his Horch was pounced on by three Allied fighters, dive-bombed and strafed. His driver was killed and Rommel was wounded so seriously in the head that he was unconscious for a week.

Just two days before, Rommel had sent "one last warning" to Adolf Hitler to "end the war." If that failed, the *Schwarze Kapelle,* the ultra-secret group dedicated to ridding Germany of the Führer, would take action. Hitler had begun to suspect that Rommel was involved in the conspiracy.

Rommel made a miraculous recovery. Two months after he was

wounded, two generals in Hitler's entourage arrived at the marshal's home in Herrlingen. Rommel was given a choice: take poison or be arrested and put on public trial for treason. If he took poison, Lucie Maria and son Manfred would not be harmed. Otherwise . . .

Erwin Rommel went upstairs to bid a hurried goodbye to his wife. A half-hour later his body was delivered to the Army Reserve Hospital in nearby Ulm.

After the Normandy debacle, Field Marshal Gerd von Rundstedt was relieved of his post as Commander in Chief, West. Hitler sent a staff lieutenant colonel with a letter telling von Rundstedt that he was being booted out. Before leaving his post he had told Rommel: "I thank God I won't be in command during the coming catastrophe."

During the time Lightning Joe Collins' corps was attacking Cherbourg, Field-Marshal Bernard Montgomery's British forces were engaged in a bitter siege of the old university town of Caen, 10 miles inland along the Calvados coast. For three weeks Montgomery had hammered against heavy concentrations of German panzers which had been sent to his front by Hitler, fearful of a breakthrough to Paris.

Montgomery took a great deal of heat in the media for his "failure" to capture Caen. But General Eisenhower could not publicly exonerate the British commander by pointing out that he was pinning down the bulk of German armor in Normandy. It would have tipped off the Germans that the main Allied effort in Normandy was to seize the port of Cherbourg. In that event the Wehrmacht would have rushed panzers from in front of Montgomery to confront General Collins in the peninsula campaign.

Montgomery brought down part of the criticism upon himself by announcing periodically during the battle how important Caen was to the Allies, Actually, the old city, then a mass of crumbled masonry, had no particular significance in the greater scheme of things.

All morning long on July 25, the air throbbed overhead with the throaty roar of Allied warplanes just west of the ancient citadel of Saint-Lô, now a pile of smoking ruins after the 29th Infantry Division captured the key traffic center in a bitter fight. After being bottled up in the *bocage* country of the Cotentin Peninsula for seven weeks, the U.S. First Army was making a maximum effort to break loose. A rectangle three miles long and one and a half miles deep was established along the Saint-Lô-Périers road and into this confined space 1,500 heavy bombers, 396 mediums, and 350 fighter-bombers were dropping their lethal cargoes.

Several hundred American foot soldiers were killed by shorts, but the massive bombing had shaken loose the German defenses. General Joe Collins, whose VII Corps spearheaded the First Army attack, poured through his tanks. Before the forward momentum of the Allies ground to a halt in September at the gates of the Third Reich, the German army in the West had been virtually wiped out.

Appendix I

Tables of Equivalent Ranks

U.S. Army	German Army
General of the Army	Field Marshal (Generalfeldmarschall)
General	Colonel General (Generaloberst)
Lieutenant General	General (General)
Major General	Lieutenant General (Generalleutnant)
Brigadier General	Major General (Generalmajor)
Colonel	Colonel (Oberst)
Lieutenant Colonel	Lieutenant Colonel (Oberstleutnant)
Major	Major (Major)
Captain	Captain (Hauptmann)
First Lieutenant	Lieutenant (Oberleutnant)
Second Lieutenant	Lieutenant (Leutnant)

SS Rank	German Army Equivalent
Reichsfuehrer SS (Himmler)	Commander-in-Chief of the Army*
None	Field Marshal
Oberstgruppenfuehrer	Colonel General
Obergruppenfuehrer	General
Gruppenfuehrer	Lieutenant General
Brigadefuehrer	Major General
Oberfuehrer	None
Standartenfuehrer	Colonel
Obersturmbannfuehrer	Lieutenant Colonel
Sturmbannfuehrer	Major
Hauptsturmfuehrer	Captain
Obersturmfuehrer	First Lieutenant
Untersturmfuehrer	Second Lieutenant

---

*This post was held by Adolf Hitler from December 1941 until the end of the war.

Appendix II

German Units, Ranks, and Strengths

Unit	Rank of Commander*	Strength†
Army Group	Field Marshal	2 or more armies
Army	Colonel General	2 or more corps
Corps	General	2 or more divisions
Division	Lieutenant General/ Major General	10,000–18,000 men 200–350 tanks (if panzer)
Brigade‡	Major General/ Colonel	2 or more regiments
Regiment	Colonel	2–7 battalions
Battalion	Lieutenant Colonel/ Major/Captain	2 or more companies (approximately 500 men per infantry battalion; usually 50–80 tanks per panzer battalion)
Company§	Captain/Lieutenant	3–5 platoons
Platoon	Lieutenant/ Sergeant Major	Infantry: 30–40 men Panzer: 4 or 5 tanks
Section	Warrant Officer/ Sergeant Major	2 squads (more or less)
Squad	Sergeant	Infantry: 7–10 men Armor: 1 tank

*Frequently, units were commanded by lower-ranking men as the war went on.
†As the war progressed, the number of men and tanks in most units declined accordingly. SS units usually had more men and tanks than Army units.
‡Rarely used in the German Army.
§Called batteries in the artillery (4 or 5 guns per battery).

Bibliography

Alanbrooke, the Viscount, *Diaries,* London: Collins, 1957.

Ambrose, Stephen E., *The Supreme Commander,* New York: Doubleday, 1970.

Bauer, Eddy, *Encyclopedia of World War II,* New York: Marshall Cavendish Corp., 1970.

Bekker, Cajus, *The Luftwaffe War Diaries,* New York: Doubleday, 1969.

Bennett, Ralph, *Ultra in the West,* New York: Charles Scribner's Sons, 1979.

Blumenson, Martin, *The Patton Papers,* Boston: Houghton Mifflin, 1974.

Blummentritt, General Guenther, *Von Rundstedt,* London: Oldham's, 1952.

Bradley, General Omar, *A Soldier's Story,* New York: Henry Holt & Co., 1951.

Brown, Anthony Cave, *Bodyguard of Lies,* New York: Harper & Row, 1975.

Buckmaster, Maurice, *They Fought Alone,* New York: W. W. Norton, 1958.

Butcher, Harry C., *My Three Years With Eisenhower,* New York: Simon & Schuster, 1946.

Collins, General Joseph L., *Lightning Joe,* Baton Rouge: Louisiana State University, 1979.

Carell, Paul, *Invasion—They're Coming!,* Boston: Little, Brown, 1964.

Collier, Richard, *Ten Thousand Eyes,* New York: E. P. Dutton, 1958.

Eisenhower, Dwight D., *Crusade in Europe,* New York: Doubleday, 1948.

Farago, Ladislas, *Patton—Ordeal and Triumph,* New York: Obolensky, 1964.

Gavin, General James M., *On to Berlin,* New York: Viking, 1978.

Harrison, Gordon A., *Cross-Channel Attack,* Washington, D.C.: Department of the Army, 1951.

Hart, B. H. Liddell, *The Rommel Papers,* London: Collins, 1953.

Hayn, Friedrich, *Die Invasion—von Cotentin bis Falaise,* Heidelberg: Kurt Vowinckel Verlag, 1952.

Irving, David, *The War Between the Generals,* New York: Congdon & Lattes, 1981.

Keitel, Field Marshal Wilhelm, *The Memoirs of Field Marshal Keitel,* New York: Stein and Day, 1965.

Killen, John, *A History of the Luftwaffe,* New York: Doubleday, 1968.

Lewin, Ronald, *Ultra Goes to War,* New York: McGraw-Hill, 1978.

Majdalany, Frederick, *The Fall of Fortress Europe,* New York: Doubleday, 1968.

Mittelman, *Eight Stars to Victory,* Privately Printed, 1948.

Montgomery, Field Marshal the Viscount, *Memoirs,* London: Collins, 1958.

Morison, Samuel Elliott, *The Invasion of France and Germany,* Boston: Little Brown, 1957.

Patton, General George S. Jr., *War As I Knew It,* Boston: Houghton Mifflin, 1947.

Rapport, Leonard, and Northwood, Jr., *Rendezvous With Destiny,* Privately Printed, 1948.

Ridgway, General Matthew B., *Soldier,* New York: Harper, 1956.

Ruge, Admiral Friedrich, *Rommel in Normandy,* San Rafael, Cal.: Presidio Press, 1979.

Speidel, General Dr. Hans, *Invasion 1944,* Chicago: Henry Regnery & Co., 1945.

Stagg, J. M., *Forecast for Overlord,* New York: W. W. Norton & Co., 1972.

Taylor, General Maxwell D., *Swords and Plowshares,* New York: W. W. Norton & Co., 1972.

Warlimont, General Walter, *Inside Hitler's Headquarters,* New York: Praeger, 1964.

Westphal, General Siegfried, *The German Army in the West,* London: Cassell, 1951.

Winterbotham, F. W., *The Ultra Secret,* New York: Harper & Row, 1974.

MISCELLANEOUS
U.S. VII Corps history of operations in Europe, 1944–45.
Utah to Cherbourg, U.S. Department of the Army.
The Carentan Causeway Fight, a post-battle study for the U.S. Army, Colonel S.L.A. Marshall.

Index